CW01035411

Heroes & Monsters:
The Unofficial Companion to
The League of Extraordinary Gentlemen

monkeybrain, inc.

HEROES & MONSTERS

THE UNOFFICIAL COMPANION TO
THE LEAGUE OF EXTRAORDINARY GENTLEMEN

BY **JESS NEVINS**

INTRODUCTION BY
ALAN MOORE

COMMENTARY BY
KEVIN O'NEILL

Heroes & Monsters:
The Unofficial Companion to
The League of Extraordinary Gentlemen
Copyright © 2003 Jess Nevins

The League of Extraordinary Gentlemen
TM and *© Alan Moore & Kevin O'Neill*

Cover illustration and design © 2003 John Picacio

Introduction © 2003 Alan Moore

A MonkeyBrain Publication
www.monkeybrainbooks.com

All of the characters in this book are ficticious, and any resemblance to actual
persons, living or dead, is purely coincidental.

No part of this book may be reproduced or transmitted in any form or by any
means, graphic, electronic, or mechanical, including photocopying, record-
ing, taping, or by any information storage or retrieval system, without the
permission in writing from the publisher.

MonkeyBrain, Inc.
P.O. Box 200126
Austin, TX 78720
info@monkeybrainbooks.com

ISBN: 1-932265-04-X

Printed in the United States of America

A Note on the Type

The cover typography was set in Treacherous Corners and Curves, a typeface
produced and licensed by Comicraft. For this font and other fabulous font
designs, please contact:

Comicraft
Richard Starkings, President
8910 Rayford Drive
Los Angeles, CA 90045
www.comicbookfonts.com

Additional cover typography was set in Adobe Woodtype Ornaments,
a typeface licensed by the Adobe Corporation.
For this font and more, please see: www.adobe.com

TABLE OF CONTENTS

ACKNOWLEDGEMENTS
7

INTRODUCTION BY ALAN MOORE
11

FOREWORD BY THE AUTHOR
15

ANNOTATIONS TO THE LEAGUE OF EXTRAORDINARY GENTLEMEN
21

ARCHETYPES
153

ON CROSSOVERS
175

YELLOW PERIL
187

INTERVIEW WITH ALAN MOORE
207

Acknowledgements

No book is written in isolation, this one most especially.

Thanks are due, first of all, to the various contributors to the annotations and the book: Zimrah Ahmed, Mitch Albala, Giles Anderson, Robin Anderson, Paul Andinach, Pierce Askegren, Astro Citizen, Peter Ayres, Trevor Barrie, Sean Barry, Richard Bell, Ruth Berman, Joël Berthomier, John Walter Biles, Chris Blakely, Steve Bolhafner, Chris Borthwick, Jerry Boyajian, Peter Briggs, Adrian Brown, Mark Brown, Michael Brown, Peter Brulls, Geoffrey Burmester, Gail Campbell, Mark Cannon, Olivier Cantinelli, Loki Carbis, Jonathan Carter, Tim Chapman, Terence Chua, Brenda Clough, Nancy Collins, Park Cooper, Steven Costa, Greg Coveney, Kieran Cowan, David Crowe, Paul Crowley, Ian Culbard, Adam Cummins, Bryn Davies, Chris Davies, Simeon Davies, Drew Dederer, Ron Dingman, Dave Van Domelen, John Dorrian, Johanna Draper, James Enelow, Owen Erasmus, Taina Evans, Dr. Eric Fennessey, Frederic Ferro, Rodolfo S. Filho, Carl Fink, Richard Flanagan, Steven Flanagan, Rev. Terry Fleming, Jason Fliegel, Philip Flores, Nick Ford, Richard Fulton, Joe Gallagher, Shawn Garre, Stephen Geigen-Miller, Nat Gertler, Andrew Getting, David Goldfarb, James Goldin, Joe Gottman, Heath Graham, P. Graves, Steve Green, Jim Gunnee, Fred Hadley, Sarah Hadley, Mags Halliday, Scott Hamilton, Brian Hance, J. Keith Haney, Peter Hardy, Fiona Harvey, Pat Healy, Warren Hedges, Lea Hernandez, Dale Hicks, Steve Higgins, David Hollander, Bryan Hollerbach, James D. Hudnall, Brian Jacobson, Bill Jennings, Andrew Johnston, Stephen Johnston, Regg Kashi, John Klima, Jacque Koh, Keith Kole, Ivan Kristofferson, Duncan Lawie, Yeechang Lee, David Leggatt, Ken Lemons, Jim Lesher, Chick Lewis, Kathy Li, Steve Lieber, Barb Lien, Martin Linck, Henry A. Lincoln, Jeff Lipton, Joe Littrell, Myles Lobdell, Jean-Marc Lofficier, Kiralee Macauley, Mike McConnell, Steve MacDonald, Dwayne

Macduffie, Jim McGill, Dave McKenna, Andrew McLean, T. Troy McNemar, Don MacPherson, Marc Madouraud, Maureen Maker, Rafael Marin, Kevin J. Maroney, Emilio Martin, Drew Melbourne, Jon Meltzer, Bala Menon, Kevin Mowery, Dr. Rainer Nagel, Stuart Nathan, Gabriel Neeb, Andrew Ness, Daniel Nogly, Michael Norwitz, Paul O'Brien, Clarrie O'Callaghan, John O'Neil, Garry Osborne, Joe Pacheco, Eric Padget, Kate Paice, Alvin Pang, Cory Panshin, Andrea L. Peterson, Bradly E. Peterson, Rob Petrone, tphile, T.E. Pouncey, Charles Prepolec, Colin Rankine, Jess Ray, Robert Reay, Pedro Gutiérrez Recacha, Bob Redmond, Michael Reese III, Alasdair Richmond, Giles Robinson, Josiah Rowe, Steven Rowe, Mike Schiffer, Greg Dean Schmitz, Martin Schroeder, Chris Schumacher, Michael Seery, Ashley Sekhon, Christopher Sequeira, David Serchay, Robert W. Sharp, John Sherman, Brian Showers, Stu Shiffman, Danny Sichel, Alan Sinder, Marc Singer, Rick Slater, Aaron Smith, Daniel Smith, Zack Smith, Henry Spencer, William Stoddard, Bill Svitavsky, Jonathan Swerdlow, Anthony Tan, Dominic Tavassoli, Robert Taylor, Kelly Tindal, Geoffrey Tolle, Jason Tondro, Ed Toschach, Alan Trewartha, Steve Trout, Christopher L. Tumber, Pedro Valente, Todd VerBeek, Jason Verbitsky, Fabrice Vigne, Jamie Ward, Lawrence Watt-Evans, S. Wayment, Silas Wegg, Kurt M. Wilcken, Ian Wildman, Gregory A. Wilson, Paul Wilson, R. Winninger, and Giles Woodrow.

Special thanks are due to Steve Higgins, Damian Gordon, and Scott Hollifield.

For the book, thanks to Win Eckert, Jean-Marc Lofficier, Steve Holland, and the Victoria-L, Alan Moore, NWNMS, and Fictionmags mailing lists for helpful information. For years of friendship, thanks to Ronald Byrd, Mark Coale, Regina Garcia, Erica Goldsmith, Kerry LaMare, Michael Norwitz, Dan Shoemaker, Karen Stevens, and Noah & Connie. Thanks to my parents and family for their patience and love. Thanks to Elena, Maggie, and Susanna, just 'cause. Thanks to Abe, il miglio fabbro.

Thanks to Chris Roberson for having faith in me and this book. Thanks to Alan Moore and Kevin O'Neill for their generosity with their time, and of course for creating League.

And, of course, to Alicia. "For thirty years, ten months and four days, she was the light of my life, my whole ambition. Anything else I did was just the fire for her to warm her hands at....she was the beat of my heart for thirty years. She was the music heard faintly at the edge of sound. It was my great and now useless regret that I never wrote anything really worth her attention, no book that I could dedicate to her." This may not be worth your attention, but...this one's for you, love.

INTRODUCTION

I am afraid both for and of Jess Nevins. He has, for no discernible reason other than sheer enthusiasm, chosen to wade out into the same incredibly deep and complex literary swamp that the estimable Mr. O'Neill and myself are being paid good money to immerse ourselves in. I think it's fair to say that we're all in way over our heads and probably won't be coming back from this one in precisely the same shape as we set out, but that isn't the point. Kevin and I have been in this industry for nearly fifty years between us. We're a mess of psychological scar-tissue and cauterised synapses that can more or less do whatever we want, simply because we're too traumatized to care that much about our mental health and well-being; Jess Nevins, on the other hand, is still a young man. And he's a civilian.

As for Kevin and myself, neither of us had the first idea precisely what this landscape would be like when first we ventured hence. The sole idea we'd started out with was that a Victorian super-hero team of previously existing characters might be something fun to work on. Then we thought it might he interesting if we worked some of the era's architectural fancies and fictions, or its technologically wild ideas, into our fantasy environment. It was probably during the Rue Morgue sequences of the first issue that it started to dawn upon us just exactly what the possibilities for such a strip might be; exactly how compendious and far reaching we might be in our reference. This was the start of our obsessive and demented stage, a phase which, worryingly, shows no signs of yet abating. We decided that, from that point on, all characters or names referred to in the strip would have their origins in either fictions written during or before the period in hand, or else in elements from later works that could be retro-engineered into our continuity by the invention of a father, grandfather or other predecessor. Since this hadn't sent us mad enough by issue six of the first volume, we elected to include in volume two an almanac that detailed all the world's fictitious places in a sprawling gazetteer that stretched made-up pole to made-up pole. Volume three might well expand this notion from the geographical to the historical, giving genealogies for England's royal family tailored to include a Dark Ages King Arthur, a sixteenth century Queen Gloriana and even the constitutional disaster that placed an oversized American named Ralph upon the throne during the 1990s. Now, that would have to be some considerable time after the collapse of the repressive "Big Brother" period of Government established after the second world war, but before the Americans find the monolith on the moon in 2001. And then, not long after that, the Daleks invade...

You begin to see, I hope, the endless, bottomless intricacy of this literary Sargasso that we've beached ourselves intentionally upon. At that very moment, for example, I'm distracted by the current chapter of the New Traveller's Almanac, this being the installment dealing with Asia and the Australias. Can I legitimately claim that Kaloon is an alternate spelling or a mispronunciation of K'un Lun? After all, they're both mountains somewhere in Asia ruled by an amoral and immortal Queen, so could Hsi Wang Mu, the Royal Mother of the West, be some guise of Ayesha? And I think I can tie in that vague offhand reference made in the Africa chapter to Orlando having known Prester John at some point in the past, maybe with a journey running from Alcina's Island off Japan to Central Asia and the inland sea-bound island of Pentexiore. And then... and then...

This stuff drives you mad. I'm serious. And it's not the kind of mad that knowing every corner of, say, Marvel comics continuity for the last sixty years can drive you. This is continuity extending back to the fourth century B.C., and hopelessly attempting to take in all of the fictions that have been created in that time, be they in literature, theatre, film or music. This is big-time mad. Imagine our surprise then when we heard that someone was attempting to give annotations to the work as it progressed. We may at first have been quite scornful of the notion... probably were, in fact. That sounds like us... but then began to feel alarm when we were told that this possibly dangerous cyber-stalker had even identified the fictitious publishers, Meesons, that we'd given on the back of the first issue to the imprint publishing the memoirs of our Campion Bond character, as originating in the work of H. Rider Haggard. Then this person identified Rosa Coote (from English Victorian stroke pamphlet *The Pearl*) in issue two and even the oblique *Eastenders* reference in issue six, which we'd been sure would throw him. Could nothing stop this implacable monster, surely sent by our Dark Master to harrow and purge our wretched souls?

It was only when someone finally conveyed these internet postings to me in a form that I feel comfortable about reading (on tree-bark, in their own urine, if you're interested) that I began to understand the invaluable asset that Jess represented (you'll notice that by now we'd begun calling him Jess instead of "Infernal Whelp of Baphomet" or "that psycho American guy who probably just drifts eerily in a flotation tank all day with a reference library wired directly into his brain-stem"). I realised that if we had some clearly gifted and dedicated person like Jess tracking down all of the references for the readers, then we could be as obscure and far-reaching as we wanted, safe in the knowledge that everyone, if they wanted to, would be able to "get it" and enjoy all of the rich texture that the League's world has to offer. I'd like to think that we have a nice little symbiotic relationship going on here, that might benefit everybody. That the reader might benefit has been born out by stories that Jess has passed on of people being guided to Flann O'Brien's sublime *The Third Policeman* by a mention in the annotations. That Kevin and I benefit personally has been verified, for me at least, by the immense amount of pleasure and new information I've received from thumbing through notes and annotations. Often Jess has brought to light some fact that I had missed or else forgotten, such as Stevenson's indications in *Dr. Jekyll and Mr. Hyde* that Hyde was indeed growing bigger, which I'd assumed was a perhaps unfounded intuition of my own and was delighted to find had been confirmed in the original work. The patient work contained within this current volume has played an important part in the construction of this vast, imaginary global edifice that we're constructing, and will certainly be an invaluable guide to any reader, no matter how knowledgeable they may like to think themselves, when it comes to finding their way around inside the structure.

So, hats off, then, to Jess Nevins. Unless Jess would rather leave his hat on, the better to conceal the hideous exo-brain and insect-like antennae sprouting from his cranium, in which case that's fine by us. Oh, and in volume three we're planning to include characters that have been created by our seven year old nephews in the course of junior school compositions and which nobody but us has ever seen. We're gonna get *you,* sucker.

I hope everyone enjoys the following as much as I'm going to, and I'll look forward to seeing you all back here for volume two.

Peace,

Alan Moore
Northampton,
17th January, 2003.

FOREWORD

Alan Moore has been a favorite of American comic book fans since 1984, when he began writing *Swamp Thing* for DC Comics. That was before the World Wide Web, and so most of us had never heard of Moore, but word spread quickly, with *Swamp Thing* winning fan awards and industry awards and even attention from the mainstream media. In 1986 Moore assured his place in the pantheon of comic book immortals with *Watchmen*, one of the most perfectly constructed and executed comic book series in the history of the medium.

His work in the 1990s did nothing to diminish his popular or critical evaluation. His superhero titles, 1963, *W.I.L.D.Cats*, and the wonderful Superman homage *Supreme*, were fan favorites. Outside of superhero comics, Moore wrote *The Voice of the Fire, From Hell*, and *A Small Killing*. All of these were popular with both fans and critics. So when Moore's fans first heard about his new series in the spring of 1998, it was a cause for celebration and no small amount of interest. The news that Kevin O'Neill was to illustrate the series added to the anticipation. O'Neill's work on *Nemesis* and *Marshal Law* had made him a cult favorite among fans, and the idea of O'Neill illustrating a Moore-written Victorian adventure story was a tantalizing one.

The product of the collaboration was *The League of Extraordinary Gentlemen*, a six issue comic book miniseries set in 1898 and starring a number of familiar figures from Victorian literature. *League* features no costumed superheroes and has lead characters from literary works rather than comic books, but the series sold surprisingly well, with higher sales than a number of industry mainstays. In trade paperback form *League's* sales are very high, and the comic has been translated into several languages and is sold in 30 countries. Beyond mere sales, however, the series has proven to be popular with audiences beyond ordinary buyers of comic books. A significant number of fans of *League* are men and women who don't buy other comic books, including authors, editors, literature students and literature professors. The attention paid to the book has come from a variety of venues, from *Entertainment Weekly* to *The Library Journal*. The series has even drawn praise from groups who would not ordinarily pay attention to comic books, from Sherlockians to the H. Rider Haggard Appreciation Society. The concept has proven attractive enough that it caught the attention of Hollywood, with 20th Century Fox commissioning scriptwriter Alex Ayres and director Stephen Norrington to produce a film version of *League*, with Sean Connery as Allan Quatermain and debuting in July, 2003.

I heard about the series at the same time most of the other online fans did, in the spring of 1998, and was immediately taken with the concept. I'd been a fan of Moore's since my friend Abe Binder made me read "The Anatomy Lesson," *Swamp Thing* #21. I'd been a faithful reader of Moore's work ever since, and was a fan of Kevin O'Neill's art, so I knew I'd be buying *League*. And I knew, given the premise and the track record of Moore and O'Neill, that it would be highly entertaining.

What I didn't know (until the first issue) was how complex and layered the references would be. I knew from the previews who the main characters would be, but I had no idea that there would be visual nods to Aubrey Beardsley, or that C. Auguste Dupin would appear, or that reference would be made to a Zola character. Nor did I have any idea that Moore and O'Neill would be creating a world in which all of these characters, and many others, would co-exist.

This concept appealed greatly to me, as I was a fan not just of many of the characters in their original stories but also of crossovers, especially ones like Philip Jose Farmer's "Wold Newton" stories and Kim Newman's "Anno Dracula" stories. But as I spoke with fans and as I read online messages from fans about *League* I realized that not only did many readers lack knowledge of Victorian literature, but also that I didn't know the subject nearly as well as I thought I did, or as well as Moore and O'Neill did.

So I began writing down notes on League, and when I had enough of them I posted them on an Internet message group, *rec.arts.comics.misc*, in January, 1999. The response was overwhelming. I had annotated comic book series before, including the densely-referenced *Kingdom Come*, and my efforts had been received well, but I had gotten nowhere near the positive feedback, nor the amount of it, that I got for my *League* annotations. As each issue of *League* came out I wrote down notes on the issue and posted them on various newsgroups and then on my web site. I received many suggestions for corrections and additions, and even after the first *League* series ended in July 2000 e-mails continued to arrive with further things to add.

I never thought about publishing the notes, though. I was surprised (and pleased) when Chris Roberson suggested it to me. And now that the notes are in book form, I'm very pleased with them, and I hope you find them as enjoyable to read as they were to write.

A few notes about the annotations:

The page numbers next to the entries ("Page 7. Panel 1.") are for the hardcover edition of the *League*. The original annotations had page numbers by issue, but more people will read the League in its collected form than in its original form.

When possible, I describe panels from left to right and top to bottom.

In general I try not to spoil any of Moore and O'Neill's surprises in my annotations, so occasionally I will defer revealing information until the appropriate time.

The individual issues of *League* had some material which does not appear in the collected editions. This material included reproductions of advertisements which appeared in Victorian magazines and newspapers, fake ads written by Moore and drawn by O'Neill, and letters to the editor. I have included the notes to these at the end of the annotations, under the "Material not included in the League hardcover" section.

I use *"League"* and *"LoEG"* interchangeably to refer to *The League of Extraordinary Gentlemen.*

As can be seen from some of Kevin O'Neill's comments on my notes, occasionally too much has been read into some panels. O'Neill's comments arrived too late to be incorporated into my notes.

I've left my erroneous annotations in because they might amuse even if they won't edify.

Jess Nevins
January, 2003

ANNOTATIONS

Front Cover: The title of the comic and the name of the group may come from a few sources. Moore may only have been trying to come up with a Victorian-sounding name for the group, something like "the Justice League" or "the Avengers" but a name which would also fit with one of the series' central conceits, that this is the kind of group/team-up comic book which would have been written in a world which had no superhero comic books. However, there are also precedents for the comic and team name, examples which may have influenced Moore's choice.

In Baroness Emmuska Orczy's *The Scarlet Pimpernel* (1905), the Scarlet Pimpernel and a group of young British noblemen rescue endangered French royalty from the Terror of the French Revolution. The group is called "the League of the Scarlet Pimpernel." In John Boland's *The League of Gentlemen* (1958), a group of retired military men carry out a bank robbery. The book was made into a 1960 film with Richard Attenborough. (Interestingly, two of the characters in Boland's book are Hyde and Mycroft, names of significance in *League*). The guitarist Robert Fripp, best known for his work with the progressive rock group King Crimson, formed a side group, the League of Gentlemen, which released two albums, "God Save the King" (1985) and "Thrang Thrang Gozinbulx" (1996). And in 1995 four British comedians, Reece Shearsmith, Mark Gatiss, Steve Pemberton, and Jeremy Dyson, formed the "League of Gentlemen" comedy troupe. They are best known for their self-titled radio and television shows.

The image on the front cover of the *League* hardcover collection is an excerpt from the back cover. The back cover image will be addressed later, after the other contents of the hardcover.

Page 2. "The Bloomsbury Quintet - Simplicissimus."

The drawing is done in the style of the English illustrator Aubrey Beardsley. Beardsley (1872-1898), a leading exponent of art nouveau, contributed illustrations to the controversial periodical *The Yellow Book*. Had he lived he might well have provided illustrations for *Simplicissimus* (see below). The silhouettes, the very large hat, the strongly emphasized mouth, the extended little fingers, and the positioning of the roses in the foreground are all Beardsley trademarks. The hands holding the knife may be a direct quote from a Beardsley drawing; there are certain similarities to Beardsley's "Oriental Dancer" (1897). The knife itself is visually similar to Beardsley's paper-knife, an implement of controversial origin.

Kevin O'Neill notes:
> I love the work of Aubrey Beardsley but any visual similarity
> is quite by accident, not design.

In real life the Bloomsbury Group was a collection of writers and critics including Clive Bell, Vanessa Bell, E.M. Forster, Roger Fry, Duncan Grant, John Maynard Keynes, Desmond MacCarthy, Thoby Stephen, Adrian Stephen, Lytton Strachey, Saxon Sydney-Turner, Leonard Woolf, and Virginia Woolf. They were notable for their efforts to challenge the social and artistic norms of the Victorian era. Although none of the League would be at ease in their company, the League members are all social outcasts of one kind or another and are in their own way a kind of Bloomsbury Group–hence the title "The Bloomsbury Quintet." Additionally, as seen on Page 50, the headquarters of the League is the British Museum, which is located in Bloomsbury, London.

Simplicissimus was a satirical German magazine, similar to the English *Punch*. *Simplicissimus* was founded in Munich in 1896 and ran for almost forty years. It was graphic-heavy and liberal in tone, and presumably this sort of illustration would have appeared there.

Page 3. This device is the container of Cavorite, the material from H.G. Wells' *The First Men in the Moon* which plays a key role in the series. It is first seen on Page 92, Panel 1.

Page 4. The credits shown here are in the style of a Victorian theater placard, as are the titles given to Alan Moore, Kevin O'Neill, Benedict Dimagmaliw, William Oakley, and Scott Dunbier.

Page 5. "My Message To Our Readers" is a parody of the messages that editors of British story papers, such as the *Boys' Own Paper* and the *Boys' Friend*, wrote to their readers. Several issues of *League* had Letters Pages with similar messages from the series' putative editor; these messages will be discussed below, after the other contents of the hardcover.

Alan Moore (the bearded, smoking gentleman) and, presumably, Kevin O'Neill can be seen in the middle of the page, entering Ivanhoe House through the Tradesmen's door.

Kevin O'Neill notes:
> "Bearded gent is Alan, I'm holding comic pages, Ben Dimagmaliw is wearing red cap back to front, and Bill Oakley is holding sack with LTG (lettering) written on it.
>
> Sign on gate originally read:
> "NOW PLAYING PULP OR BE DAMNED. SOLD OUT."
> A reference to issue #5 being pulped. Wildstorm felt pulp reference might irritate DC!!
>
> Baboon bothering the cockatoo is an obscure reference to Tiger Tim and the Bruin Boys and their antics in The Rainbow Comic and elsewhere.

Page 6. The name of the publisher of Bond's book is a reference to H. Rider Haggard's *Mr. Meeson's Will* (1888), a crime novel about Mr. Meeson, an unscrupulous publisher.

Page 7. Panel 1. Dover is the point in England which is closest to France. Dover is famous for its white cliffs, which can be seen in the background of this panel and in the image on Page 6.

Panel 2. The figure on the cigarette case is Harlequin. The character of Harlequin first appeared in the Italian *Commedia dell'Arte* (Italian street theater) in the Sixteenth century, as Arlecchino, a quick-witted servant. As time passed he became a buffoon, but when the English pantomime, or harlequinade, developed, Harlequin became the figure of the persecuted lover who could turn himself invisible, frustrate the tricks of the Clown, and rescue Columbine, Harlequin's lover. The Harlequin's presence on the case may be symbolic of the cigarette case's owner's view of himself, as a kind of trickster who frustrates the schemes of his enemies.

The image itself is taken from the Aubrey Beardsley drawing "The Scarlet Pastorale," which first appeared in *The London Year Book* in 1898.

Panel 3. The hansom cab is a constant in Arthur Conan Doyle's Sherlock Holmes stories. Its appearance here is not coincidental, for reasons which will eventually become apparent.

Panel 5. "John Bull" is the name of the unofficial icon of England in much the same way that "Uncle Sam" is the name of the unofficial icon of the United States. John Bull first appeared as a character in John Arbuthnot's *The History of John Bull* (1712) but became widely known thanks to cartoons drawn by Sir John Tenniel for *Punch*, the British humor magazine, in the mid- and late Nineteenth century.

Bryant and May have been British matchmakers since 1861.

Panels 6-7. This is the first appearance of two of the main characters of *League*. The woman is "Wilhelmina Murray," but as is seen on Page 9 this is not the name by which she is most recognizable.

The gentleman is "Campion Bond." Moore has described him as a dandy, like Sergey Pavlovich Diaghilev (1872-1929), the Russian ballet impresario who was responsible for the revival of ballet as a serious art form. Diaghilev was famous for getting the best out of the men and women he worked with, a group which included Vaslav

Nijinsky, Anna Pavlova, Henri Matisse, Georges Braque, Maurice Utrillo, Jean Cocteau, Igor Stravinsky, Maurice Ravel, and Erik Satie. Moore's invocation of Diaghilev's name with regard to Campion Bond may give a hint as to Bond's true nature.

Bond's name has a familiar ring to it, but the character, Campion Bond, is an original one. Moore has stated that he needed a character to play a particular role in *League*, but that there was none available who qualified, so he made one up. Moore further said that Bond's name was designed to lend an air of familiarity to the character. Campion Bond's last name is the same as James Bond, Ian Fleming's British secret agent, and the opening sequence of this issue is similar to a sequence in the 1962 James Bond film *Doctor No*. The first issue of *League* begins with Campion Bond taking his cigarette case from his jacket, removing a cigarette from the case, and lighting it. Campion Bond's face is not revealed until the end of the sequence. In *Doctor No*, in the casino scene in which James Bond is introduced, Sean Connery, playing Bond, takes a cigarette and lights it while playing baccarat. Connery's face remains hidden until the woman he is playing against asks his name, at which point the camera reveals his face while Connery utters the famous line, "Bond. James Bond." (The second *League* series contains a further hint linking Campion Bond to James Bond; in *The League of Extraordinary Gentlemen* v2 #2 the head of Campion Bond's cane has the Morse Code symbol for "007").

Bond's first name, Campion, is a dual reference. A "campion" is a small flower often found on the sides of roads, as the scarlet pimpernel flower is. And the British mystery author Margery Allingham published over two dozen novels about the detective and British government agent Albert Campion.

Page 8. This panel is our first indication that the England seen in *League* belongs to an alternate reality. The massive structure that Bond and Murray stand upon is, as can be seen from the plaque, the "Channel Causeway," that is, a bridge across the English Channel linking England and France. The idea of connecting France and England goes back at least to 1750, when the Academy of Amiens held a competition for the best way to improve cross-Channel travel. Nicolas Desmarest, an engineer, suggested a tunnel. A similar scheme was considered by Napoleon in 1802. But the idea of a bridge across the Channel was not seriously considered until the mid-1850s, when several schemes for bridging the Channel were put forward, including one involving a bridge with 4000-ft spans 500 feet apart and 500 feet above the water. No such link between England and France was built during the Nineteenth century, for political reasons (England's distrust of France through most of the Nineteenth century was marked), business reasons (a cross-Channel bridge would pose a serious nuisance to ship navigation), and technological reasons (the machinery needed to construct a bridge of the size seen here was not available in 1898). However, the idea of a cross-Channel bridge has appeared in science fiction books, notably Michael Moorcock's *The Runestaff* (1969).

It might be assumed that the reason for such a difference between the real world and the world of the *League* is that personalities from Victorian-era fiction, such as Sherlock Holmes, the fictional Thomas Edison, and Dr. Moreau, made a difference in the course of history, and so made England more technologically-advanced than it otherwise was. This being the case, *The League of Extraordinary Gentlemen* is properly described as "steampunk." Steampunk is a subgenre of science fiction in which science fictional events take place against the backdrop of the Nineteenth century, usually late nineteenth-century London. Some notable steampunk works are K.W. Jeter's *Morlock Night* (1979), Paul Di Filippo's *The Steampunk Trilogy* (1985), and Bruce Sterling & William Gibson's *The Difference Engine* (1990).

The partially-completed statue of the helmeted woman is of Britannia, the personification of the British Empire. The first known instance of the use of this figure to represent Britain was on a Roman coin, circa 150 AD; the figure was revived in 1665 during the reign of Charles II.

The statue of the lion appears because the lion is one of the traditional symbols of England. The Royal Arms of England, "Gules three lions passant guardant or," show three lions in "passant gardant," walking and showing the full face, as the lion here does.

"Albion Reach," seen on the stand below the lion, is a dual pun. "Albion" is a term for England dating to the Tenth century, deriving from both the Latin "albus" (white), and the white cliffs of Dover. So "Albion Reach" puns not only on "all beyond reach"--that is, England being beyond the reach of the world--but also on "reach" in the meaning of "England's grasp"--that is, England, by linking itself via the bridge with France, has France, and perhaps the world, within its grasp. A further meaning of the phrase lies in the definition of "reach" as a length of water which lies between two bends. A bridge connecting England and France would naturally be located at "Albion Reach."

Note the pun on the crane's side, a reference to the Albert Hall.

The placard on the side of the support announcing the delay in the completion date of the Causeway is probably a reference to the many delays which plagued the construction of the Channel Tunnel.

Page 9. **Panel 1**. "Wilhelmina Murray" is Mina Harker, of Bram Stoker's *Dracula* (1897). In the novel "Murray" was Mina Harker's maiden name, "Mina" being short for Wilhelmina. In *Dracula* Mina Harker was the wife of Jonathan Harker, the putative protagonist for the novel. Mina and Jonathan, along with Dr. Abraham van Helsing, come into conflict with Dracula and eventually triumph, although not before Mina is bitten by Dracula and forced to drink his blood. At the end of the novel, however, Mina is again human. The novel's epilogue contains a cheerful note about Mina and Jonathan's married happiness and their son Quincey. Mina's divorce from her husband Jonathan is Moore's invention.

Panel 2. For an explanation of Bond's "inflammation of the brain" comment, see Page 17, Panel 3, below.

Panel 3. Bond's "ravished by a foreigner" comment is a reference to Mina's being bitten by Dracula. For more on this, see the notes to

Page 118, Panel 3, below.

Page 10. Panel 1. Campion Bond's words here imply that he works for a British intelligence agency, perhaps the British Secret Service. This is a further hint on Moore's part of Campion Bond being a familial predecessor to James Bond.

In Arthur Conan Doyle's Sherlock Holmes stories Mycroft Holmes is Sherlock Holmes' older, fatter, and more intelligent brother. It was established in the Holmes stories that, just as Sherlock had occasion to render Her Majesty certain services, so too did Mycroft, but on a more regular basis. In "The Adventure of the Bruce-Partington Plans" (*The Strand Magazine*, December 1908), Holmes and Watson have this exchange:

> "It recalls nothing to my mind. But that Mycroft should break out in this erratic fashion! A planet might as well leave its orbit. By the way, do you know what Mycroft is?"
>
> I had some vague recollection of an explanation at the time of the Adventure of the Greek Interpreter. "You told me that he had some small office under the British government."
>
> Holmes chuckled.
>
> "I did not know you quite so well in those days. One has to be discreet when one talks of high matters of state. You are right in thinking that he is under the British government. You would also be right in a sense if you said that occasionally he is the British government."
>
> "My dear Holmes!"
>
> "I thought I might surprise you. Mycroft draws four hundred and fifty pounds a year, remains a subordinate, has no ambitions of any kind, will receive neither honour nor title, but remains the most

indispensable man in the country."

"But how?"

"Well, his position is unique. He has made it for himself. There has never been anything like it before, nor will be again. He has the tidiest and most orderly brain, with the greatest capacity for storing facts, of any man living. The same great powers which I have turned to the detection of crime he has used for this particular business. The conclusions of every department are passed to him, and he is the central exchange, the clearing-house, which makes out the balance. All other men are specialists, but his specialism is omniscience. We will suppose that a minister needs information as to a point which involves the Navy, India, Canada and the bimetallic question; he could get his separate advices from various departments upon each, but only Mycroft can focus them all, and say offhand how each factor would affect the other. They began by using him as a short-cut, a convenience; now he has made himself an essential. In that great brain of his everything is pigeon-holed and can be handed out in an instant. Again and again his word has decided the national policy. He lives in it. He thinks of nothing else save when, as an intellectual exercise, he unbends if I call upon him and ask him to advise me on one of my little problems."

Mina's statement that Bond's superior is known as "Mr. M" is a reference to both fictional and real spymasters. In Ian Fleming's James Bond books "Mr. M" is Bond's superior and the Head of the British Secret Service. In real life the two main departments of the British Secret Service are MI5, which is the Security Service responsible for counterespionage activities within the borders of the United Kingdom, and MI6, which is responsible for foreign intelligence. The tradition of the heads of the British Secret Service calling themselves by a single initial dates back at least a century. Although there are persistent stories within the intelligence community that Sir Francis Walsingham, a member of Queen Elizabeth's Privy Council and the head of her intelligence agency, referred to himself as "M," the first documented example of a head of the British Secret Service being known by a single initial was Captain Sir Mansfield Cumming, who was appointed director of the British Secret Intelligence Service, then known as MI1c, in 1909. Captain Sir Cumming's name was never officially made public, and he was generally known by the initial "C." Captain Sir Cumming's successors at MI6 carried on the tradition of calling themselves "C," although none of their names began with that initial. Major General Sir Vernon Kell, the founder of MI5 in 1909 and its first head, referred to himself on official documents as "K," which resulted in that initial becoming synoymous with the head of MI5. In the years between the wars Max Knight, the head of B5(b), MI5's section dealing with subversives, called himself "M" in imitation of MI6's "C." Finally, in John Pearson's *The Authorized Biography of 007* (1973), Mycroft Holmes, his lifespan extended by a treatment involving Royal Bee pollen–the same pollen that various pastiches have used to explain Sherlock Holmes' great age–approaches Bond and offers the treatment to him, also explaining that he, Mycroft, was a former head of the British Secret Service.

Panel 3. "We live in troubled times, where fretful dreams settle upon the Empire's brow." Bond says this in 1898, only a year after Queen Victoria's Diamond Jubilee, an event of great self-celebration on the part of the British. But despite the boasting and hubris of the Diamond Jubilee, the general mood among British leaders and opinion-makers in 1898 was pessimistic. France was re-emerging as a world power and expansionist European rival, newly-united nations like Germany and Italy were disturbing the familiar world order, British exports were falling, the country no longer maintained a trade surplus, and the supremacy of the British manufacturing and commercial empire was being threatened by Germany and the United States. Finally, Britain's diplomatic isolation, which Lord Salisbury approvingly called the "splendid isolation" in 1896, had grown increasingly uncomfortable. Britain had no reliable allies in 1898, and it was disliked by many in Europe and America, not least for its actions in maintaining the Empire, such as the Jameson Raid in South

Africa in 1895, which was a failed attempt to overthrow the Afrikaner government. All of these are reasons why Bond would feel troubled about the future.

Page 11. Panel 2. This is an opium den, and those long instruments the men are holding and smoking are opium pipes.

Guide: "Who's staying here, Miss?"

Panel 3: Guide: "Whom are you seeking here?"

Murray: "Thank you for your great help."

Page 12. Panel 2. Ms. Murray is speaking to Allan Quatermain, the hero of fourteen of H. Rider Haggard's books, the most famous of which was the first, *King Solomon's Mines* (1885). Quatermain was one of the prototypical square-jawed Great White Adventurers, journeying among native races in remote locations on Earth. Through Allan Quatermain Haggard had an enormous amount of influence on later pulp and adventure fiction; characters from Edgar Rice Burroughs' John Carter and George Lucas' and Philip Kaufman's Indiana Jones can trace their lineage to Allan Quatermain.

In Quatermain's second appearance, *Allan Quatermain* (1887), he dies of a lung injury. Haggard went on to write a dozen more novels featuring Quatermain, but all of them were retrofitted into Quatermain's career before he died. His appearance here in a Cairo opium den is another of Moore's changes to the fates of the original characters. The explanation for the change is given in Chapter 1 of "Allan and the Sundered Veil," on Page 157.

Panel 11. Mina: "Get off!"

Guide: "Come here, woman! We are not that ugly. That's just a glass. You won't feel a thing."

The meaning of the word "glass," in this context, is unclear.

Panel 12. Fat Guy: "Come on...be nice to us."

Page 13. **Panel 1**. Slim Guy: "You are going to like this. We are his darlings."

Panel 3: Slim Guy: "...yes, that's better."

Panel 4: Slim Guy: "I swear to God."

Panel 5: Quatermain: "That's enough!"

Panel 6: Quatermain: "...leave her alone or I'll crack your heads open."

Panel 7: Fat Guy: "...he's exaggerating ...just look at him. He's a destroyer."

Presumably "destroyer" is idiomatic for being an opium or drug addict.

Slim Guy: "You live like a dead man. Among gnats."

Panel 8: Slim Guy: "I'll make a gnat out of you."

Panel 9. Quatermain's revolver, seen clearly in this panel, is unusual. It has nipples protruding from the rear of each chamber, which indicates that the gun is a black-powder weapon; each chamber must be manually loaded with powder and ball, as opposed to having individual cartridges loaded into it. The weapon has nine chambers, where most revolvers have six. And, finally, the revolver has two barrels, with the lower barrel being as wide as the first.

The only revolver with all of these features is a LeMat, an unusual and rare revolver developed in 1860 by Dr. François A. Le Mat. Over a thousand were sold to the Confederate Army during the American Civil War. Its presence here is curious as the Le Mat was archaic by 1898, cased ammunition having been introduced in the 1870s, and in the list of guns which Quatermain brings on the expedition in *King Solomon's Mines* the only handguns included are Colts. But Quatermain encounters Edgar Rice Burroughs' John Carter, a Confederate veteran, in "Allan and the Sundered Veil" (see below), and it's possible that Carter gave Quatermain a Le Mat before leaving.

Kevin O'Neill notes:

> The anachronistic revolver I chose as something Quatermain would carry for protection having sold his own weapons to fuel his drug habit.

> The John Carter/Confederate connection is another accident, but an amusing one.

Panel 12: Fat Guy: "Son of a bitch, you killed my brother... I´ll tear your heart apart."

Page 14. Panel 1. Fat Guy: "You damned English...dirty..."

Panel 2: Fat Guy: "Son of a whore!"

Panel 3: Fat Guy: "You'll not stay tired. You are going to..."

Panel 4: Fat Guy: "...die?"

Panel 8: Fat Guy: "My friends, they have killed me! ....don´t let them escape!"

Page 16. This is the *Nautilus*, the submarine of Jules Verne's Captain Nemo. This is not, however, what the original *Nautilus* looked like, but rather is Kevin O'Neill's design. Verne describes the *Nautilus*, in *Twenty Thousand Leagues Under the Sea*, as "a huge fish of steel" with a "blackish back...smooth, polished, without scales...made of riveted plates." In *The Mysterious Island* the *Nautilus* is described as "a long cigar-shaped object...similar in shape to an enormous whale...about 250 feet long, and rose about ten or twelve above the water."

This newer version differs from the original in several ways. There is the presence of the symbol between the *Nautilus'* "eyes" that resembles the question mark *leitmotif* of the *League*. There are the tentacles, which on Page 99 are shown to be more than just decorative. (The nautilus, a mollusk, does have tentacle-like arms.) There is the lack of the triangle-shaped spur on the nose of the *Nautilus*, which in *Twenty Thousand Leagues Under the Sea* allowed the submarine to sink ships and kill the "cruel, mischievous" cachalots. And there is the overall squid-like design, a possible reference to the Cthulhu Mythos stories of H.P. Lovecraft (1890-1937), in which aquatic imagery and design are the hallmark of the evil alien god Cthulhu.

The *Nautilus* of *Twenty Thousand Leagues* and *Mysterious Island* was scuttled at the end of *Mysterious Island*. It may be that the *Nautilus* of *The League of Extraordinary Gentlemen* is a second submarine which Nemo has built.

Kevin O'Neill notes:
> Yes, this is a new Nautilus to replace original. The question mark symbol between the eyes is in fact "Vishnu's conch-shell signifying the primordial sound of the origin of existence." (*Forms of the Formless: The Hindu Vision*, Alistair Shearer, Thames and Hudson LTD, London, 1993)

> On the upper deck of the Nautilus is a trident. This is "Shiva's trident (trishula) symbolizing the three-in-one at the heart of creation." (*Forms of the Formless*, Shearer)

> I designed the Nautilus to resemble a giant (rather Nautiloid-like) squid encircling a sperm whale. The design allows the craft to separate into two distinct (squid or whale) craft. This facility has yet to be shown.

Page 17. Panel 3. This is Captain Nemo, from Jules Verne's *Vingt Mille Lieues Sous les Mers* (Twenty Thousand Leagues Under the Sea, 1870), *L'Île Mystérieuse* (The Mysterious Island,1875), and *Voyage à Travers l'Impossible* (Journey Through the Impossible, 1882).

The popular image of Captain Nemo is of an older white man. More people are familiar with Captain Nemo through the various film versions of *Twenty Thousand Leagues* than through Verne's books, and in the films Nemo has always been played by white actors, most notably James Mason in the 1954 movie version of *Twenty Thousand Leagues*. Verne originally intended Nemo to be a wealthy Polish count whose daughters had been raped and whose wife and father were killed by the Russians during the 1863 Polish insurrection. However, Russia had proved to be a very lucrative market for Verne's stories, and Pierre-Jules Hetzel, Verne's publisher, legitimately feared that Czar Alexander II would ban *Twenty Thousand Leagues* if it portrayed Nemo as a Polish nationalist. Verne reached a compromise with Hetzel and kept Nemo's ethnicity nebulous. In *Twenty Thousand Leagues* Nemo is described in this way:

> The second unknown man deserves a more detailed description. A disciple of Gratiolet or Engel could read his open physiognomy. I immediately recognised his dominating qualites: his confidence, for he held his head nobly on an arc formed by the line of his shoulders, and his black eyes looked at me with a cold assurance; his calm, for his skin, pale rather than colored, exhibited the quietness of his blood; his energy, which was seen in the quick contraction of his muscles; and finally his courage, for his great respiration implied a big heart.

> I judged that this man could be trusted, for his close looks and his calm seemed to reflect deep thoughts, and that the homogeneity of expressions in the gestures of the body and face, following an observation of his physiognomy, resulted an inscrutable frankness.

> I felt myself involuntarily reassured in his presence, and this augured well for our interview.

> This person had thirty-five or fifty years, I was unable to judge more closely. He was tall, with a

> wide forehead, a straight nose, a clearly drawn
> mouth, magnificent teeth, fine hands, a lengthy and
> eminent body...all of which seemed worthy to serve
> such a high and fascinated soul. This man formed
> certainly the most admirable type that I had ever
> met.

The image of Nemo which accompanied this passage in the first edition of *Twenty Thousand Leagues* was drawn by Alphonse de Neuville, and clearly shows Nemo to be a white man.

However, when Verne wrote *The Mysterious Island* from 1871-1873, he changed that. The Nemo of *Island* is an Indian, driven to misanthropy by British injustice. Verne, in *The Mysterious Island*, describes Nemo's origin in this way:

> Captain Nemo was an Indian, Prince Dakkar, the
> son of a rajah of the then independent territory of
> Bundelkund and a nephew of the Indian hero,
> Tippu-Sahib. His father sent him to Europe when
> he was ten years old so that he would receive a
> thorough education and with the secret hope that
> he would fight one day with equal arms against
> those whom he considered to be the oppressors of
> his country...
>
> In 1857, the great Sepoy revolt erupted. Prince
> Dakkar was its soul. He organized the immense
> upheaval. He put his talents and his riches to the
> service of this cause. He sacrificed himself; he
> fought in the front lines; he risked his life like the
> humblest of those heroes who had risen up to free
> their country; he was wounded ten times in twenty
> battles but could not find death when the last soldiers
> of the fight for independence fell under English
> bullets.

Bundelkhand–Verne wrote "Bundelkund" in error–was, during the British rule, located in the eastern section of the Central India Agency. Today it is a part of Madhya Pradesh, in north central India.

"Tippu-Sahib" is Tipu Sultan (1753-1799), one of India's more interesting figures. Tipu, the Sultan of Mysore, was a vocal supporter of the principles of the American and French Revolution while also owning a mechanical tiger which he used to torture his enemies. He was also the first man known to use rockets in war. Tipu Sultan was the son of Haidar Ali (1721-1782), who took the throne of Mysore in 1761, fought the British in the First Mysore War (1766-1769), and forced them to sign a treaty of mutual assistance. Haidar Ali received no support from the British in his own war with the Marathas, another powerful Indian ethnic group, and so allied himself with France and attacked the British in the Carnatic in 1780 in the Second Mysore War. Haidar Ali was killed in 1782 and Tipu Sultan was forced to make peace with the British in 1783 when French aid to Mysore ceased. In 1789 Tipu Sultan attacked the city of Travancore, starting the Third Mysore War, but he was defeated in 1792 by Lord Cornwallis. In 1799 Tipu, deep in correspondence and negotiation with the French, refused to cooperate with the British Governor General, Richard Wellesley, in his efforts to suppress French influence in India. The British sent two armies into Mysore and drove Tipu into Seringapatam, his capital, and took it by storm. Tipu died, bravely fighting in a breach in the walls.

The great Sepoy revolt, also known as The Great Mutiny, was the culmination of years of Indian dissatisfaction with British rule. The sepoys were the Asian troops in the armies of the British East India Company, which was, for all intents and purposes, the reigning British military power in India. There were some regular British Army units in India in 1857, but they were outnumbered by the East India Company sepoys by around seven to one. But the sepoys were commanded by a British officer corps, most of whom were incompetent and/or venal and/or cruel, and there was a great deal of unrest in the native armies who felt that their religion was disrespected by their British overlords and who were generally poorly treated by the British officers. The Minié rifle cartridge was introduced at this time. The cartridge had to be bitten for loading, and a rumor spread among the disaffected elements of the army that the grease used in the cartridge included the fat of cows and pigs. This rumor—which later investigations showed had some truth to it—was immensely offensive to both Hindus, for whom the cow was a sacred creature, and to Muslims, to whom the pig is an unclean animal. When eighty-five sepoys in Meerut refused to accept the new cartridges, they were disgraced and imprisoned. An Indian regiment released them and killed as many Europeans as they could, prompting fourteen months of massacres and counter-massacres. The Great Mutiny left a deep mark on the British psyche, with heated debate following as to the cause of the mutiny. Conservatives such as Prime Minister Disraeli, who argued that the East India Company's reforms had led to the Mutiny, won the debate, and the British administration in India became markedly more conservative in tone.

Besides Nemo's ethnicity and personal history, there are other inconsistencies and contradictions between *Twenty Thousand Leagues Under the Sea* and *The Mysterious Island*. *Twenty Thousand Leagues* is set between 1867 and 1868, while *Island* begins in 1865 and ends in 1867, although in *Island* Nemo claims to have been living on Lincoln Island for ten years. Similarly, the racial make-up of the crew of the *Nautilus* changes from mixed in *Twenty Thousand Leagues* to Indian in *The Mysterious Island*.

The League of Extraordinary Gentlemen further exacerbates at least one of these discrepancies. Bundelkhand, Prince Dakkar's home, did not come under British control until 1817. If Dakkar was sent away from Bundelkhand by his father, the Rajah, at age 10, Nemo would have to be at least 91 at the time of *League*. Kevin O'Neill draws Nemo as being some decades younger than this.

By joining Nemo, Mina Murray and Allan Quatermain in the same story, Moore is working within the tradition of inter-textual crossovers. As seen in the "Crossovers" essay, the idea of the characters of different creators intermingling in one story was not a new one in 1898.

The shell on the front of Nemo's turban is a nautilus, the sea mollusk after which Nemo's submarine is named.

"Memesahib," or "Mem-Sahib," is a Hindi word used by Hindus and Muslims in colonial India when addressing or speaking to a European married woman or one of social or official status; "sahib" is the word used when addressing a male.

Nemo's reluctance to "have women on my ship" is a reference to the centuries-old superstition among sailors that a woman's presence on board a ship brought bad luck to the ship.

On Page 9, Panel 2, Campion Bond makes reference to Nemo's "inflammation of the brain." The Victorians often blamed behavior they disapproved of on pseudo-physical ailments, so that a woman acting in "manly" ways would be described as having "hysteria" brought on by "tilting of the womb," as Dr. Jekyll describes Mina on the back cover of Issue #5. Eccentric behavior would be attributed to "inflammation of the brain." In the late Nineteenth century this phrase was used as a synonym for meningitis, but also as a catch-all explanation for eccentric and anti-social behavior. Dr. Robson Roose, the personal physician of Lord Randolph Churchill, stated in 1875 that "chronic inflammation of the brain attacks persons of exhausted habits, brought on by excesses and irregular living."

There is no specific textual reference in *Twenty Thousand Leagues* or *The Mysterious Island* to Nemo suffering from a brain inflammation, but it does work as a Victorian explanation for some of Nemo's peculiar behavior. In Chapter 21 of *Twenty Thousand Leagues,* Nemo is "plunged in a musical ecstasy" so that he cannot hear what is said to him. And in Chapter 21 of *Twenty Thousand Leagues,* Nemo, angered by something, undergoes what might be called a fit:

> Captain Nemo was before me, but I did not know him. His face was transfigured. His eyes flashed sullenly; his teeth were set; his stiff body, clenched fists, and head shrunk between his shoulders, betrayed the violent agitation that pervaded his whole frame. He did not move. My glass, fallen from his hands, had rolled at his feet.

Panel 4. "Mohammedan" is an English term for Muslims that came into usage in the Eighteenth century. By the late Eighteenth century it was one of several terms, including "Muhammadan" and "Muhammedan," used to describe those of the Muslim faith. It is in character for Nemo, who is not just an Indian but a Sikh and a Hindu (see Panel 5 below), to be contemptuous of Muslims; relations between Muslims and Sikhs and Hindus in India have traditionally been fractious.

Panel 5. Man: "Don't let the white devils escape...the damned tall one...isn't he..."

The "isn't he" is presumably the pursuing man recognizing Nemo.

The Captain Nemo of *The League of Extraordinary Gentlemen* is the first Nemo to be shown wearing Indian clothing. His depiction here may have been influenced by the Captain Nemo seen in the Japanese anime *Fushigi no Umi no Nadia* (Nadia: The Secret of the Blue Water, 1990), a television series about an orphan searching for her father at the start of the Twentieth century who is rescued at sea by Captain Nemo. Although the Nemo of *Fushigi no Umi* is white, his jacket is similar to the one Nemo wears in *The League of Extraordinary Gentlemen*.

The issue of Nemo's ethnicity is one that Moore clearly put some thought into. Moore has said in interviews that he originally thought of Nemo as looking like James Mason until Kevin O'Neill pointed out to him that Nemo was an Indian. In *League* Nemo is portrayed as a Sikh and a Hindu. Moore has said in interviews that Nemo must be a Sikh, the most warlike of the Indian peoples. This is represented visually, in O'Neill's choice of the turban, which is mandatory for all orthodox Sikhs. Nemo's long hair and beard are hallmarks of the Sikhs, the majority of whom are *kes-dhari*, "one who wears hair uncut." And as can be seen on Page 21, Panel 1, Nemo is also a Hindu, having a statue of Siva-Nataraja(the Hindu god of the dance) on board the *Nautilus*.

It might seem impossible for Nemo to be both Hindu and Sikh, as the two are separate faiths. Moreover, Tipu Sultan was a Muslim, which means that Nemo, his nephew, should have followed the same faith. But there are several examples in Indian history of Moghul (Muslim) princes and kings marrying the daughters of Rajput (Hindu) kings, as Akbar the Great (1542-1605) did. The purpose of these marriages was often to solidify alliances between kingdoms in order to face a perceived common enemy, which the British would certainly have qualified as in Tipu Sultan's eyes.

There are also historical examples of Indians being both Hindu and Sikh. In the Punjab region of India, the home to most Sikhs, Hindu families sometimes initiate their eldest son into the Sikh faith; Sikhism is seen as a martial religion and those who follow the faith are seen as defenders of the land. Too, Sikhism evolved from Hinduism and shares some of the same rituals, such as the *shradh*, a ceremony designed to aid deceased forbears, so that by the Nineteenth century it was not uncommon to find Sikhs worshiping in Hindu temples and vice versa.

Kevin O'Neill notes:
> Regarding Nemo's appearance, I have never seen *Nadia: The Secret of the Blue Water* TV series. Nemo's image grew from re-reading Verne and telephone conversations with Alan- and our desire to stress Nemo's ethnic and spiritual origins.

Panel 6. Man: "You will tell us..."

Page 19. Panel 5. Nemo's response here is an echoing of Nemo's response in Chapter 10 of *Twenty Thousand Leagues*, when Professor Arronax, the novel's narrator, asks Nemo his name. Nemo's response is, "I am nothing to you but Captain Nemo; and you and your companions are nothing to me but the passengers of the *Nautilus*."

Nemo is not the character's real name. Nemo is Latin for "no one," and the Captain's use of this pseudonym in *Twenty Thousand Leagues* is most likely a reference by Verne to Ulysses' ploy in *The Odyssey* to deceive the Cyclops Polyphemus. When Polyphemus asks Ulysses' name, Ulysses says his name is "Noman."

Page 20. Panel 3. The scars on Quatermain's belly may have come from the lion attack Quatermain mentions in Chapter 1 of *King Solomon's Mines*, the attack which left him with a recurring pain in his left leg.

Kevin O'Neill notes:

> Yes, I read all the Haggard Quatermain stories I could find to illustrate his ravaged body as accurately as possible. Strictly speaking he should walk with a limp, and perhaps be less nimble than I've indicated – but then our Quatermain did not die and is in pretty good physical shape for a man of his age.

Page 21. Panel 1. The "diamond mines" Quatermain raves about are King Solomon's, which Quatermain found after many fierce adventures. "Umslopogaas" was Quatermain's brave and noble Zulu companion, whose final fate is revealed in *Allan Quatermain* and is referred to in "Allan and the Sundered Veil."

The steering wheel of the Nautilus, seen behind Nemo and Murray, is a statue of the god Siva (Shiva) in his identity as Siva-Nataraja, the god of the cosmic dance. Siva is the Hindu god of destruction and of the cosmic dance, and one of the three most important deities of the Hindu religion. It makes a certain amount of sense that Nemo, who is both warrior and philosopher/scholar, would worship Siva, who embodies those characteristics. Plus, as Moore pointed out in an interview, making the steering wheel of the *Nautilus* into a statue of the dancing Siva is good design sense. This is another deviation from the description of the *Nautilus* in the Verne novels.

Panel 2. In the American Old West certain gunfighters and explorers read about their exploits in the pulp press, with William Cody living to read Ned Buntline's "Buffalo Bill" stories. This occurred to Sherlock Holmes in "The Valley of Fear," and apparently, in the world of *League*, Verne's novels about Nemo and Haggard's novels about Quatermain were available.

Panel 4. Mina's pointing at her neck while being evasive about her "qualifications" is a perhaps unconscious hint on her part about what her real qualifications are. Her experience with Dracula has hardened her to the point where she is more than the equal of the other members of the League.

Page 22. Panel 1. The elaborate Parisian cityscape is a reference by Moore and O'Neill to Jules Verne's *Paris in the Twentieth Century*. *Paris* was written by Verne in 1863 but was not published until 1995; Pierre-Jules Hetzel, Verne's publisher, believed the novel to be an unrealistic failure and rejected it. *Paris* is a remarkable feat of anticipation, predicting overpopulation, skyscrapers, electric street lights, streets crowded with internal-combustion-powered automobiles, elevated driverless mass transit, an electric lighthouse at the location of the future Eiffel Tower, fax machines, and photocopiers. What O'Neill has drawn here is a steampunk landscape lifted from *Paris*.

Kevin O'Neill notes:
> I wanted Paris to be more adventurous in design than London, reflecting the general British reluctance to embrace outré style.

Panel 3. The "'Mysterious Island' affair" is a reference to Verne's book of the same name.

Page 23. Panel 1. The Chevalier C. Auguste Dupin was created by Edgar Allen Poe and appeared in three stories: "Murders in the Rue Morgue" (*Graham's Lady's and Gentlemen's Magazine*, Apr. 1841), "The Mystery of Marie Roget" (*Snowden's Lady's Companion*, 2 Nov. 1842), and "The Purloined Letter" (*The Gift*, 1844). Dupin is a brilliant French amateur detective whose place in the history of detective literature is an important one. Through Dupin and his stories Poe created and established many of the conventions of detective fiction, including the locked room mystery, the impossible crime, the armchair detective, the use of a secondary narrative voice to which the Great Detective can voice his conclusions, the primacy of deduction in solving a crime, and most significantly the figure of the Great Detective himself, the brilliant and solitary crime-solver.

Like Conan Doyle's Sherlock Holmes, Dupin was modeled on a real person. Dupin took his name and insightful mind from André-Marie-Jean-Jacques Dupin (1783-1865), a well-known legal expert who was reputed to be a walking encyclopedia. Dupin took his hobby and interest in crime from Eugène François Vidocq (1775-1857), a French criminal who rose from an informer for the Parisian police to the head of the Sureté, the Parisian police force in 1812. Vidocq wrote his autobiography, the *Mémoires de Vidocq* (1828-1829), a heavily fictionalized account of his own exploits. The *Mémoires de Vidocq* was very popular and created the stereotype in French literature of the Great Detective.

Arthur Conan Doyle actually referred to Dupin in a Holmes story. During "A Study in Scarlet" (*Beeton's Christmas Annual*, 1887), Holmes astounds Watson by correctly deducing a number of facts about him just through careful observation. Watson responds as follows:

> "It is simple enough as you explain it," I said, smiling. "You remind me of Edgar Allan Poe's Dupin. I had no idea that such individuals did exist outside of stories."

> Sherlock Holmes rose and lit his pipe. "No doubt you think that you are complimenting me in comparing me to Dupin," he observed. "Now, in my opinion, Dupin was a very inferior fellow. That trick of his of breaking in on his friends' thoughts with an apropos remark after a quarter of an hour's silence is really very showy and superficial. He had some analytical genius, no doubt; but he was by no means such a phenomenon as Poe appeared to imagine."

Doyle intended this to be tongue-in-cheek; his own opinion of Poe and Dupin was much higher than Holmes', and Holmes himself breaks in on Watson's thoughts on more than one occasion.

It might be questioned how Dupin could still be alive, given that his first appearance was in 1841. But if he were thirty years old in "Murders in the Rue Morgue," he'd be in his late eighties during the events of *League*, leaving him elderly but not extraordinarily so.

Panels 5-6, Page 24 Panels 1-2. Dupin is recounting the events of "Murders in the Rue Morgue."

Panel 4. The "Whitechapel fiend" is Jack the Ripper, who preyed on the women of London's Whitechapel district.

Panel 5. Anna "Nana" Coupeau was created by Emile Zola and appeared in *L'Assommoir* (1877) and *Nana* (1880). Anna Coupeau is a woman who is driven to prostitution by the alcoholism of her parents and becomes, to use one of Zola's images, a golden fly that rises from the dunghills of society to enter the windows of palaces and infect their inhabitants; Nana's rise and fall parallels that of the French empire itself.

Panel 6. A "demi-mondaine" is a prostitute, more specifically a kept woman.

Page 25. Panel 3. Although it is never overtly stated in this *League* series, Mina's reluctance to remove her scarf is due to the lasting scar left on her throat by Dracula's bite. As is seen in the second *League* series, the scar is not two clean puncture marks, but rather horrid jagged slashes, caused by Dracula's teeth, which are saw-like, as a real vampire bat's are.

Page 27. Panel 8. Dupin: "Excuse me, ma'am."

Panel 9. Streetwalker: "Good evening, Daddy. You again?"

Dupin: "I'm looking for a woman. A small brunette. She was with a client..."

Page 28. Panel 1. Streetwalker: "Yeah, I saw her steal my client! She went in that direction with Henry the Englishman not two minutes ago!"

Dupin: "This Henry is a strapping man, yes? A true gorilla?"

Panel 2. Streetwalker: "Henry? He's a small Englishman. He has a place on the corner."

Dupin: "Thank you, ma'am, you were very helpful."

Panel 5. The object thrown out the window is an umbrella stand made out of an elephant's foot, a grotesque piece of furniture which was in vogue during the Victorian era.

Page 30. "Edward" is Edward Hyde, of Robert Louis Stevenson's *The Strange Case of Dr. Jekyll and Mr. Hyde* (1886). In the novel the good but repressed Dr. Jekyll uses drugs to separate his "libertine side," his id, from his normal self. This leads to the emergence of Jekyll's evil side, Edward Hyde, who indulges himself in various unspecified depravities.

In the book Hyde is younger than Jekyll. Hyde is also stunted and nimble, unlike the monstrous and huge Hyde of *League*. However, by the end of the novel Hyde's size has increased. In "Henry Jekyll's Full Statement of the Case," Jekyll says

> That part of me which I had the power of projecting, had lately been much exercised and nourished; it had seemed to me of late as though the body of Edward Hyde had grown in stature, as though (when I wore that form) I were conscious of a more generous tide of blood; and I began to spy a danger that, if this were much prolonged, the balance of my nature might be permanently overthrown....

Hyde dies at the end of *Dr. Jekyll and Mr. Hyde*, committing suicide rather than face the gallows. Hyde's continued existence and monstrous size are Moore's deviations from the original source material. (Jekyll himself makes note of the change in Hyde's size on Page 134, Panel 3.)

Dr. Jekyll and Mr. Hyde admits of many interpretations; it has been interpreted as, variously, a story about the struggle between id, ego, and super-ego, an allegory of the struggle between the proletariat and the bourgeoisie, and even an allegory of *fin-de-siècle* homosexual panic. A further interpretation is that the novel is an allegory of evolution, with the very proper Jekyll being quite human and the unrepressed and spontaneous Hyde being monkey-like and therefore a step down the moral and evolutionary ladder.

Hyde's notably simian appearance in *League* may be a reference to Gustav Klimt's "Beethoven Frieze" (1902). The painting, an allegory about man's search for happiness, is about a knight's quest for the Holy Grail; he finds it in the arms of a woman after defeating the "Hostile Powers." One of the Powers, the giant Typhoeus, is visually similar to Kevin O'Neill's Hyde.

The heavy cane which Hyde carries is the same kind which he used to kill Sir Danvers Carew in *Dr. Jekyll and Mr. Hyde*:

> He had in his hand a heavy cane, with which he was trifling; but he answered never a word, and seemed to listen with an ill-contained impatience. And then all of a sudden he broke out in a great flame of anger, stamping with his foot, brandishing the cane, and carrying on (as the maid described it) like a madman. The old gentleman took a step back, with the air of one very much surprised and a trifle hurt; and at that Mr. Hyde broke out of all bounds, and clubbed him to the earth. And next moment, with ape-like fury, he was trampling his victim under foot, and hailing down a storm of blows, under which the bones were audibly shattered and the body jumped upon the roadway...
>
> It was two o'clock when she came to herself and called for the police. The murderer was gone long ago; but there lay his victim in the middle of the

> lane, incredibly mangled. The stick with which the
> deed had been done, although it was of some rare
> and very tough and heavy wood, had broken in the
> middle under the stress of this insensate cruelty;
> and one splintered half had rolled in the
> neighbouring gutter - the other, without doubt, had
> been carried away by the murderer.

This cane is visually similar to the cane Frederic March used as Hyde in the Rouben Mamoulian-directed *Dr. Jekyll and Mr. Hyde* (1931). That film also made plain the evolutionary allegory between the Jekyll-to-Hyde transformation, with Frederic March's Hyde being particularly simian in appearance and becoming increasingly monstrous with every transformation. In the film, as in *League*, any sort of stress triggers the change from Jekyll to Hyde.

The "Edison/Teslaton" insignia on the junction box is a clue to the source of the advanced science of *League*'s England. Thomas Edison (1847-1931) was a brilliant inventor and self-promoter who in 1879, with his associates and employees, developed and created carbonized cotton thread as a filament for conducting electricity. This eventually led to the development of the electronic vacuum tube, and was directly responsible for electric lamps and lighting.

Edison's electronic inventions were powered by direct current, that is, an electric current flowing in one direction only and constant in value/power. Nicola Tesla (1856-1943) was an electrical engineer who worked for Edison and later became his rival. In 1888 Tesla invented the alternating current induction motor, which made possible the universal transmission and distribution of electricity. Alternating current is electric current which reverses its direction at regularly recurring intervals; Tesla's alternating current generators are the basis for the modern electrical power industry.

Kevin O'Neill notes:

> Hyde's simian appearance was developed from the [first
> issue's original] back cover (originally drawn as a
> promotional ad) image of a monstrous Hyde hand dwarfing
> the others. Our Hyde is physically intimidating and morally

complicated. The only similarity to Gustave Klimt's "Beethoven Frieze" image is his dark colouring, which was Ben Dimagmaliw's choice.

In real life Tesla had a difficult time persuading people to make use of alternating current, for Edison was much more popular and well-known at the time, and Edison felt that alternating current was dangerous to human beings and used his position to discredit Tesla. In the world of *League*, however, a way was seemingly found to combine the two, with the obvious result of technology becoming much more advanced than it really was.

Page 31. Panels 1-4. The narrative frame here and on page 37 is Mina's letter to Campion Bond. The narrative of *Dracula* is similarly framed, with journal and diary entries, letters, and memoirs being the vehicle through which the story is told.

Panel 4. The gun Dupin shoots Hyde with is a pepperbox revolver. Introduced in the early 1800s, the pepperbox was a type of revolver which had a number of barrels bored in a circle in a single piece of metal similar to the cylinder of a modern revolver. The pepperbox worked in much the same way as an ordinary revolver, with the entire cylinder revolving to bring each barrel under the hammer for firing. However, pepperboxes were clumsy, unreliable, and muzzle-heavy, and fell out of style after the 1840s, although they were still being made in the 1860s. Mark Twain wrote about the pepperbox in *Roughing It*:

> It was a cheerful weapon...sometimes all six barrels would go off at once, and then there was no safe place in all the region round about it, but behind it.

However, the pepperbox is quite appropriate as Dupin's weapon, being from the same era as he.

Page 35. Panel 2. Laudanum originally meant any preparation in which opium was the main ingredient, but by the late Nineteenth century it meant a mixture of opium and alcohol, usually wine.

Page 36. Panel 4. Moore and O'Neill's policy for the dating of events in the world of *League* is that the events of a story or novel occurred in the year in which the story or novel was published. By this method *Dracula* took place in 1897, which is why Dupin says that Mina's "certain events" took place "last year."

However, the final Note in *Dracula* states that "seven years ago we all went through the flames," and mentions Mina's and Jonathan's son Quincey.

It can be reasoned, though, that just as Dr. Watson was an unreliable narrator, fudging certain facts in his accounts of Holmes' doings, so too were certain pieces of information in *Dracula* deliberately obscured or altered.

Page 37. Panel 2. Note Hyde's prehensile toes.

Page 38. The "OXO" on the dirigible in the upper right is a British brand of liquid meat extract; originally created by Dr. Justus Liebig, it was marketed in Britain as "Liebig Company's Extract of Beef" starting in 1865, becoming OXO brand in 1899. It is still sold today as just-add-water beef stock cubes.

The presence of the elephant being slung ashore is curious. There were a few elephants in Victorian literature, from the steam-powered elephant-shaped vehicle of Jules Verne's *Le Maison à Vapeur* (The Steam House, 1881), visible on the back cover of the *League* hardcover, to the elephant-shaped aircraft of Francis T. Montgomery's *The Wonderful Electric Elephant* (1903) and *On a Lark to the Planets* (1904).

Similarly, the locomotive being hauled ashore draws comparisons to other locomotives of the era, including the Cannonball Express, the fastest train in the world in 1900 and the train for which Casey Jones is known, and the titular train of Rudyard Kipling's ".007" (*The Day's Work,* 1898). The number 5 on the side of the train rules out both of those trains, as the Cannonball Express was #382 and Kipling's engine was #.007. A likelier source for engine #5 is *The*

Wild Wild West, an American television show created by Michael Garrison and airing from 1965-1970. *The Wild Wild West* was a steampunk Western in which two American Secret Service agents used a technologically-advanced railroad car to adventure through the American West. The railroad car's engine was #5.

Kevin O'Neill notes:
> The elephant being hoisted ashore simply lends character and scale to the scene. Elephants were also very popular in Victorian and Edwardian England. For similar reasons I showed a steam locomotive being unloaded.

Page 39. Panel 1. "Inspector Donovan" is Dick Donovan, the creation of James Edward Preston Muddock (1843-1934). Muddock was a journalist and writer who produced dozens of works of fiction and non-fiction, including over fifty detective novels and short story collections. Muddock used "Dick Donovan" as his pseudonym. "Dick Donovan" was also the narrator of many of Muddock's stories and the protagonist in about half of them. Donovan appeared in fifteen short story collections from 1888 to 1899, starting with *The Man-Hunter: Stories from the Note-Book of a Detective* (1888). As a detective Donovan was a direct descendant of Inspector Bucket, from Charles Dickens' *Bleak House* (1853), and Sergeant Cuff, from Wilkie Collins' *The Moonstone* (1868). Donovan is a stolid and dogged detective who brings down criminals through persistence and cunning rather than through flights of deductive genius.

Panel 2. The "Hetty Duncan murder" was solved by Inspector Donovan in the 1890 short story, "Who Poisoned Hetty Duncan?"

Panel 3. "The Great Detective" is the title commonly given to Sherlock Holmes. Holmes "died" with Professor Moriarty in the story, "The Adventure of the Final Problem" (*Strand Magazine*, December 1893). As mentioned in the note to Page 36, Panel 4, the dating method for *League* is that the events of a story or novel occur in the year in which the story or novel was published. But "The Final Problem" is quite specifically dated by Doyle as occurring in April and May of 1891, which is why Campion Bond dates Holmes' death as taking place "seven years ago."

Moore and O'Neill's method of dating creates a further discrepancy regarding Holmes. In "The Adventure of the Empty House" (*Collier's*, September 26, 1903), Holmes returns, seemingly from the dead. The story is dated by Doyle in the spring of 1894. But in *League*, set in 1898, everyone believes that Holmes is still dead.

In this case it must just be accepted that in the world of *League* "The Final Problem" takes place in 1891 when the story says it does and that "The Adventure of the Empty House" takes place in 1903 when it was published.

"Robur" is the creation of Jules Verne and appeared in two books: *Robur le Conquerant* (Robur the Conqueror, 1886) and *Maître du Monde* (Master of the World, 1904). In *Robur the Conqueror,* Robur, a brilliant engineer and vehement proponent of heavier-than-air travel, invents a technologically advanced "flying machine," the *Albatross*, and uses it to kidnap several partisans of lighter-than-air travel and take them around the world. In *Master of the World,* Robur returns, now a dangerous megalomaniac intent on conquering the world.

Robur's "hidden stronghold" is in the Great Eyry, an inaccessible mountain in the American Appalachians. *League* is set after the events of *Robur*, when Robur has become misanthropic and insane.

"Prime Minister Plantagenet Palliser" is from Anthony Trollope's seven Palliser or Political novels. Palliser first appeared as a minor character in *The Small House at Allington* (1864) and then debuted as a major character in *Can You Forgive Her?* (1865). Plantagenet Pallier, one of Trollope's "perfect gentlemen," is a politician and is the heir to the Duke of Omnium. He eventually gains the dukedom and becomes the Prime Minister in *The Prime Minister* (1876). In real life the British Prime Minister in 1898 was Robert Arthur Talbot Gascoÿne Cecil, the third Marquis of Salisbury, but, again, history in the world of the *League* is somewhat different than it is here.

Panel 4. "The astronomer Lavell" is a reference to H.G. Wells' *The*

War of the Worlds (1898). In Book One of *War,* "Lavelle of Java" is said to have "set the wires of the astronomical exchange palpitating with the amazing intelligence of a huge outbreak of incandescent gas" on Mars. This presages the imminent arrival of the Martians on Earth. The events of *War* are portrayed in the second *League* series.

"Reverend Septimus Harding" is from Anthony Trollope's seven Barsetshire books. Harding debuted in the first of the novels, *The Warden* (1855), and went on to appear in each of the Barsetshire novels. Harding is a gentle innocent, a long-suffering and good-natured old clergyman who is the warden of an almshouse.

"Miss Coote" is a reference to Rosa Belinda Coote, the creation of William Dugdale (1800-1868), the Professor Moriarty of Victorian back-alley pornography. Coote first appeared as the supposed author and narrator of Dugdale's *The Convent School, or Early Experiences of A Young Flagellant* (1876), a pornographic novel about flagellation, especially with birch wands. Letters from "Rosa Coote" then appeared in *The Pearl* from July 1879 to December 1880. *The Pearl* was one of the more notorious of the pornographic Victorian magazines. Rosa's letters, appearing in "Miss Coote's Confessions, or the Voluptuous Experiences of an Old Maid," were about her experiences being birched and as the granddaughter of Sir Eyre Coote, the general famous for his actions in East India. Finally, Rosa appeared as the heroine of anonymously-written pornographic novel, *The Yellow Room* (1891). "Coot" is an English word which in the Seventeenth century meant "to copulate."

Page 40. Panel 2. For information on "Hawley Griffin," see Page 41, Panel 3.

"Mann, Crossman & Paulin" is a kind of British ale; its brewery was not far from the Tower Bridge, in London's East End on Whitechapel Road, which may be the road Mina and Campion Bond are walking down.

Panel 3. Mina again touches her scarf, perhaps unconsciously, when thinking about her past.

Panel 4. The "Prospect of Whitby," located on Wapping Wall Road along the Thames, is one of London's oldest and most famous pubs, dating back to 1520. It is also the location of much of the action in *Dracula*, which is why Mina is upset by the site of the pub.

Page 41. Panel 1. Being loaded on to the *Nautilus* are a mine, at the top of the panel, and a torpedo or missile, on the right of the panel.

Presumably the men working on the *Nautilus* are its crew. In *Twenty Thousand Leagues* the crew of the *Nautilus* were multi-ethnic outcasts of many nations. In *Mysterious Island* the crew, now solely Indian in background, have passed away, leaving Nemo "the solitary survivor of all those who had taken refuge with him in the depths of the ocean." In between the events of *Mysterious Island* and *League* Nemo obviously formed a new crew. We will meet two of them on Page 79.

Panels 3-4. "Hawley Griffin" is the lead character from H.G. Wells' *The Invisible Man* (1897). In that novel "Griffin," a scientist, discovers a process to make himself invisible. Due to his greed and criminal nature he uses his invisibility for petty crimes, and is ultimately killed by a crowd.

In *The Invisible Man,* Griffin's first name is never given; Griffin is only referred to as "Griffin" or "Mr. Griffin." The first name of "Hawley" is Moore's invention. Moore has stated in interviews that he gave Griffin the first name of Hawley as a reference to the murderer Dr. Hawley Crippen, who poisoned his wife in 1910 and became one of the most notorious of England's pre-WWI murderers.

In *The Invisible Man,* Griffin is "almost an albino... a pink and white face and red eyes." The reason his university records do not confirm this is given below, on Page 50, Panel 3.

Panel 7. The painting or tapestry behind Nemo is Kali, the dread Black Woman. In the Hindu religion Kali is the goddess of destruction and of motherhood; Kali is motherhood in its destructive aspect, the mother who kills and devours the life she produces. Nemo has been shown to be a Hindu, and a statue of Siva-Nataraja can be seen Page 17, Panel 5. From this it might be guessed that Nemo is a Saivite, a worshiper of Siva, but the presence here of Kali in her most terrible aspect might indicate that Nemo is a worshiper of destruction in whatever form.

Page 42. Panel 1. The "Correctional Academy for Wayward Gentlewomen" appeared in Rosa Coote's stories in *The Pearl*; see the note for Panel 3 below.

"Schadenfreude" is a German word meaning, roughly, "malicious joy in one's heart at another's downfall."

Panel 3. "Miss Flaybum," like Rosa Coote, was a recurring character in Victorian pornography. Miss Flaybum predated Rosa Coote, however, first appearing in 1760 in the pornographic novel entitled *Sublime of Flagellation; in letters from Lady Termagant Flaybum, of Birch-Grove, to Lady Harriet Tickletail, of Bumfiddle-Hall : in which are introduced the beautiful tale of La coquette chatie, in French and English: and The boarding-school bumbrusher : or, The distresses of Laura*. Flaybum proved to be a popular character, appearing in a cartoon by the noted caricaturist and painter James Gillray, *Lady Termagent Flaybum going to give her Step Son a taste of her Dessert after Dinner, a Scene performed every day near Grosvenor Square to the annoyance of the neighbourhood* (1786). *Sublime of Flagellation* was reprinted, quite successfully, in 1872 as issue #6 of the *Library Illustrative of Social Progress*, a vehicle for new and reprinted pornography. When *The Pearl* began its run in 1879 Lady Flaybum appeared in it as the operator of the "Correctional Academy for Wayward Gentlewomen" which Rosa Coote attended to "further her education."

The name on the cab, "Barkas and Sons," is a reference to Barkis, from Charles Dickens' *David Copperfield* (1850). In the novel Barkis is a carrier who becomes Copperfield's friend and eventually marries the nurse Clara Peggotty.

Panel 5. A "punkah-wallah" is an Anglo-Indian compound word used during the years of the Raj in India. A "punkah" was a portable fan, and a "wallah" was, roughly, "a man who does something," and a "punkah-wallah," in colloquial usage, was a household servant who operated a portable fan.

Quatermain's words here are a joking reference to the stereotypical and possibly apocryphal advice given by Victorian mothers to their daughters, that the best way to endure the horrors of sex was to "lie back, close your eyes, and think of England."

Page 43. Panel 2. "Olive Chancellor" is from Henry James' *The Bostonians* (1886). In the novel Olive is a strong-willed American "new woman" who tries and fails to help her protegé Verena Tarrant. Some critics have seen a marked lesbian subtext in *The Bostonians*, which gives her presence here an added frisson.

Panel 3. "Katy Carr" is the heroine of Susan Coolidge's *What Katy Did* (1872), *What Katy Did At School* (1873), and *What Katy Did Next* (1886). Katy Carr is a head-strong and naughty child who falls from a swing and injures her back. Wheelchair-bound, she is at first despondent but through the "School of Pain" eventually learns to walk again and to accept domestic discipline.

Panels 4-5. "Becky Randall" is the title character of Kate Douglas Wiggin's *Rebecca of Sunnybrook Farm* (1903) and its sequel *More About Rebecca* (1907). Rebecca Rowena Randall is an orphan who grows up in Sunnybrook Farm but is eventually sent to Riverboro, Maine to stay with her two elderly, unmarried aunts. In Riverboro she makes friends, sells soap to help a poor family, and eventually meets her future husband.

Page 44. Panel 3. "Peine forte et dure," directly translated, means "pain, strong and hard." In England it was an official sentence of torture, beginning with the reign of Henry IV in the early Fifteenth century and continuing through 1772. This method was occasionally used in Scotland and Ireland and only rarely in America, most notably during the Salem (Massachusetts) witch trials of 1692. "Peine forte et dure" consisted of a great weight, usually stone blocks, being placed on the chest of the victim, and increasing amounts of the weight being placed there until the victim confessed or, in some cases, until the victim died, regardless of his or her statements. Inscribed at a bed's headboard it takes on a different meaning.

Page 45. Panel 1. Quatermain's wife is mentioned at the end of *Allan Quatermain* (1887), in Quatermain's final diary entry, where he writes about "the sweetest and most perfect woman that ever gladdened this grey earth." But Haggard gave no further details about her until *Allan's Wife* (1889), the story of how Quatermain and his childhood friend Stella Carson were reunited, how she saved his life, the pair fell in love, married, and then how she died giving birth to their son Harry.

Quatermain's son Harry is referred to in several of the Quatermain books, beginning with the first, *King Solomon's Mines* (1885), in which Quatermain states that Harry is one of the reasons why he writes down his adventures. Harry's death, from smallpox contracted while working in a hospital, is described in *Allan Quatermain*. Harry's death takes place "two years ago and more" before the events of *Allan Quatermain*, which take place about three years before the novel was published, while Stella's death, coming as it does at Harry's birth, must have occurred around twenty-five years before Harry's. So in the world of *League,* Stella's death took place around 1857, while Harry's took place at about 1882.

Panel 6. "Polly Whittier," better known as "Pollyanna," is the heroine of Eleanor H. Porter's *Pollyanna* (1913) and several sequels, only the first of which, *Pollyanna Grows Up* (1915), by Porter. In the first novel Pollyanna goes to live with her spinster aunt Polly after Pollyanna's father dies. Aunt Polly is very ill-tempered, but Pollyanna's resolutely cheerful disposition, even in the face of temporary paralysis, helps melt Aunt Polly's cold facade.

Pollyanna, in *Pollyanna*, is never called "Polly," only Pollyanna.

Page 46. Moore, perhaps anticipating objections to the rape scenes in *League*, had this to say about them in an interview in the November 1998 issue of *Tripwire*:

> I think that when you take the sex scene with Pollyanna that takes place in the second issue, you'll see that there is a lighthearted element to it. The scene where the Egyptians try to rape Mina is nasty but comical though. Rape is serious, the idea of rape is a horrible thing and there's no intention of trivialising it. However, one of the unspoken pillars of Victorian fiction was the notion of 'the fate worse than death.' Human sexuality, screwed up as it is, is a big part of Victorian fiction, as is the racism. When you see the Arabs in the first issue and when you see the Chinese in #3, I'm sure they'll be portrayed in the same way. This is what we wanted. We're not talking about real Arabs, real Chinamen, or even real women.
>
> I suppose people could accuse me of wallowing in those elements under the guise of postmodernism and they'd probably be right. I don't think that you get an unpleasant atmosphere after reading the stories. It's more British attitudes that are being pilloried rather than the targets of those attitudes. What makes it funny is the absurdity of the Victorian vision, this idea of a supremacist Britain that ruled the entire world. It's one of the bits that I'm most enjoying, to explore all those Victorian attitudes. In the girl's school in issue #2, there's plenty of flogging scenes and this is because the Victorians believed that corporal punishment was good for the character.

Page 49. Panel 2. "Lord and Lady Pokingham" are from "Lady Pokingham; Or They All Do It," another piece of Victorian-era erotica that appeared in *The Pearl*.

Page 50. Panel 2. "Ayesha," a.k.a. "She Who Must Be Obeyed," appears in H. Rider Haggard's She books: *She: A History of Adventure* (1886), *Ayesha: The Return of She* (1904), *She and Allan*

(1919), and *Wisdom's Daughter: The Life and Love Story of She-Who-Must-Be-Obeyed* (1922). Ayesha was a 2000-year-old goddess worshiped in the African city of Kôr. She died at the end of *She* but returned for *Ayesha*, with the events of *She and Allan* and *Wisdom's Daughter* occurring before the events of *She*. *She and Allan* chronicles Allan Quatermain's trip to Kôr and his meeting with She, which is why Quatermain pays special attention to the relics in this panel.

Panel 4. The giant skull that Nemo is examining likely belonged to a Brobdingnagian, one of the rustic giants from Jonathan Swift's *Gulliver's Travels* (1726). The skull in the glass case on the far right of the panel is from a Yahoo, one of the vicious brutes in human form in *Gulliver's Travels*. The display case with the tiny figures probably contains either live or stuffed Lilliputians, the very small people of *Gulliver's Travels*.

Page 51. Panel 4. In *The Strange Case of Dr. Jekyll and Mr. Hyde*, Jekyll initially needs a drug to turn into Hyde, as Bond states in this panel. As time passes Jekyll needs more of the drug to facilitate the change:

> The power of the drug had not been always equally displayed. Once, very early in my career, it had totally failed me; since then I had been obliged on more than one occasion to double, and once, with infinite risk of death, to treble the amount; and these rare uncertainties had cast hitherto the sole shadow on my contentment.

However, by the end of the novel matters have changed:

> Now, however, and in the light of that morning's accident, I was led to remark that whereas, in the beginning, the difficulty had been to throw off the body of Jekyll, it had of late gradually but decidedly transferred itself to the other side. All things therefore seemed to point to this: that I was slowly losing hold of my original and better self, and becoming slowly incorporated with my second and worse.

59

Both of the objects on the wall are references to Jules Verne's *Voyage au Centre de la Terre (*Journey to the Center of the Earth, 1864). In that novel a German professor, Otto Lidenbrock, finds a book from a sixteenth-century Icelandic alchemist, Arne Saknussemm (whose name is partially visible on the upper plaque). In the book Saknussemm claimed to have journeyed to the center of the Earth. Intrigued, Lidenbrock follows Saknussemm's path, using his "AS" markers, as seen on the top plaque here, to guide him. Among the other things that Lidenbrock finds are an underground sea, the "Lidenbrock sea" mentioned on the bottom plaque, and various "prehistoric" animals such the ichthyosaur seen here.

Page 52. Panel 2. "Professor Selwyn Cavor" is from H.G. Wells' *The First Men in the Moon* (1901). Professor Cavor is the inventor of "cavorite," a gravity-canceling alloy ("this possible substance opaque to gravitation") which Cavor and his friend Mr. Bedford, the narrator of the novel, use to travel to the moon. In the novel Cavor is described as "a short, round-bodied, thin-legged little man, with a jerky quality in his motions; he had seen fit to clothe his extraordinary mind in a cricket cap, an overcoat, and cycling knickerbockers and stockings."

Panel 3. In *The First Men in the Moon*, Cavor and Bedford's lunar expedition takes place in late March or early April, 1900.

Page 53. Panel 1. Despite Bond's statement the idea that England might be the victim of aerial bombing was not unthinkable to Victorian writers. Aerial bombardment was something of a staple of Victorian science fiction, beginning with Alfred, Lord Tennyson's "Locksley Hall" (1842), which spoke of "the nations' airy navies grappling in the central blue." Herman Lang, in 1859, wrote *The Air Battle*, a novel set in 6900 A.D. in which future civilizations war over slavery, using vast air navies of enormous aircraft which are powered by new energy sources and armed with superexplosives. In 1872 the Hungarian novelist Mór Jókai published *A Jovo Szazad Regeneye* (A Novella of the Coming Century), in which a Hungarian scientist uses the wonder metal "ichor" to build a super-airship and then impose peace on Earth, using the ship's advanced weapons to suppress rebellion, including an uprising in London. Dime novel boy inventors such as Luis Senarens' Frank Reade, Jr. built steam- and electric-powered aircraft and used them to bomb warlike natives and even enemy cities. George Griffith's *The Angel of the Revolution* (1893) told of the anarchist Natas and his organization, Terror, seizing control of the world and building a utopia. During the novel the French and Russians bomb the British into submission with their aerostats, or war balloons. And E. Douglas Fawcett's *Hartmann the Anarchist* (1893) featured the titular anarchist and his group of terrorists bombing and strafing London from their superpowered airship *Attila*.

"Captain Mors" is the lead character of *Der Luftpirat und Sein Lenkbares Luftschiff* (The Pirate of the Air and his Navigable Airship), a German *heldroman* (dime novel) published from 1908-1911. The creator of Captain Mors is unknown, but it is likely that several well-known German science fiction writers of the era, such as Oskar Hoffman, were involved. Captain Mors, the "Man with the Mask," is a Captain Nemo-like character, fleeing from mankind with a crew of Indians and involved in a prolonged fight against tyranny and evil, both on Earth and on Venus, Mars, and the rest of the solar system.

Panel 2. This grouping is an earlier League assembled by the British Secret Service; the second *League* series provides more information about them. The members of this League, the 1787 League, are as follows:

- Lemuel Gulliver is the ship's cook, explorer, and world-traveler from Jonathan Swift's *Gulliver's Travels*. Gulliver was born in 1660, according to the internal chronology of *Gulliver's Travels* (1726), so the decrepit Lemuel Gulliver seen here is 127 years old. At Gulliver's feet can be seen one of the Lilliputian cattle Gulliver brought back after his first voyage.

- Mr. & Mrs. P. Blakeny, otherwise known Sir Percy Blakeney and Lady Marguerite Blakeney, are from Baroness Emmuska Orczy's *The Scarlet Pimpernel* (1905) and its ten sequels. Sir Percy Blakeney was a foppish British nobleman during the years of the French Revolution. His alter ego, the Scarlet Pimpernel, was a daring hero who rescued many innocent members of the French royalty from Robespierre and the Terror. Lady Marguerite Blakeney, his wife, was "the cleverest woman in Europe" and an able partner to the Pimpernel. Their presence together as husband and wife in a 1787 portrait is somewhat incongruous with the events of *The Scarlet Pimpernel*; in the novel the pair married in 1790 or 1791, and Sir Percy became the Pimpernel in response to the Terror in 1792.

- The Reverend Dr. Syn is from Russell Thorndike's *Doctor Syn* (1915) and its six prequels. In *Doctor Syn* the kindly and genial Reverend Doctor is the vicar of Dymchurch at the turn of the Nineteenth century. Syn is also the notorious pirate and smuggler Captain Clegg, also known as the Scarecrow. His pose here, hunched beneath a broad-brimmed hat and with both guns crossed, is likely a deliberate evocation of the pulp hero The Shadow.

- Mistress Hill is the bawdy heroine of John Cleland's *Fanny Hill, Or, Memoirs of a Woman of Pleasure* (1749). *Fanny Hill*, one of the most notable early works of English pornography, tells of Mistress Hill's erotic exploits. Although Mina's history is not nearly as scandalous as Fanny Hill's, both of them would be seen by proper society as fallen women.

- N. Bumpo is Natty Bumppo, from James Fennimore Cooper's five Leatherstocking novels, the most famous of which is *The Last of the Mohicans* (1826). Bumppo, aka "Hawkeye," aka "Leatherstocking," is a white man adopted by Chingachgook, who with his son Uncas are the titular last of the Mohican tribe; Bumppo grows up to be a mighty hunter and woodsman.

"Montagu House," written along the bottom of the label, was the Seventeenth century mansion on whose site the British Museum was later built.

Panels 3-4. The man Bond is describing is Dr. Fu Manchu. Fu Manchu was created by Sax Rohmer, a.k.a. Arthur Sarsfield Ward, and first appeared in a series of short stories in *The Story-Teller* in 1912. These stories were collected and published in 1913 as *The Insidious Dr. Fu Manchu*. Fu Manchu is an evil Chinese mastermind with world-conquering aims, and is the most prominent example of the Yellow Peril stereotype. (For a history of this character type, see the "Yellow Peril" essay.)

Fu Manchu is never named in the pages of *League* for copyright reasons. While the earliest of Rohmer's Fu Manchu novels are in the public domain, the character himself is trademarked, so his use in *League* would require a licensing agreement with the Sax Rohmer estate.

The comment that he's "regarded as Satan" is a reference to Nayland Smith's famous description of Fu Manchu in Chapter Two of *The Insidious Dr. Fu Manchu*: "Imagine a person, tall, lean and feline, high-shouldered, with a brow like Shakespeare and a face like Satan..."

Page 54. Limehouse, a dockfront section of London's East End, is the location of one of Fu Manchu's bases in *The Insidious Dr. Fu Manchu*. Long before the first appearance of Fu Manchu, however, Limehouse was notorious among the British for being the home of Chinese immigrants.

The Chinese began emigrating to London in the late Eighteenth century, initially as employees of the East India Company. By 1850 they were settling in Limehouse and Liverpool, arriving as seamen or ships' launderers. By 1890 sailors from Shanghai were settled in Pennyfields, Amoy Place, and Ming Street, while Cantonese and sailors from southern China took up residence in Gill Street and Limehouse Causeway. At the turn of the Twenty century there were only 545 Chinese officially in London, but the unofficial number of illegal immigrants was as much as ten times higher, and most of them were concentrated in Limehouse. By 1914 there were, officially, thirty Chinese businesses in Limehouse, which by then had become known as "Chinatown."

While immigrants from China also settled in other areas of London, Limehouse became associated with the Chinese and with opium smoking in the British popular imagination during the Victorian era. In 1868 the Prince of Wales visited an opium den located in the house of a Chinese-English couple, a visit given coverage in the London press. Charles Dickens, who as a child sang to the customers in a pub in Limehouse, opened *The Mystery of Edwin Drood* (1870) with a scene in a Limehouse opium den. In *The Picture of Dorian Gray* (1890), Oscar Wilde has Dorian Gray go to Limehouse to smoke opium. In Arthur Conan Doyle's "The Man with the Twisted Lip" (*Strand Magazine*, December 1891), Dr. Watson goes into a Limehouse opium den to rescue a family friend. And after the turn of the century Thomas Burke's Limehouse stories, including his "The Chink and the Child" (*Colours*, October 1915), the source of the very popular 1919 D.W. Griffith film *Broken Blossoms*, extensively explored Limehouse and East London.

This panel is another example of Moore and O'Neill's satire of British stereotypes of foreigners. The real Limehouse was populated by immigrants, no more or less criminal than any other group of English. Opium smoking was seen by the Chinese as simply a part of their daily ritual, rather than something criminal and dangerous. Yet the Limehouse in *League* is the Limehouse of the popular imagination: a dangerous warren of criminal dives, opium dens, and brothels.

Fu Manchu is shown wearing the style of mustache popularly associated with him. But in the Rohmer novels Fu Manchu is hairless; in *The Insidious Dr. Fu Manchu* Nayland Smith describes his "wicked, hairless face." It was only in 1931, when Warner Oland played Fu Manchu in *Daughter of the Dragon*, that Fu Manchu was portrayed with a mustache.

The image of Fu Manchu's face in the sky may be a reference *The Vengeance of Fu Manchu* (1968). At the end of this movie, in which Christopher Lee played Fu Manchu, Fu Manchu's face appears in the sky, vowing, "The world shall hear from me again."

Kevin O'Neill notes:
> Image of Oriental in sky is not a movie reference, more a classic comic device for suggesting a brooding presence over a scene.

Page 55. **Panel 1**. A further indication of how far Mina Murray has fallen from the Victorian ideal of "proper" womanhood is seen here: she is smoking. Women simply did not smoke in "proper" Victorian society. Although some few women smoked, it was customarily done in secret with a female friend; a woman who smoked was considered "fast." Similarly men never smoked or even asked to smoke in the "company of the fair;" one always excused oneself from their presence to enjoy a cigar or pipe.

Panel 2. Griffin here echoes his own words, from Chapter 27 of *The Invisible Man*:

> The game is only beginning. There is nothing for it now, but to start the Terror. This announces the first day of the Terror. Port Burdock is no longer under your Queen, tell your Colonel of Police, and the rest of them; it is under me--the Terror! This is day one of year one of the new epoch,--the Epoch of the Invisible Man. I am Invisible Man the First.

Page 56. The words on the planks of the table around which the League sits are references to Robert Louis Stevenson's *Treasure Island* (1883). "Hispaniola 1760" is a reference to the *Hispaniola*, the name of the ship on which Jim Hawkins sails. "Skeleton island" is the destination for which the *Hispaniola* sailed, with Jim Hawkins, Long John Silver, and the rest of the crew. Although the exact dates of the events of *Treasure Island* are not given, they occur after 1745, as seen in the text, and 1760 seems a likely year for those events.

Page 57. In Chapter 23 of *The Invisible Man,* Griffin breaks into a theatrical supply store and steals certain supplies which he uses to pass among humans. Presumably this is where he learned the trick of coating himself in greasepaint.

Page 58. Panel 4. The "eruptions on Mars" occur in the first chapter of Wells' *War of the Worlds*. The "well-known astronomer" Ogilvy believes that the eruptions could be volcanic in nature, or the impacts of a meteor shower on Mars, but they are, rather, the precursor to the Martian invasion of Earth.

Page 59. Panel 1. The first banner, on the far left, reads "Geography," as in the academic subject. The second banner to its right reads "Book."

The script used in this and succeeding panels is the simplified modern script of Putonghua Mandarin Chinese introduced by the People's Republic of China in 1954.

Panel 2. The script on the wall reads, "Doctor."

Panel 3. Quong Lee was the creation of Thomas Burke. Lee appeared in *The Song Book of Quong Lee of Limehouse* (1920), a collection of poems, and in the short-story collections *The Pleasantries of Old Quong* (1931) and *Dark Nights* (1944), all part of Burke's Limehouse series of stories about the Chinese enclave. Quong Lee, loosely based on Burke's childhood friend Quong Li, is the wise, gentle, compassionate, elderly operator of a tea shop.

The sign reads, in the Cantonese dialect, "Quong Lee, Eastern Fine Tea Supplier."

Page 60. Panel 1. The sign next to Quong Lee reads, "Tea."

Page 62. For more information on Rotherhithe and the "Rotherhithe Bridge," see Page 69, Panel 3 below.

Panel 5. The sign on the bridge, "Fry's," is a reference to J.S. Fry & Sons, a British chocolate and confectionary maker. In 1847 Fry & Sons sold a "Choclat Delicieux a manger," thought to be the first chocolate candy bar. In 1919 Fry's merged with Cadbury's.

The sign on the bus, "Pears," is a reference to Pears Soap, an English soap produced by the Pears family from 1789 through 1914 and still sold today.

Page 63. Panel 2. "Ho Ling" is a character from various Thomas Burke poems and short stories, including "The Song of Ho Ling"

(1921). In Burke's work Ho Ling runs a fantan parlor, fantan being a Chinese gambling game.

In *The Insidious Dr. Fu Manchu,* the opium den which leads Petrie and Nayland Smith to Fu Manchu is called Singapore Charlie's.

Panel 5. Stella Carson, mentioned with more detail in the notes to Page 45, Panel 1, was Quatermain's second wife. His first wife, Marie Marais, appears in H. Rider Haggard's *Marie* (1912). Marie Marais was Quatermain's first great love. In the novel he meets, woos, and marries her, but she dies saving Quatermain's life. Allan says of Marie, "She was my first wife, but I beg you not to speak of her to me or to anyone else, for I cannot bear to hear her name."

Page 64. Panel 1. The exterior of Shen Yan's shop, as seen here, is similar to its description in Chapter Six of *The Insidious Dr. Fu Manchu*.

The Chinese script on the sign reads, "Shen Yan, Barber Shop." The word on the side of the building to the left of Shen Yan's reads, "Killer."

In Chinese mythology the four-toed dragon, called the "mang," is a symbol of high rank, and is used by the nobility, officials, and the gentry. That such a creature is used by Shen Yan outside his shop is indicative of his high position.

Panel 2. Apart from the three stairs in front of the door the interior of Shen Yan's shop is not similar to Rohmer's description in the book.

Page 65. Panel 2. The rhythm of the dialogue and the words chosen in this panel and the rest of the scene indicate that Mandarin rather than Cantonese is being spoken.

Angry Man: "The boss needs more brushes. These are melting. Look at this. It's useless."

Panel 3: Angry Man: "I want another one."

Frightened Man: "All right, quickly, the boss is waiting."

Panel 4: Frightened Man: "Please forgive me. I have a new brush here."

The vessel seen here is a *chueh*, a bronze vessel used for heating and drinking wine as well as for the ritual pouring of libations to the spirits. *Chueh* were buried in the tombs of nobility from the time of the Shang dynasty, circa 1600 B.C.E.

Panel 5. Angry Man (presumably): "Hurry up, idiot, the boss is writing poetry!"

The words etched on the man's chest, reading from right to left and up to down, consist of a poem:

> The stars are destiny's verse:
> A man without scars
> Is an unwritten book.

Panel 6: "Look at this! I found one!"

Page 66. Panel 1. Angry Man: "Give it to me! I'm in a hurry!"

Panel 2. Angry Man: "Finally! Next time, be quicker!"

Fu Manchu, in Chapter Two of *The Insidious Dr. Fu Manchu*, is described as having "the long, magnetic eyes of the true cat-green." In Chapter Six he is described this way:

> Of his face, as it looked out at me over the dirty table, I despair of writing convincingly. It was that of an archangel of evil, and it was wholly dominated by the most uncanny eyes that ever reflected a human soul, for they were narrow and long, very slightly oblique, and of a brilliant green. But their unique horror lay in a certain filminess (it made me

think of the membrana nictitans in a bird) which,
obscuring them as I threw wide the door, seemed to
lift as I actually passed the threshold, revealing the
eyes in all their brilliant iridescence.

Here, however, the eye seems entirely alien and not at all human.
This shot of the Doctor's eye may be meant to put the reader in
mind of another sort of eye, one "envious" and backed by an intellect
"vast and cool and unsympathetic"–a Martian's eye. Moore may be
implying that the Doctor is not human at all. Alternatively, Moore
and O'Neill may be extending their satire of Victorian British attitudes
towards the Chinese by portraying Fu Manchu as exaggeratedly non-
human in appearance.

Panel 3. Angry Man: "Who are you?"

The banner behind Quatermain reads "Doctor."

Page 67. Panel 2. Many kinds of opium are visually similar to tar,
having the same color and texture, but opium has a very distinct
sweet, pungent smell which makes it unlikely to be confused with
tar by anyone other than a novice opium smoker. This undoubtedly
adds to Quatermain's explanation that he feels foolish for having
been tricked.

Panel 4. Traditionally there have been two ways to use opium:
smoking it and eating it. Before the introduction of smoking in the
early Seventeenth century, opium, then confined to Asia, was only
eaten. After smoking spread, opium continued to be taken orally in
India, Turkey, and the West until the Nineteenth century, while it
was smoked in China, the East Indies, Vietnam and Taiwan. By 1898
opium was primarily smoked everywhere but India, where the British
government continued to produce and sell opium to be eaten, insisting
that it was medicinal and non-addictive, until World War II.

Page 69. Panel 3. Rotherhithe Road runs along the south side of
the Thames, in the area known, both during the Victorian era and
currently, as Rotherhithe. Just across the Thames from Rotherhithe

is Wapping, which is a part of Shadwell. In reality there have been two tunnels connecting Rotherhithe to Wapping.

The first Rotherhithe Tunnel, which was known in the Victorian years as the "Thames Tunnel," was successfully built in 1843 after two previous attempts, in 1798 and 1802, were abandoned due to quicksand and the Thames breaking in. The Thames Tunnel was used for foot traffic until 1863, when it was converted into a railway tunnel for the East London Railway. The Thames Tunnel still exists today, as part of the East London Underground Line.

The second, current Rotherhithe Tunnel was built from 1904-1908 and is used for automobile traffic.

In our world neither of these tunnels was under construction in the 1880s, but in the world of *League*, with technology our England did not possess, history obviously proceeded differently.

Page 72. Panel 2. Triads are, as Quatermain says, secret Chinese criminal societies. According to their own legends they were founded by the survivors of the destruction of the Shaolin temple by Imperial troops in 1674 C.E. The Triads, underground societies, which rebelled against the government and the law, used legal front organizations and businesses called "Tongs." For Chinese immigrants in the West, Tongs acted as mutual protection unions. Although the Tongs began as completely legal organizations, over time they became criminal organizations and warred on rival Tongs, just as the Triads did and do.

The first Triads arrived in America in the early 1850s, but it was not until 1890 that a Triad society was present in Limehouse. In the chronology of *League* it's quite possible that the Doctor arrived in Limehouse alongside the Triads.

Panel 4. "Alienists" were the Victorian equivalent of practicing psychologists, medical experts who specialized in the study and treatment of mental diseases. They were also occasionally called upon by the police for help in constructing personality profiles of criminals based on evidence found at crime scenes, but were more often connected with insane asylums. They were not well-regarded by most Victorians.

Mina's scornful attitude towards alienists might have something to do with her own background. In *Dracula* both Dr. Seward and Professor van Helsing were practising alienists, Seward at the asylum next to Carfax Abbey and van Helsing as Seward's teacher.

Page 73. Panel 2. Judging from the roster of names on the wall behind Quatermain, the shelter is crowded with writers of fantastic literature. These writers were responsible for the main characters in *League*:

- "oyle" is Arthur Conan Doyle, the creator of Sherlock and Mycroft Holmes.
- "Haggar" is H. Rider Haggard, the creator of Allan Quatermain.
- "Poe" is Edgar Allan Poe, the creator of C. Auguste Dupin.
- "Rohm" is "Sax Rohmer," a.k.a. Arthur Sarsfield Ward, the creator of Dr. Fu Manchu.
- "Stev" is Robert Louis Stevenson, who created Dr. Henry Jekyll and Mr. Edward Hyde.
- "Stok" is Bram Stoker, who created Mina Murray.
- "Vern" is Jules Verne, who created Captain Nemo.
- "Wel" is H.G. Wells, who created Griffin, the Invisible Man.

Page 74. Panel 8. Victorian poorhouses had sentiments just like "Are You Ready To Die" carved into their walls and ceilings, as was shown in Moore and Eddie Campbell's *From Hell*.

Page 79. Panel 1. "Mr. Mate" was the customary form of address for the first mate on a ship during the Victorian era.

Panel 2. "Call me Ishmael" is one of the most famous opening lines in all of literature, and a clear indicator of the identity of the speaker: the narrator of Herman Melville's *Moby Dick* (1851). In *Moby Dick*, Ishmael, a young man, signs on to the whaler *Pequod* and in so doing comes to witness the prolonged duel between Captain Ahab and Moby Dick, the great white whale.

Ishmael was a young man during the events of Moby Dick and survived the final events of the novel, so it is easily possible that he could still be alive for the events of *League*.

Panel 3. "Broad Arrow Jack" was created by E. Harcourt Burrage, a prolific author of penny dreadfuls, and appeared in "Broad Arrow Jack," a serial published in *The Boys' Standard* in 1866. "Broad Arrow Jack" is actually John Ashleigh, a young Englishman fallen on hard times in Australia. He becomes the notorious Robin Hood-like outlaw Broad Arrow Jack, so-called because of the arrow brand on his back. (The illustrations of Broad Arrow Jack in the penny dreadful show Jack conveniently without a shirt and thereby displaying his arrow brand.)

The "broad arrow" which Jack bears is a traditional symbol of British authority created by Henry, Viscount Sydney, Earl of Romney (1693-1702), the master-general of the ordnance. The arrow was the mark used by the British Board of Ordnance and placed on their stores.

Panel 5. Nemo is standing at an altar on which stand three statues of Siva. As seen on Page 21, Panel 1, Nemo is a worshiper of Siva, and incorporated aspects of Siva into the *Nautilus*. Here Nemo's altar can be seen. The white flowers at the foot of the altar are *pushpa*, which symbolize water and the human heart. The lamp represents fire and the human heart.

The small statue to the immediate right of Nemo is of Siva-Nataraja, Siva as the cosmic dancer. The larger, square framed statue with two hooks may be a statue of Siva-Bhairava, Siva as the Lord of Terror.

Panel 6. The statue Nemo is holding is presumably of Siva in one of his other aspects.

Page 80. "Gods of Annihilation," the title of this issue, can be used to refer to a number of the characters in *League*. Fu Manchu has referred to himself as "the Lord of the Fires" and "the Avatar of Destruction." Siva is the god of destruction in the Hindu pantheon. The title can even be applied, without too much exaggeration, to Nemo.

Page 83. Panel 3. The guard here is speaking Mandarin.

Guard: "Who are you?"

One of the customary costumes of the criminal Triad societies is an outfit of black shirt or chainmail with a red or yellow symbol on the breast, very similar to what is worn by the guards of Fu Manchu.

Panel 4. Guard: "What are you doing? This is none of your business."

Page 84. Panel 1. Guard: "Come with me! I will bring you to see the Master!"

Panel 2. Guard: "That's enough! Hand over that gun and follow me!"

Panel 3. Guard: "What did you say? What is...?"

Page 87. Panel 8. Mustached man: "What's the matter?"
Bespectacled man: "Get rid of this bastard."

Panel 9. Mustached man: "You will come with us."

Page 89. Panel 1. Guard: "Heaven protect us! He is a demon!"

Page 91. Panel 4. Shouting man: "What's happening?"
Pointing man: "There are some men fighting upstairs."

Page 93. Panel 3. Quatermain's wonderment at "the very idea of powered flight" reflects the nineteenth-century debate about which type of flight would be dominant in the future, unpowered or powered—or as it was often phrased, "heavier-than-air versus lighter-than-air." Before the 1880s most stories featuring aircraft had featured lighter-than-air flight, but in 1886 Jules Verne published *Robur the Conqueror*, in which Robur's heavier-than-air *Albatross* decisively beats the lighter-than-air crafts of the Weldon Institute. After the publication of *Robur,* stories featuring powered flight become predominant and the genre of balloon travel stories and lighter-than-air, unpowered flight dwindled.

Panel 5. Mina's statement about men being "so obsessed with mechanisms that further nothing but destruction" might be taken as a commentary by Moore on the mechanics-obsessed science fiction of the time, especially the dime novels, in which it was customary to show diagrams of inventor characters' new creations in each issue or book; these writers' obsession with new inventions and their use and destructive potential is almost fetishistic.

Page 100. Panel 3. *Mobilis in mobili* is Nemo's motto in *Twenty Thousand Leagues Under The Sea* and is engraved on all his silverware. It means, in Latin, "Mobile in the mobile (medium)."

Panel 4. "Pizzle" is the name for an animal's penis; it dates to the Sixteenth century. Hardly the language of a lady, but as has become clear Mina Murray does not see herself as a lady, at least as the Victorian elite defined the word.

Page 101. Panel 1. This building, the headquarters of MI5 (identified as such in Panel 5 below), is visually quite similar to the real MI6's headquarters in Vauxhall Cross in South London.

Two obelisks are visible here. The closer one is Cleopatra's Needle, the celebratory obelisk originally constructed for Pharaoh Tuthmosis III, ruler of Egypt's Eighteenth Dynasty from 1504-1450 B.C.E. The obelisk, one of nine which Tuthmosis III had built, was given to Britain in 1819 by the Viceroy of Egypt and placed on the Thames Embankment in London on the opposite side of the Thames to Vauxhall. Cleopatra's Needle is placed next to MI5's headquarters because it was a Freemason, Sir Erasmus Wilson, who funded the transportation of the Needle from Egypt to London. See Panel 4, below, for more on the presence of Masons in *League*.

Panels 4. The symbol above and to the left of Campion Bond is a Masonic symbol, the compass and right angle, which in Masonic lore symbolizes the instruments of both the Masons and God. (The G between the compass and right angle stands for either God or Geometry or both; as with so many other Masonic matters, the truth is unclear.) Their presence here and on Page 127, along with several other Masonic symbols, is a hint that in the world of *League* the Freemasons are in control of the British intelligence establishment. The idea that the British monarchy and/or intelligence establishment are controlled by the Freemasons is an old and established one among conspiracy theorists. If that is the case here, then Inspector Donovan's two-fingered salute, on Page 39, Panel 1, is an indication that Donovan is a Mason.

Panel 5. "Her Majesty's Military Intelligence Division 5" is a reference to "Military Intelligence 5," a.k.a. "MI5," the section of the British Secret Service which is responsible for counterespionage within the United Kingdom. In real life MI5 was formed in 1909 as a part of the British Secret Service Bureau to control counterespionage operations for the British government as well as to serve as a liaison between the War Office, the British Admiralty, and Britain's spies and agents overseas. The activities of Fu Manchu would be the purview of MI5, but Jekyll in France would be a mission for agents of MI6, the British Security Service responsible for overseas espionage.

Page 102. Panel 4. The idea that Mycroft Holmes was "M" was first mentioned in John T. Lescroart's *Son of Holmes* (1986), a Sherlock Holmes pastiche.

Panel 7. Although his surname is not given here, M's identity is confirmed in this panel. M is Professor James Moriarty. Created by Arthur Conan Doyle and appearing in only one story, "The Adventure of the Final Problem," Moriarty was the greatest opponent Sherlock Holmes ever faced, a brilliant and evil mathematician who "is the Napoleon of crime" and "the organizer of half that is evil and of nearly all that is undetected" in London. His influence and reputation greatly exceed the actual literature; he appears in "The Adventure of the Final Problem" and his influence pervades *The Valley of Fear* (1915), but he makes no other appearances in the Holmesian canon, the four novels and sixty short stories by Doyle which are the "Sacred Writings" or the official cases of Sherlock Holmes.

In "The Final Problem" Holmes sacrifices his own life to put an end to Moriarty and his organization, throwing Moriarty and himself over the Reichenbach Falls, but due to the outcry of an outraged public Doyle brought Holmes back, in "The Adventure of the Empty House." Doyle kept Moriarty dead, but successive *pasticheurs* have not.

Kevin O'Neill's drawing of Moriarty is very similar to the original Sidney Paget drawings of Moriarty in *The Strand* where "The Final Problem" first appeared.

Page 103. The title of this issue, "Some Deep, Organizing Power...," is a Holmes quote. In "The Final Problem" he is describing Moriarty when he says,

> As you are aware, Watson, there is no one who knows the higher criminal world of London so well as I do. For years past I have continually been conscious of some power behind the malefactor, some deep organizing power which forever stands in the way of the law, and throws its shield over the wrong-doer.

This scene is the final confrontation between Professor Moriarty and Sherlock Holmes from "The Final Problem," the story that Arthur Conan Doyle intended to be his last Holmes story. Doyle came to loathe Holmes, feeling that the detective was taking him away from his more serious writings, and was overjoyed to be free of him after "The Final Problem."

The Reichenbach Falls do exist; they are in Bern canton in Switzerland. May 4, 1891, was the date established in "The Final Problem" as the day of Holmes' death.

In this panel Kevin O'Neill has accurately duplicated the Sidney Paget drawing of the Reichenbach Falls which appeared with "The Final Problem" in *The Strand.*

Page 104. Panel 1. In "The Final Problem" Holmes and Watson are walking on the path seen on Page 103 when Watson, a doctor, is summoned back to the hotel by a note requesting his help in consoling an Englishwoman dying of consumption. The note is a ruse, as Holmes states here.

Panel 2. This style of conversation, where the thought processes of Moriarty and Holmes are the same, and they independently reach the same conclusions, is seen in "The Final Problem."

The Holmesian Canon contains several internal contradictions and discrepancies, not the least of which is the matter of Dr. Watson's wives. The names of his wives and the years in which he was married to them are contradictorily given in various stories. In *Sherlock Holmes of Baker Street* (1962), the noted Sherlockian William S. Baring-Gould states that Dr. Watson was married to Mary Morstan in May 1889, the date of "The Sign of Four." According to "The Final Problem," Watson was married at some point not long before 1891, the time of the story. Textual hints in "The Final Problem" seem to point to 1888 or 1889 as the year in which Watson married. This would make his marriage two years old at the time of Holmes' "death," making Holmes' statement that Watson was "newly married" somewhat curious.

(As an aside, the textual evidence in "The Sign of Four" points to the story taking place in 1889. However, certain Sherlock Holmes stories, like "The Five Orange Pips," are set in 1887 or 1888 and either refer to Watson's wife or to "The Sign of Four." These discrepancies have led to numerous theories about Watson's wives; as Dorothy Sayers said in 1944, "there is a conspiracy theory afoot to provide Watson with as many wives as Henry VIII.")

Panel 4. The idea that "there's nothing personal in this" is expressed by Moriarty in "The Final Problem," although not in so many words.

Panel 6. Moriarty's joy in the "golden, mathematic logic of it all" is a reference to his background. Moriarty is described in "The Final Problem" as

> a man of good birth and excellent education, endowed by nature with a phenomenal mathematical faculty. At the age of twenty-one he wrote a treatise upon the binomial theorem, which has had a European vogue. On the strength of it he won the mathematical chair at one of our smaller universities, and had, to all appearances, a most brilliant career before him.

Moriarty's joy in the setting and scenery, and his statement, on Page 105, Panel 1, that the setting and the clash are "Olympian," reflect the portrayal of Moriarty and Holmes as a Dionysian and Apollonian pair. The German philosopher Friederich Nietzsche, in his *The Birth of Tragedy* (1872), described what he called the two central principles in ancient Greek culture: the "Apollonian" and the "Dionysian." Apollonian, derived from the sun god Apollo, represents an analytical, structured, and detached approach. Dionysian, coming from Dionysus, the god of the arts and of wine, represents emotion, enthusiasm, and ecstasy. In this scene Holmes is Apollonian: calm, detached, and logical, giving measured responses and, during the fight on Pages 105 and 106, wearing a calm expression. Moriarty, for his part, is Dionysian: instinctive, moody, emotional, and taken with the beauty of his surroundings. During the fight with Holmes Moriarty's face is savage with anger. Moreover, Moriarty is associated with the Freemasons, who are also called the "Dionysian Architects." These traits were not seen in "The Final Problem" and "The Adventure of the Empty House," and are Moore and O'Neill's interpretation of the Holmes-Moriarty pair.

Panel 7. The note that Holmes is writing is his farewell to Watson, given in full in "The Final Problem:"

My dear Watson:

I write these few lines through the courtesy of Mr. Moriarty, who awaits my convenience for the final discussion of those questions which lie between us. He has been giving me a sketch of the methods by which he avoided the English police and kept himself informed of our movements. They certainly confirm the very high opinion which I had formed of his abilities. I am pleased to think that I shall be able to free society from any further effects of his presence, though I fear that it is at a cost which will give pain to my friends, and especially, my dear Watson, to you. I have already explained to you, however, that my career had in any case reached its crisis, and that no possible conclusion to it could be more congenial to me than this. Indeed, if I may make a full confession to you, I was quite convinced that the letter from Meiringen was a hoax, and I allowed you to depart on that errand under the persuasion that some development of this sort would follow. Tell Inspector Patterson that the papers which he needs to convict the gang are in pigeonhole M., done up in a blue envelope and inscribed "Moriarty." I made every disposition of my property before leaving England and handed it to my brother Mycroft. Pray give my greetings to Mrs. Watson, and believe me to be, my dear fellow,

Very sincerely yours,

Sherlock Holmes

Page 105. Panel 2. In "The Final Problem," Watson describes "the silver cigarette-case" which Holmes is handling here. It, along with the note for Watson, is all that Watson finds when he returns to the Reichenbach Falls in search of Holmes at the end of "The Final Problem."

"The Final Problem" does not, however, mention the design on the case. This is the Question Mark Man, which appears at various points in *League* and seems to be the *de facto* symbol of the League.

Page 106. Panel 1. Doyle described the final fight between Holmes and Moriarty in "The Adventure of the Empty House," the story in which Doyle brought Holmes back. In "The Adventure of the Empty House," Holmes says that Moriarty "drew no weapon, but he rushed at me and threw his long arms around me." Holmes, of course, may be misremembering the events of Reichenbach Falls.

Panel 2. In "The Adventure of the Empty House," Holmes describes how he saved himself:

> We tottered together upon the brink of the fall. I have some knowledge, however, of baritsu, or the Japanese system of wrestling, which has more than once been very useful to me. I slipped through his grip, and he with a horrible scream kicked madly for a few seconds, and clawed the air with both his hands.

Page 107. Panels 1-3. In "The Adventure of the Empty House" Holmes says this of Moriarty's fall:

> With my face over the brink, I saw him fall for a long way. Then he struck a rock, bounded off, and splashed into the water.

Page 108. Panels 1-4. In "The Adventure of the Empty House," Holmes says,

> I stood up and examined the rocky wall behind me. In your picturesque account of the matter, which I read with great interest some months later, you assert that the wall was sheer. That was not literally true. A few small footholds presented themselves, and there was some indication of a ledge. The cliff is so high that to climb it all was an obvious impossibility, and it was equally impossible to make my way along the wet path without leaving some tracks. I might, it is true, have reversed my boots,

as I have done on similar occasions, but the sight of three sets of tracks in one direction would certainly have suggested a deception. On the whole, then, it was best that I should risk the climb.

Panels 5-6. In "The Adventure of the Empty House," Holmes says, "I am not a fanciful person, but I give you my word that I seemed to hear Moriarty's voice screaming at me out of the abyss."

Panel 6. Holmes' addiction to drugs has been noted before, both in the Holmesian Canon ("The Man With The Twisted Lip," among others) and outside of it. The subject is given the most attention in Nicholas Meyer's *The Seven-Per-Cent Solution: Being a Reprint from the Reminiscences of John H. Watson, M.D.* (1974), in which Sigmund Freud helps cure Holmes of cocaine addiction and, after lengthy sessions of psychoanalysis, reveals the root of Holmes' drive to see justice done. (It involved an unhappy childhood and his father murdering his mother.)

However, the allegation that Holmes is a sodomite was (for obvious reasons) never made in the Canon and has rarely been made since then. In some ways it is a reasonable deduction: Holmes' distaste for all women (with the notable exception of Irene Adler) is well-known, and his close friendship with Watson is a given. But there is no evidence within the canon for Holmes being of a Uranian disposition, although Billy Wilder's *The Private Life of Sherlock Holmes* (1971) seems to hint at it. Holmes is sexless; he is a dispassionate character who would never give in to primal feelings like lust.

Page 109. Panel 2. "Moran" is Colonel Sebastian Moran. Colonel Moran appears in "The Adventure of the Empty House" and is mentioned in "His Last Bow" (*Strand Magazine*, September 1917). Described by Holmes as "the second most dangerous man in London," Moran served as Professor Moriarty's Chief of Staff and, in "The Adventure of the Empty House," attempted to avenge Moriarty.

Panel 6. In "The Final Problem," Holmes, on the verge of capturing Moriarty and already having survived two attempts on his life, shows a fear of "air-guns." He may have been speaking of Moran's "air-rifle," which is described in "The Adventure of the Empty House": "'An admirable and unique weapon,' said he, 'noiseless and of tremendous power: I knew Von Herder, the blind German mechanic, who constructed it to the order of the late Professor Moriarty.'"

In "The Adventure of the Empty House," Holmes survives an attack with a boulder:

> A huge rock, falling from above, boomed past me, struck the path, and bounded over into the chasm. For an instant I thought that it was an accident, but a moment later, looking up, I saw a man's head against the darkening sky, and another stone struck the very ledge upon which I was stretched, within a foot of my head.

Panel 7. In the Holmesian Canon it is never established or even implied that Col. Moran is an agent of British Intelligence. However, the idea that he worked for them is a reasonable deduction. In "The Adventure of the Empty House," Moran's biography is briefly sketched, and he is described as having served in "Jowaki Campaign, Afghan Campaign, Charasiab (despatches), Sherpur, and Cabul." He is also credited as the author of *Heavy Game in the Himalayas* (1881) and *Three Months in the Jungle* (1884). In the 1870s and 1880s a number of British men in Afghanistan, India, Tibet and the Himalayas were involved in the Great Game of espionage against the Russians. It is therefore a logical assumption that Moran, with his experience in those areas, was an agent of British Intelligence.

The brief of Military Intelligence Group Five, a.k.a. MI5, is counterespionage, while MI6 is in charge of overseas intelligence work. However, this is an alternate universe, and MI5, which was formed years before the real MI5, apparently has different duties than its real world counterpart.

Page 110. Panel 1. The presence of the question marks here might indicate that Question Mark Man, which had formerly been seen in *League* only with League members, may instead be a code or symbol denoting an agent of British Intelligence.

The motorized streetsweeper is a steampunk version of vehicles currently in operation in London.

Panel 2. Three names are visible on the sheets of paper on Moriarty's desk.

The first is "Blake," a reference to Sexton Blake, "the schoolboy's Sherlock Holmes." Blake was created by Harry Blyth and debuted in the story paper *Halfpenny Marvel* #6 (December 20, 1893). Blake began as a standard intelligent, successful detective, but within a few years was transformed into a copy of Sherlock Holmes, which is how he achieved his greatest success, and how he remained for over 3000 stories and over fifty years.

The second name is "Klimo," a reference to the hero of Guy Boothby's "The Duchess of Wiltshire's Diamonds" (*Pearson's Magazine*, February 1897). Klimo is a brilliant detective, influenced by Holmes in certain ways, who is so bored with the lack of opposition that he devises and carries out the theft of the titular diamonds simply to give himself something to do. Klimo is actually the gentleman thief Simon Carne, who uses the identity of Klimo to aid his thefts. Carne, who went on to appear (as himself) in a series of stories, was the first notable gentleman thief in fiction, predating E. W. Hornung's Raffles by two years and Maurice LeBlanc's Arsène Lupin by eight years.

The third name, partially obscured as "ikola," is a reference to Doctor Nikola. Doctor Nikola was created by Guy Boothby and appeared in five novels, beginning with *A Bid for Fortune, or Doctor Nikola's Vendetta* (1895). Doctor Nikola is a Moriarty-style criminal mastermind with plans to conquer the world.

Moriarty is apparently making a list of names of people who might be Sherlock Holmes in disguise. Although the rest of the world, including the members of the League, believes Holmes dead at this time, Moriarty knows he is still alive.

Moriarty's autobiography is similar to that of a number of real-life spies, including the notorious Kim Philby, who while still in college were recruited by various intelligence organizations, American, British, and Soviet. However, such a practice did not exist in the Nineteenth century, at least in real life. Moriarty's college years would have been in the 1850s or 1860s, thirty to forty years before the events of *League*. In the 1850s and 1860s the British intelligence apparatus consisted solely of the Topographical and Statistics Department of the British War Office and was widely viewed, not without reason, as being "harmless but rather useless." The Topographical and Statistics Department was very much a shoestring operation run by well-meaning amateurs without the funds or organization to carry out any recruiting. At this time and up through the mid-1890s, the general Victorian opinion of intelligence assessment and gathering was quite low. The various intelligence groups succeeding the Topographical and Statistics Department were seen by the military and by Cabinet members as carrying out work unworthy of gentlemen. It was not until 1896 when Sir John Ardagh became the Director of Military Intelligence of the British Intelligence Department that modern tactics, such as recruiting spies, were instituted.

Page 111. Panel 7. Battersea is a suburb of London on the south bank of the Thames, opposite Chelsea. Although there is a tradition of fairs in Battersea on the weekends, the Battersea Fun Fair, a permanent amusement park originally known as the "British Pleasure Gardens," was built in the Battersea Park in 1951 and run until 1972, long after the events of *League*.

Panel 8. It is fitting that Moriarty, the "Napoleon of Crime," would have a bust of Napoleon in his office.

Pages 112-113. Griffin's murder of the policeman here is an illustration of Griffin's own words in Chapter 24 of *The Invisible*

Man:

> We have to consider all that invisibility means, all
> that it does not mean. It means little advantage for
> eavesdropping and so forth--one makes sounds. It's
> of little help, a little help perhaps--in housebreaking
> and so forth. Once you've caught me you could
> easily imprison me. But on the other hand I am
> hard to catch. This invisibility, in fact, is only good
> in two cases: It's useful in getting away, it's useful
> in approaching. It's particularly useful, therefore,
> in killing. I can walk round a man, whatever weapon
> he has, choose my point, strike as I like. Dodge as
> I like. Escape as I like.

Page 115. Panel 4. The news on the placards is a reference to one
of the true curiosities of Victorian literature. In 1898 Morgan
Robertson wrote the novel *Futility*, about the cruise of the *Titan*,
the largest and most opulent liner ever built. In *Futility* the *Titan*
cruises the North Atlantic in April carrying the elite of society as
passengers. One April night the *Titan* strikes an iceberg and sinks,
taking most of the passengers and crew with it. When news emerges
of the tragedy, society is outraged, for the makers of the ship had
deemed it "unsinkable" and had put in far too few lifeboats, enough
to save only a fraction of the passengers. The similarities between
Futility and the actual sinking of the *Titanic* are numerous and
uncanny. *Futility* was not the first novel to predict a *Titanic*-like
disaster, however; in 1892 W.T. Stead wrote *From the Old World to
the New*, a novel about a White Star ship, the *Majestic*, coming to
the aid of another liner which has collided with an iceberg. Stead
himself died on the *Titanic*.

Page 118. Panel 3. Nemo is referring to the events of *Dracula* and
its aftermath.

As someone who had been partially turned into a vampire, and then
returned to mortality, Mina would be seen by Victorian society as
having been soiled, and so deserving of being divorced by her husband
and enduring considerable social opprobrium. It wasn't easy to

acquire a divorce in England in the 1890s. Most people went to Scotland for an easy divorce rather than subject themselves to the lengthy and arduous English legal process. Women were not wholly without rights in England in 1898; the Married Woman's Property Act of 1883 granted women property and the right to earn their own money, and in 1898 a judge ruled that a husband never had the right to beat his own wife, so women's liberation had made some inroads in society at this time. Nonetheless, a woman could not divorce her husband unless he had committed bigamy, incest, cruelty, or bestial acts in addition to adultery, while a husband could divorce his wife for simple adultery. A divorced woman was seen as scandalous, and divorce was fatal to a proper woman's reputation, regardless of the cause. Nor would being unwillingly violated by Dracula mitigate Mina's situation in any way. A common Victorian belief was that a proper Englishwoman could not be raped against her will. Someone publically known to have been violated, as Mina would have been, would be seen as damaged and flawed. To have been raped by a foreigner, as Mina was, meant to Victorians what the historian George Trevelyan said of Sir Hugh Wheeler's daughter, who survived the Indian Mutiny and married the sepoy who saved her, that she "was by no means of pure English blood."

However, as is seen in the second *League* series, it is Mina who is more in favor of the divorce than Jonathan, rather than the other way around.

Page 119. Panel 3. Mina's vehemence when she says, "I won't have you two keeping me in the dark about everything," may be related to the moment in *Dracula* when Dr. van Helsing, Jonathan Harker, and Dr. Seward keep Mina "in the dark" about their plans concerning Dracula. Their intent is to protect Mina, but her isolation leaves her vulnerable to Dracula's attack. Due to her past Mina is undoubtedly sensitive to being patronized in this way.

Page 120. Panel 3. Griffin's dance here is a reference to Claude Rains' Invisible Man, who does a similar dance in the 1933 *Invisible Man* film.

Page 121. Panel 2. Griffin's description of Moriarty is similar to Holmes', in "The Final Problem:"

> He is extremely tall and thin, his forehead domes out in a white curve, and his two eyes are deeply sunken in his head. He is clean-shaven, pale, and ascetic-looking, retaining something of the professor in his features. His shoulders are rounded from much study, and his face protrudes forward and is forever slowly oscillating from side to side in a curiously reptilian fashion. He peered at me with great curiosity in his puckered eyes.

Mina's response, "Pray continue," is one of Holmes' catchphrases.

Page 122. Panel 5. The *Pequod* was the ship on which Ishmael, Queequeg, and Captain Ahab sailed in *Moby Dick*. At the end of *Moby Dick* Ahab is found clinging to the coffin of his friend Queequeg; the box seen here might be Queequeg's coffin.

Page 124. Panel 2. The "Fogg" just visible on the side of the traveling case at the far left side of the panel is a reference to Phileas Fogg, the explorer from Jules Verne's *Le Tour du Monde en Quatre-Vingt Jours* (Around the World in Eighty Days, 1873).

The *New Lincoln Herald* was the newspaper published by the colonists on Lincoln Island, the titular island of Jules Verne's *The Mysterious Island*.

The sheet of gibberish writing is actually in code. It is from Jules Verne's *La Jangada* (Eight Hundred Leagues on the Amazon, 1881), a mystery involving a cryptogram and a dead man. In the novel the identity of the traitor is revealed in a coded confession. The extract seen here is only part of the whole, which reads:

Ph yjslyddf dzxgas gz zqq ehx gkfndrxu ju gi
ocytdxvksbx bhu ypohdvy rym huhpuydkjox ph etozsl
etnpmv ffov pd pajx hy ynojyggay meqynfu q1n
mvly fgsu zmqiz tlb qgyu gsqe uvb nrcc edgruzb
l4msyuhqpz drrgcroh e pqxu fivv rpl ph onthvddqf

hqsntzh hh nfepmqkyuuexkto gz gkyuumfv ijdqdpzjq
syk rpl xhxq rym vkloh hh oto zvdk spp suvjhd.

The key to the cipher is the number 432513; to decode the message, you must take the fourth letter before p, the third letter before the h, the second letter before the y, the fifth letter before the j, the first letter before the s, the third letter before the l, and repeat the process for the entire message.

The decoded message reads

Le véritable auteur du vol des diamants et de
l'assassinat des soldats qui escortaient le convoi,
commis dans la nuit du vingt-deux janvier mil
huit-cent vingt-six, n'est donc pas Joam Dacosta,
injustement condamné à mort, c'est moi, les misérable
employé de l'administration du district diamantin,
out, moi seul, qui signe de mon vrai nom, Ortega.

In English:

The real author of the robbery of the diamonds and of
the murder of the soldiers who escorted the convoy,
committed during the night of the twenty-second of January,
one thousand eight hundred and twenty-six, was thus not Joam Dacosta,
unjustly condemned to death; it was I, the wretched
servant of the Administration of the diamond district;
yes, I alone, who sign this with my true name, Ortega.

Panel 5. The "Dr. Samuel Ferguson Expedition" occurred in Jules Verne's *Cinq Semaines en Ballon* (Five Weeks in a Balloon, 1863), one of Verne's first works and one that set much of the tone for his later "Voyages Extraordinaire" stories. The balloon of the book's title is the *Victoria*, and Samuel Ferguson is an English doctor, who with his Scottish friend Dick Kennedy and his manservant Joe, crosses Africa in the *Victoria*.

Page 125. Panel 1. Although most and perhaps all of the non-speaking background characters in *League* are not references to anything, it is quite possible that the child pickpocket might be the titular child from Arthur Morrison's *Child of the Jago* (1896), a realistic and depressing account of life in the Jago, a fictionalized version of London's East End. The titular child is a boy doomed to a short, unhappy life by a bad family and a crooked fence.

Page 126. Kevin O'Neill notes:
> Image of St. Paul's Cathedral is based on Wren's great model rather than dome as built.

Page 127. Panel 2. The Sergeant's uniform has three major Masonic symbols.

The noose around the Sergeant's neck is used as a part of the initiation ritual into the First Degree of Masonry, although in the ritual the noose hangs behind the initiate. In a Masonic initiation the candidate swears secrecy on peril of being "buried in the sand of the sea at low water mark, or a cable's length from shore." The noose symbolizes the link between all Masons as well as the "cable tow" which awaits all apostate Masons.

The compass and right angle are the tools of the Masonic trade as well as being the instruments that God used to measure and circumscribe the boundaries of the universe. The square also reminds Masons to square their actions, to keep them socially acceptable, while the compass tells Masons to circumscribe their desires and to keep their passions restricted.

The eye in the pyramid, which also appears on the American dollar bill, represents the All-Seeing Eye of God and of the Freemasons.

Page 128. "The Day of Be-With-Us" is an occult phrase for the Apocalypse or the end of time. Initially it was simply "the day of Yahweh" (Amos 5:18), meaning the Day of the Judgment, but in medieval Christian usage it became "the day of God-Be-With-Us." Helena Blavatsky, the founder of the Theosophy, wrote about the apocalyptic "Day of Be-With-Us" in *The Secret Doctrine* (1888).

Page 129. Panel 3. The aged thief is the Artful Dodger, from Charles Dickens' *Oliver Twist* (1838). In the novel the Artful Dodger is John Dawkins, a very adept young thief. The Dodger seen here is sixty years older and has become like Fagin, his former mentor in thievery. The boys with the Dodger are his attempt to emulate Fagin and bring together his own group of child thieves.

The Dodger, despite his age, has lost none of his wits. When confronted with a new and horrible concept, air war, he immediately strikes upon the same answer that Londoners did during the Blitz in World War Two: head for underground (and Underground) tunnels.

Panel 4. Mitchell, from Panel 3, and Master Watts, from this panel, are references to Grant Mitchell and "Dirty Den" Watts from the British soap opera *Eastenders* (1985-present). Mitchell, in *Eastenders*, is bald, just like his Victorian ancestor seen here.

Page 131. Panel 3. The woman kneeling behind Fu Manchu is Fah Lo Suee, Fu Manchu's daughter.

Pages 132-133. This scene may be a reference to H.G. Wells' *The War in the Air* (1908), a novel about the creation of efficient, heavier-than-air aircraft, which leads to countries creating air armadas, which eventually clash in a massive aerial world war. Some relevant quotes from *War in the Air* follow:

> If the Germans had three hundred airships all together in the world, the score of Asiatic fleets flying east and west and south must have numbered several thousand. Moreover the Asiatics had a real fighting flying-machine, the Niais as they were called, a light but quite efficient weapon, infinitely superior to the German drachenflieger. Like that, it was a one-man machine, but it was built very lightly of steel and cane and chemical silk, with a transverse engine, and a flapping sidewing. The aeronaut carried a gun firing explosive bullets loaded with oxygen, and in addition, and true to the best tradition of Japan, a sword... The wings

of these flyers had bat-like hooks forward, by which they were to cling to their antagonist's gas-chambers while boarding him...

The Japanese and Chinese have joined in. That's the great fact. That's the supreme fact. They've pounced into our little quarrels.... The Yellow Peril was a peril after all! They've got thousands of airships... And now Asia is at us all, and on the top of us all.... It's mania. China on the top....

The Asiatic airship was also fish-shaped, but not so much on the lines of a cod or goby as of a ray or sole...

It was not in their airships, but, as I have said, in their flying-machines proper, that the strength of the Asiatics lay. Next only to the Butteridge machine, these were certainly the most efficient heavier-than-air fliers that had ever appeared. They were the invention of a Japanese artist, and they differed in type extremely from the box-kite quality of the German drachenflieger. They had curiously curved, flexible side wings, more like bent butterfly's wings than anything else, and made of a substance like celluloid and of brightly painted silk, and they had a long humming-bird tail. At the forward corner of the wings were hooks, rather like the claws of a bat, by which the machine could catch and hang and tear at the walls of an airship's gas-chamber.

Page 133. Panel 4. Mina's question, "Can London survive this?" was often asked by the British during the aerial bombardments of London in World War II.

Page 134. Panel 3. Jekyll's comment, "Do you know, I was once taller than he was?" is a reference to Hyde's original, diminutive and ape-like stature in *Dr. Jekyll and Mister Hyde*.

Page 140. Panel 2. Mina's horror at the carnage Nemo's automatic harpoon gun produces, and her comments that the gun is "inhuman" and "unsporting," reflect a certain confused strain of late Victorian thought regarding sportsmanship and warfare.

The Victorians felt that there were certain standards of behavior in war that should not be violated. Observation dirigibles, steel helmets, snipers–these were all things that were "Not Done" by proper English soldiers, or so the public thought. "Fair Play" was one of the guiding principles of the Empire. When British soldiers killed wounded Mahdists during the campaign to avenge Gordon's death, and when the British Army made a practice of burning Boer farms and rounding up Boer civilians and placing them in concentration camps, the British public objected in great numbers, because such acts fell below the standards to which all Englishmen should adhere. Despite the lessons of the American Civil War and the Crimean War, the British public did not understand the nature of modern warfare until World War One, in large part because accounts of the battles were heavily edited and bowdlerized before they appeared in British newspapers. To this way of thinking Nemo's use of the automatic weapon on the charging soldiers would indeed be "unsporting."

But the British public had long been aware of the existence of the Gatling, Mitrailleuse, and Maxim guns, and were aware of the slaughter they could cause. Even with newspaper accounts which held only the barest details of battles in Afghanistan, India, the Sudan, and South Africa, the public was well aware that the basis for British imperial and military supremacy was superior technology. As Hillaire Belloc wrote, "Whatever happens, we have got/The Maxim gun and they have not." The Maxim gun, the first modern machine gun, was adopted for use by the British army in 1889 and saw its first use against the enemy in 1893. In 1898 the Maxim, the "devil's paintbrush," was in large part responsible for the horrific slaughter at the Battle of Omdurman in the Sudan, where the British killed 11,000 Dervishes and lost only fifty-nine. This was seen by the British public as a great victory and a triumph for Christendom. (In fairness, there were some dissenters, including Winston Churchill, who saw the use of the Maxim at Omdurman as "unfair.") What Nemo does in this sequence is what the British did to the Mahdists and the many other native peoples they fought during the "small wars" of Queen Victoria's reign: use an automatic weapon to massacre dozens of charging enemies.

Despite this awareness of the facts of the Empire, however, the public and the military were resistant to new technology and innovations. Many of the British attitudes towards fair play were self-serving and derived from Napoleonic-era notions of how war should be fought. The idea of weapons which would render these notions outdated, from automatic weapons to high explosive artillery, was offensive to many, regardless of the fact that maintaining the Empire relied on these very weapons. The idea of combat tactics which would negate these notions, like the Boers' guerrilla warfare and angular attacks rather than frontal charges because of the lethality of automatic weaponry, was equally offensive. Mina's objection to Nemo's gun comes from this adherence to a world-view which was outdated but still common in 1898.

Finally, Mina's horror contains a racial element. British soldiers customarily used the Maxim to mow down hundreds of non-white natives, and while this was "unsporting" it was also to be expected, on some level, because the natives were not civilized and the British soldiers were spreading the light of Empire and Christianity. But the use of automatic weaponry on whites was an entirely different matter. Tactics which would not have caused comment if used against the Zulus or Afghans led to public outcries when applied to the Boers. Whites were to be treated differently on the battlefield, and unsporting weapons and tactics were not to be used. This attitude held true until World War I. So it is to be expected that Mina, seeing white soldiers slaughtered by an Indian, would find the moment and the weapon particularly horrifying.

Page 142. Panel 3. There's no textual support in *Dracula* for Mina being seen as a lesbian; her close friendship with Lucy was typical of many Victorian women, for whom passionate "romantic friendships" were quite common.

But the word "lesbian" was certainly common enough to be flung at

Mina by Moriarty. The common understanding of the word "lesbian" as dating only to 1870 is based on the *Oxford English Dictionary*'s entry for the word. However, the editors of the *Oxford English Dictionary* have traditionally deliberately excluded sexual slang from their dictionary and instead relied upon literature rather than diaries, pamphlets, newspapers, and the other kinds of writings in which slang is recorded. Other, less common dictionaries, such as the *1811 Dictionary of the Vulgar Tongue* (1811) and Farmer & Henley's *Slang and its Analogues* (1890-1902), provide numerous terms to describe women-loving women, including "fricatrice," "lesbian," "sapphist," "sucker," "suckster," "tom," "Tommy," and "tribade." The latter term was often used, appearing in *The Pearl*, in the story "An Adventure with a Tribade," as well as in Oscar Wilde's *Teleny* (1893) and in *My Secret Life* (1894), a noted work of Victorian pornography. Professor Moriarty, being a classically educated scholar as well a familiar of the criminal classes, would undoubtedly have known most if not all of these terms, but as a classicist Moriarty would be most likely to use the words "lesbian," with its connotations of the island of Lesbos, "sapphist," with its connotations of the poet Sappho, or "tribade," with its provenance from the erotic classics of Martial and Ovid. Its use here, therefore, is not an anachronism.

Page 143. Panel 5. If Holmes did refer to Quatermain as a "weakling," it was probably due to Quatermain's drug addiction. Given that Holmes himself was a casual drug user, if not an addict, this seems rather hypocritical as well as ungracious. It may be that Holmes thought Quatermain a weakling for succumbing to the lure of opium while he, Holmes, was able to function despite his drug use.

And while such a statement by Holmes would be ungracious, it would not be entirely out of character. As mentioned in the note to Page 23, Panel 1, Holmes, in "A Study in Scarlet," calls Poe's Dupin "a very inferior" fellow. In that same story Holmes describes Emile Gaboriau's Monsieur Lecoq as "a miserable bungler." Gaboriau was a French novelist and journalist whose novels have a place of significance in the history of mystery fiction; they are a coalescence of many different traits and are, in many ways, the first modern mystery novels. Monsieur Lecoq appeared in five of Gaboriau's novels, beginning with *L'Affaire Lerouge* (The Widow Lerouge, 1865). Lecoq is an energetic and clever young French policeman who is aided in his crime-solving by the elderly Pére Tabaret, an eccentric amateur detective with a great skill at taking in all the details of a crime scene at a glance and then being able to give police detailed descriptions; these features have led critics to see Gaboriau as influencing Arthur Conan Doyle. Holmes' scorn for Lecoq is a joke by Doyle towards a writer who he openly admired, but it is also an example of Holmes' poor attitude towards other major fictional detectives. In this light Holmes' "weakling" comment would be in character for him, if he did in fact say it, and Moriarty is not simply being cruel to Quatermain.

Page 144. Panels 4-5. Moriarty falling into the sky may be an homage to H.P. Lovecraft's "The Other Gods" (*The Fantasy Fan*, November 1933), in which prophet Barzai the Wise scales the mountain Hatheg-Kla in order to look on the faces of the gods. In this story, written during Lovecraft's Lord Dunsany phase, Barzai sees the faces of the gods, as well as, "The other gods! The gods of the outer hells that guard the feeble gods of Earth!" Barzai's last words are, "Merciful gods of earth, I am falling into the sky!"

Page 146-147. Kevin O'Neill notes:
Falling man is wearing corset as advertised in earlier issue.

Page 149. Panel 1. The two characters on the left are "Weary Willy" and "Tired Tim." This pair of amiable tramps was created in 1896 by the cartoonist Tom Browne and was based on a pair of tramps he had spotted on the Thames Embankment. Weary Willy and Tired Tim debuted in the British comic *Illustrated Chips* in 1896 and appeared there for decades. After Browne died in 1910 their adventures were written by, among others, Herbert Allingham, the father of Margery Allingham, the creator of Albert Campion (see the note to Page 7, Panels 6-7 above).

The character on the far right is Ally Sloper. Ally Sloper, a British comic character like Weary Willy and Tired Tim, was created by

Charles Ross and Marie Duval and first appeared in *Judy* in 1867. He was regularly featured in *Ally Sloper's Half-Holiday* from 1884 through 1914. Ally Sloper was one of the first rogues in British comics to be featured as a hero. His name comes from the practice of avoiding the rent collector by "sloping" down an alley, and his personality is a combination of cheerful insolence and naked, unashamed self-interest.

Panel 2. The broken walking stick on the wall is Professor Moriarty's.

Panel 3. The bust at the far left side of the panel is of Karl Friedrich Hieronymus, Baron von Münchhausen (1720-1797). Baron Münchhausen is best known for his extraordinarily tall tales. A collection of his tales first appeared in 1781-1783, under the title *Vademecum fur Lustige Leute* (Manual for Merry People), but Münchhausen developed into the epitome of the European tall tale teller with the 1785 publication of *Baron Munchhausen's Narrative of His Marvellous Travels and Campaigns in Russia*. It is interesting that MI5 should have a bust of a notorious braggart and teller of lies in its headquarters, but as is shown in the second *League* series, the Baron was a member of a previous League.

The mustached man is Dick Donovan, last seen on Page 51, Panel 3 interrogating Hyde.

The balloon is the *Victoria* from Verne's *Five Weeks in a Balloon*, as mentioned in the note to Page 124, Panel 5. Moore originally intended to use the balloon from Verne's *Around the World in 80 Days*, but a balloon was used only in the 1956 David Niven film of *Around the World*, rather than in the book, and so plans were changed.

The portly man is Mycroft Holmes, Sherlock Holmes' smarter brother, mentioned in the notes to Page 10, Panel 1. His non-committal response to Mina's condolences is due to the fact that he alone knows that Sherlock Holmes is still alive. As mentioned, Holmes "died" in "The Final Problem," which was published in 1893 and set in May 1891. Doyle brought Holmes back in "The Adventure of the Empty House," published in 1903 and set in the spring of 1894. The period of time between May 1891 and spring 1894, when Holmes was alive, but not active in London, is known to Sherlockians as "The Great Hiatus." Doyle dropped hints in "The Empty House" about Holmes' activities during this time: he visited Tibet, Mecca, Khartoum, and Montpellier, France. During this time only one man knew Holmes was still alive: his brother Mycroft.

For the possible identity of the policeman, see the note to Panel 4, below.

The box on the right, dated 1657, is the box that Cyrano de Bergerac used to fly to the moon in his *Histoire comique des États et Empires de la Lune* (History of the States and Empires of the Moon, 1657). In this novel Cyrano travels into space and finds different alien societies.

Panel 4. The metal object to the right of Mina is the "Huge Hunter," from Edward S. Ellis' "The Huge Hunter, or, the Steam Man of the Prairies" (*Irwin P. Beadle's American Novels* #45, August 1868). The Huge Hunter is a steam-powered engine in the shape of a man which its inventor, the hunch-backed dwarf Johnny Brainerd, used to draw a cart. "The Steam Man of the Prairies" was the first story to feature an Edisonade (boy inventor) character and established several features of the genre, which was to last well into the Twentieth century with characters like John Blaine's Rick Brant and Harriet Stratemeyer Adams' Tom Swift, Jr.

The policeman on the right side of the panel has the collar insignia #49. This may be a reference to Police Constable Archibald Berkeley-Willoughby, PC 49, from the eponymous British radio serial (1947-1953), two films and various comic strips. In the radio serial and films, PC 49 is an ordinary "bobby on the beat" who patrols the streets and docks of all of London, rather than just the West End.

Kevin O'Neill notes:
> Yes, this is a PC 49 reference and to his left is Baltimore Gun Club's capsule.

Panel 5. The winged woman in the glass bottle is one of the Cottingley faeries. Arthur Conan Doyle, later in his life, took refuge in various eccentric spiritual beliefs, including "spirit photography," the fraudulent practice of taking pictures which supposedly revealed the ghost of a recently deceased relative or loved one. In 1917 Elsie Wright and Frances Griffiths, two young Yorkshirewomen from Cottingley, copied illustrations of faeries on cardboard and then had their pictures taken next to the cardboard cut-outs. The pair then played a practical joke on their parents by claiming that they had been playing with five faeries. In 1919, when news of the photographs spread, they were taken seriously by a number of people, including Arthur Conan Doyle, who was heartbroken over the deaths of his brother, son, brother-in-law, and two nephews in World War I.

Page 150. The descending bullet-shaped objects are the Martian cylinders making their initial landing in Woking, from Chapter Two of H.G. Wells' *The War of the Worlds*, the novel that serves as the backdrop for the second *League* series.

The sitting gentleman picking at his feet wears the traditional costume of John Bull, the unofficial icon of England.

The purple mushrooms in the lower right corner of the panel may be a reference to H.G. Wells' "The Purple Pileus" (*Black and White*, Christmas Number, 1896), a story about a shopkeeper who eats a strange purplish mushroom and undergoes a complete change in personality.

Kevin O'Neill notes:
> Scene of descending Martian cylinders takes some license with H.G. Wells who describes them landing one at a time (this is corrected in Volume Two).

> Purple mushrooms in corner had no significance at time.

Page 153. The *Boys' First-Rate Pocket Library* was a real magazine. As shown at the bottom of this page, it was published by the Aldine

Publishing Company of London and ran for 472 issues from 1890 to 1905. The *Pocket Library* was a boys' story paper, a magazine publishing fiction aimed at boys. The stories in the *Pocket Library* were reprints from American dime novels, featuring characters like the cowboy vigilante Deadwood Dick, the Huge Hunter (see the note to Page 149, Panel 4), and Happy Hans, "the Dutch Vidocq." The stories were very similar to "Allan and the Sundered Veil," albeit not as well written. The covers of the *Pocket Library* were similar to the cover shown here.

The figures on the cover will be identified as they appear in the story.

Page 154. Many story papers in the late Victorian and early Edwardian years contained advertisements for other story papers published by the same publisher. This advertisement is very authentic-looking and is likely a reproduction of an actual ad. *The Rival* was a story paper published from October 1897 to August 1899 by Aldine. There were three story paper authors by the name of Henry T. Johnson, one of whom wrote widely for the story papers. (Each issue of the first and second *League* series had one or two fake ads, prepared in a properly Victorian style by Moore, O'Neill, William Oakley, and Todd Klein. These ads are covered below, in the "Material Not Included In The League Hardcover" section.)

Kevin O'Neill notes:
> Penny Dreadful ad for *The Rival* is a genuine ad that appeared on the back cover of *The Aldine Library of Invention, Travel, & Adventure: Jack Wright's Search for Captain Kidd's Gold* (No. 237) It appears unaltered. And is from a handful of Penny Dreadfuls I've managed to find.

Page 155. "Allan and the Sundered Veil" is written in a rococo, lush, and over-ripe style. In other words, it is a deliberate recreation of the style of *fin-de-siècle*, Yellow Nineties Decadent writers like Robert Chambers, Arthur Machen, and M.P. Shiel, as if one of them had written a boys' magazine story starring Allan Quatermain.

"...those abandoned ornamental gardens sprawled out among the castle ruins. Turrets fallen to a scree of brick and warped spines of collapsing battlement lay abject and senescent in the lunar sickle's cool, diluted silvering, so that even the dead man caught his breath: he had not thought the place to be so changed since his demise."

Allan is looking at Ragnall Castle, which he first visited in *The Ivory Child* (1916). Haggard describes it as "a splendid old castle with brick gateway towers, that had been wonderfully well restored and turned into a most luxurious modern dwelling."

Page 156. "Lady Ragnall is expecting you."
Lady Ragnall was created by H. Rider Haggard and appeared in three of Haggard's Allan Quatermain books: *The Ivory Child*, *The Ancient Allan* (1920), and *Allan and the Ice Gods* (co-written by Rudyard Kipling, 1927). Her maiden name was Luna Holmes; she became Lady Ragnall on her marriage to Lord Samuel Savage. In the course of *The Ivory Child* she meets Quatermain and then, years later, is kidnaped by a group of Africans who worship her as the incarnation of the priestess of their goddess/statue, the Ivory Child. Quatermain eventually rescues her. In *The Ancient Allan* she and Quatermain experiment with taduki, an herb which when smoked gives one visions of both past and future lives. In one vision he experiences his life as the Egyptian nobleman Shabaka. In *Allan and the Ice Gods,* Quatermain is told Lady Ragnall has died and has left him a casket full of taduki which he smokes, experiencing his life as Wi, a caveman of the Upper Paleolithic.

"More troubling still, how could it be that his dear former friend and patron Lady Ragnall yet resided here."
In *Allan and the Ice Gods* the friendship between Quatermain and Lady Ragnall founders because he "did not wish for more adventures in which women were mixed up," and because "it is extremely awkward to foregather with an imperial woman who is firmly convinced that she was once your wife, so awkward that, in the end, it might have proved necessary to resume what she considered to be an established, if an interrupted, relationship." For these reasons Quatermain avoids Lady Ragnall and finds out second-hand that

she has died in Egypt. But Quatermain never sees her body, only speaks with the executor of her estate and receives her posthumous gift to him of the taduki.

Page 157. "They said that you were dead. I had a letter from Sir Henry's brother, George, to that effect. Apparently you died at dawn three years ago in 1886, from injuries bravely received, away in some darker-than-usual corner of the darkest continent."
In *Allan Quatermain,* Quatermain dies at dawn from a wound taken in the Battle of the Pass, in Africa. *Allan Quatermain* consists of Quatermain's diary and a post-script from George Curtis, the brother of Quatermain's friend Sir Henry Curtis. *Allan Quatermain* was published in 1887, but the internal dating of *Allan Quatermain* places Quatermain's death in 1886.

"A world enthused by Mr. Haggard's somewhat overblown and generous accounts of my adventures would not suffer me to rest; would never tolerate the thought of Allan Quatermain, now grey and doddering, pruning his roses in some leaden suburb."
The conceit that H. Rider Haggard was Allan Quatermain's biographer is one used by a number of writers in describing how an author and his or her fictional creation would interact in a fictional world, so that in several stories Arthur Conan Doyle is described as the co-writer, with Dr. Watson, of the Sherlock Holmes stories.

The image of an elderly Quatermain tending to his garden in a dull suburb may be a reference to T.E. Lawrence, the British adventurer and author who after twenty-one years in the British military, Colonial Office, and R.A.F. retired to his cottage in Dorset. His death two months later in a motorcycle accident led to widespread rumors that, unable to cope with the boredom of the "pointless existence" of post-military life, Lawrence had committed suicide. Quatermain apparently imagines a quiet life in retirement for himself, but like Lawrence, Quatermain cannot live life quietly, which is why he has come back to Lady Ragnall.

"It was all a yarn, then? All that business that George Curtis mentioned in the letter that he sent, concerning a lost kingdom called

Zu-Vendis? Why, he told me that Sir Henry Curtis was now king there and would be no more returning to these isles. He said that you were slain and so too was the Zulu friend you spoke of once. Umslopogaas, was that his name? As George reported things, your warrior companion fell heroically in battle against plotters who might otherwise have robbed Sir Henry of his life."

This is an accurate summary of the events of *Allan Quatermain*.

"Would that it were. I saw Umslopogaas myself as he was slain, hurling his enemy Lord Nasta from a parapet before he raised his bloody axe, Inkosikaas, up to his lips and kissed it, crying out 'I die, I die, but 'twas a kingly fray.'"

In *Allan Quatermain* Sir Henry Curtis is menaced by a band of assassins, and in one of the most memorable fights in all of adventure fiction Umslopogaas holds the staircase against them, killing the assassins and their leader, the wicked Lord Nasta, but taking mortal wounds in so doing.

Page 159. "There below his wraith-like feet, lush tufts of pale mauve grass grew from mud of rich indigo. A queasy hybrid vegetation, writhing blossoms neither wholly cuttlefish nor thistle, sprouted from the spectral verges."

The description of the landscape here and following is similar to the description of the decayed and dying landscape of the future Earth in H.G. Wells' *The Time Machine* (1895).

"To one side of this cheerless blaze there sat a stooped young man, lugubrious features weirdly underlit by the wan radiance of the campfire."

This figure, who introduces himself on Page 160, is Randolph W. Carter. Carter was created by H.P. Lovecraft and appeared in five of Lovecraft's stories: "The Statement of Randolph Carter" (*The Vagrant*, May 1920), "The Unnamable" (*Weird Tales* v6 n1, July 1925), *The Dream-Quest of Unknown Kadath* (1943), "The Silver Key" (*Weird Tales* v13 n1, January 1929), and "Through the Gates of the Silver Key" (with E. Hoffmann Price, *Weird Tales* v24 n1, July 1934). Carter, who Lovecraft partially based on himself, is a morose man who has adventures in various dreamlands.

"Cross-legged on the mauve turf opposite this dreamy individual sat a person stranger yet, a strongly built man decked out in the dusty grey apparel of a Southern officer of the American War between the States."

This figure, who is introduced on Page 160, is John Carter. John Carter was created by Edgar Rice Burroughs and appeared in the ten Martian novels, beginning with *A Princess of Mars* (1912). Carter is a swashbuckling Confederate veteran who travels to Mars via astral projection and finds love and adventure there among the Martians.

Page 160. "I am Randolph Carter. This is my great-uncle John."
Lovecraft never established any family links between his character and Burroughs'. Family ties between the two Carters have been created by successive *pasticheurs*. However, Lovecraft knew of a prominent Carter family in his home state of Rhode Island; the first newspaper of Providence had been established in 1762 by John Carter. Lovecraft also knew that this family had emigrated to Rhode Island from Virginia. In Lovecraft's own words, "…this transposition of a Virginia line to New England has always affected my fancy strongly." So the groundwork for a family link between Randolph Carter and John Carter, who is from Virginia, was laid by Lovecraft.

"The young man went on to describe an improbable New England of the twentieth century, a life spent in reclusive exploration of the world of dreams. During one such excursion through what the young man referred to as 'the gates of Deeper Slumber,' he had strayed unwittingly into these current psychic wastelands, previously unknown to him."

As stated, most of Carter's life is spent exploring and adventuring in the Dreamlands, often in search of his ideal "sunset city." The "Gate of Deeper Slumber" appears in *The Dream-Quest of Unknown Kadath*; it is the gateway to the Enchanted Wood of the Dreamlands.

"All I know is that I was dying in a cave and staring at the planet Mars just hanging there above me in the grey dawn sky, its strong unblinking light amidst the fading stars. Suddenly, I'm wrenched from my body, just as if the pull of Mars is drawing up my soul towards it...but instead I end up in this dismal, gaseous place...."

In *A Princess of Mars* Carter is prospecting for gold in Arizona when he and his partner are attacked by Apaches. Carter retreats into a cave, the Apaches leave, and then he leaves the cave. Looking at Mars, Carter feels the planet pull at him, and he passes out as he is "drawn with the suddenness of thought through the trackless immensity of space." Carter's adventure in "Allan and the Sundered Veil" therefore takes place in his own chronology before any of his Martian adventures.

"The swathe of emerald flame briefly illuminated something very like a monstrous centipede made of translucent gelatine, a frogspawn cluster of a dozen eyes grouped at one end that glittered momentarily in the ghastly viridian light."

Although this creature is reminiscent of some of the animals in *The Time Machine*, particularly the giant crab things which menace the Time Traveler in Chapter 11, it and several of the creatures in "Allan and the Sundered Veil" are also similar to many of the alien creatures in Lovecraft's fiction.

"The explorer gasped in disbelief as the peculiar throb of light resolved itself into a ghostly figure, seated in mid-air upon the saddle of a dazzling contraption made from brass, the man's garb not dissimilar to that of Quatermain's own era. The bright light around this new arrival and his craft seemed to alarm the squirming presences beyond the firelight's rim, prompting them to withdraw. At this, the stranger called out to the three men.

"'Climb aboard. The novelty of my arrival won't deter these horrors long.' Pausing, he thought to introduce himself.

"'I'm sometimes called the Time Traveler.'"

The Time Traveler is the lead character from H.G. Wells' *The Time Machine*. The Traveler is never named in *The Time Machine*. In the first version of *The Time Machine*, a never-completed set of short stories cumulatively called *The Chronic Argonauts*, the Traveler is named "Dr. Nebogipfel," but that name was dropped during the completion of *The Time Machine*.

Page 162. "Rising from the bleached and calceous floor not far from where their craft had come to rest, a towering and flawless statue of pure alabaster stood in sharp relief against the plush, star-sequined velvet of the night. Supine on its massive plinth the white Sphinx sprawled, its weighty feline forepaws resting one atop the other and its smoothly chiseled woman's lips creased faintly in a knowing, almost melancholy smile."

In *The Time Machine* the Traveler discovers a giant Sphinx statue. Initially he is unable to enter it; he later does but does not explore it, instead escaping from the Morlocks who hoped to trap him inside it.

Page 164. "My name is of no consequence. Suffice to say that I am an inventor, formerly residing here in London, who perfected in the last years of the nineteenth century a means of traveling in time. I had adventures in Earth's farthest future after which, following a brief farewell visit to my own day, I have dwelled here in the phantom stream of decades ever since as an explorer, much like your good self."

In *The Time Machine* the Traveler visits the Earth in the year 802, 701, sees the peaceful Eloi and the brutal troglodytic Morlocks, and then travels to Earth in its dying days. At the end of the novel the Traveler returns to London in the Nineteenth century, relates his story to the narrator (implicitly Wells), and then vanishes again. The Traveler's story here explains what he did after the novel ended.

"You will guess my horror, then, when I discovered that there seems to be a vast, near unimaginable hole torn in the fabric of Creation, and that certain atmospheres or entities are leaking through this dreadful and apocalyptic pit from somewhere else!"

This is an apt summation of the basic premise of many of H.P. Lovecraft's stories.

"Awful and shambling simian forms whose greatest horror was the faint humanity remaining in their slack albino faces shuffled through the dunes outside, uncomfortably near the undefended Time-machine.

Gaze fixed upon the shimmering crystal of his watching-glass, their host's voice burned with stifled anger as he spoke.

"'They're Morlocks, known to other eras as Mi-Go, or as abominable snowmen. While they're not the entities that I referred to, they appear to serve them.'"

In *The Time Machine* the Morlocks are an evolutionary offshoot of the human race. They are brutish, subterranean, and treat the Eloi as cattle. The "Mi-Go" are the creation of H.P. Lovecraft; they appeared in his "The Whisperer in Darkness" (*Weird Tales* v18 n1, August 1931) and were mentioned in *At the Mountains of Madness* (1936). The Mi-Go are alien beings, known to the "Nepalese hill tribes" as "the dreaded Mi-Go or 'Abominable Snow-Men'," who "lurk hideously amidst the ice and rock pinnacles of the Himalayan summits." They stay on Earth in order to mine certain minerals which they cannot find on their home planet of Yuggoth. Lovecraft describes them as being "half-fungous, half crustacean creatures" and serving the alien space gods "The Great Old Ones."

Page 167. "Allan's attention was seized by one vignette in particular: a wasted, almost skeletal old man sprawled on a pallet on what seemed to be a beige rug in an opium den, a thin pipe clasped there in his nerveless fingers. Crouching by the man, a striking woman in a long, red scarf seemed to be speaking urgently to the near cadaver. There was a sudden start of purest horror as Quatermain realized that the drugged and wretched creature slumped there in bug-haunted squalor was himself."

Quatermain is seeing his future, the start of *League*; see Pages 11-13.

"'An Aleph,' the Time Traveler sighed, almost ecstatically. 'Behold, my friends, Time's very fulcrum. Gaze, if you dare, into the diamond eyepiece of Infinity!'"

This is a reference to Jorge Luis Borges' "El Aleph" (*Sur*, September 1945). In Borges' story the Aleph is "a small iridescent sphere of almost unbearable brilliance" whose "diameter was probably little more than an inch." The Aleph is "one of the points in space that contains all other points...the only place on earth where all places are." In it can be seen the entire universe.

Page 168. The picture on the left side of this page is a melange of images from the characters' futures. The two beings in the upper left corner are John Carter, in his Martian garb, and a four-armed Martian; this fight could appear in any of Edgar Rice Burroughs' Martian novels. The image below and to the right, of a burning building, is from H.G. Wells' *War of the Worlds*; the thin black lines on the right side of this image are the legs of Martian Tripods, who presumably have just set the building alight with their heat beams. The events of *The War of the Worlds* are shown in the second *League of Extraordinary Gentlemen* series. The image in the lower left is of Mina and Allan, from Page 11, Panel 4. And the image at the bottom of the panel is of the *Nautilus*.

"Her Ladyship was not without some personal experience in feigning death so as to thwart the gross intrusions of the living, having staged her own end some years earlier to live since then in blissful undisturbed seclusion as the stately pile of Ragnall Hall fell into luscious ruin about her...."
This is a reference to Lady Ragnall's "death" in *Allan and the Ice Gods*. As mentioned above, in the last note to Page 156, Lady Ragnall's death is not witnessed by Quatermain; he finds out about it via a telegram received from Cairo.

Page 169. "He saw himself fighting for his life, aboard some great and frightful skyboat above a dark benighted city; struggling in the wind-lashed rigging with a large, impossibly-constructed gun that seemed to fire harpoon after harpoon. The woman from the earlier fragment clung against his side, her body pressing to him in the howling night."
This seems to be a somewhat inexact reference to the events on Page 142.

"Now he watched a hideous subhuman beast that was absurdly garbed in the remains of what seemed to be formal evening dress, the creature bellowing and laughing hideously as it attacked some great metallic thing that Quatermain could not make visual sense of.

More shapes moved against a fire-lit skyline, glinting metal hulks supported on what seemed the spindly legs of monstrous iron flamingos."

This is another reference to the events of the second *League* series, in which Mr. Hyde attacks one of the Martian Tripods.

"Now he saw the familiar small, determined woman clad in nothing but a dirty blanket, shrieking, overcome by horror in what looked to Allan's traveled eye like the interior of a dark and rural building, possibly in the Americas. Arcane symbols were inscribed in noxious, nameless fluids on the bare boards of the floor and on the walls, and there was something thrashing over in a distant corner of the room. Quatermain saw himself, screaming as loudly as the woman while engaged in combat with a tentacled and writhing shape that seemed to reach in some way through the walls of the dilapidated farm-house."

This is a reference to an event in Allan and Mina's future. In the second *League* series it is explained that in 1899 Mina and Allan traveled to the fictional town of Arkham, Massachusetts, and have an encounter with a creature of H.P. Lovecraft's Cthulhu Mythos. The Cthulhu Mythos is a linked series of stories which the American science fiction/horror writer H.P. Lovecraft wrote about a group of malign alien gods, the Great Old Ones, and their existence, along with their worshipers and creations, on Earth.

Page 170. "Randolph Carter, lost within his own cascade of vision, groaned with recognition and with longing as there in the jewel before him he saw the familiar vista of his native Arkham, with its gambrel rooftops gilded by the last, long rays of afternoon."

In H.P. Lovecraft's stories Arkham is a city, located on the North Shore of Massachusetts, which is the home to Miskatonic University. Arkham is a fictional city based on Salem, Mass.

"The elder Carter crouched nearby and gazed in wonderment at scenes of strange red deserts, almost-naked ruby-clad princesses and green, towering men that had too many arms...."

John Carter is seeing parts of his future. The red deserts, near-naked princesses (in this case, Dejah Thoris, Carter's future wife), and large, multi-armed "men" are all seen in Edgar Rice Burroughs' Martian novels; at this point in time Carter has not yet reached Mars.

Page 172. "They called it Yuggoth. They perceived it, variously, as a planet, as a god, or as a state of mind."
In Lovecraft's Cthulhu Mythos stories "Yuggoth" is the Mi-Go's name for the planet Pluto.

"The myriad lesser notions which comprised this hive-like meta-being were in turn seen as subsidiary deities, who functioned both as avatars and envoys to the central, hideously animate conceptual core. These individual agents were collectively termed 'Lloigor'...."
This is a reference to the Lloigor, a creature which has appeared in several stories making use of H.P. Lovecraft's Cthulhu Mythos. The Lloigor, an alien space god, was first mentioned in "Lair of the Star-Spawn," by August Derleth and Mark Schorer (1932).

Page 173. "Upon a lower, more immediate level it was the Lloigor named Ithaqqa, worshiped in the arctic regions as a demon of the upper air, or of the intellectual faculty in man. Most intimately, in as much as one might say that it was capable of understanding anything, it understood itself to be a nameless elemental of the kind known as wind-walkers, or sometimes as Wendigo."
"Ithaqqa," or Ithaqua, was created by August Derleth and first appeared in "Beyond the Threshold" (*Weird Tales*, September 1941), although two earlier stories, Algernon Blackwood's "The Wendigo" (1910) and George Allan England's "The Thing From Outside" (*Science and Invention*, April 1923), feature creatures very similar to Ithaqua, but not associated with the Cthulhu Mythos. Ithaqua, in the Cthulhu Mythos, is the "real" version of the mythological Canadian monster the Wendigo.

Page 174. "When they spoke of such they would refer to the phenomenon by a variety of names, and all these names, Marisa understood, spoke only of one thing: Great Old Ones."
In the Cthulhu Mythos stories, the Great Old Ones are alien gods of malign intent and great power.

"Wild-eyed, the tall obsidian beauty looked about her for a scrap of paper and some writing tools with which she might construct this 'Elder Sign' herself and in this manner aid the man who writhed and twisted like a landed fish upon the library floor before her."

The Elder Sign was first mentioned in H.P. Lovecraft's "The Descendant" (*Leaves* v2, 1938). The Elder Sign is a magic symbol created by the Elder Gods, ancient alien deities more powerful than the Great Old Ones, as protection against the Great Old Ones.

Page 175. The picture of the flaming Ragnall Castle is visually similar to the home of Great Uncle Baal, a supporting character in the British comic strip "Nemesis." "Nemesis," which appeared in the comic *2000AD,* was drawn at times by Kevin O'Neill, the artist for *League*.

Kevin O'Neill notes:

> Ragnall Castle being similar to my design for the Great Uncle Baal in *Nemesis the Warlock* – well, not much of a similarity, but probably highlights my love of the operatic in design.

Page 178. The format of this cover is a reference to the *Illustrated Police News*, a British sensationalist newspaper (today it would be thought of as a crime-oriented tabloid) covering the most recent, newsworthy, and horrifying crimes, disasters, and scandals. It ran from 1864 to 1938, and in its heyday had the largest circulation of any periodical in Britain. The covers of the *IPN* had drawn reproductions of crime scenes around a center sketch or sketches of the individuals involved, just like this image.

This cover is not just an homage to the *Illustrated Police News*-style cover illustrations, but also a satire of several Victorian attitudes. Despite its focus on crimes and scandals the *IPN* also often carried vividly illustrated stories about monsters and strange animals in foreign locations. The "Egyptians Beset" panel is an example of this, showing a bizarre monster attacking a foreign port.

Similarly, the *IPN*, in true tabloid style, pandered to the biases of its readers by portraying foreigners in very stereotyped ways. The

"Affront To Womanhood" panel portrays rapacious and hook-nosed Arabs threatening a white woman with rape, the "fate worse than death," a persistent subtext in much Victorian writing. The image of the white woman imprisoned in an Eastern harem was common among British accounts of Turkey and India in the Eighteenth century, and many Gothic novels in the late Eighteenth and early Nineteenth centuries depicted English women being threatened with rape by foreigners. Emerging ideas of racial purity combined with the 1857 Indian Mutiny to produce a spate of diaries, letters, and stories and over fifty novels about innocent English women being kidnaped, imprisoned, and threatened with rape and torture by barbaric Indian men. (This, despite the fact that no evidence was ever found that English women had been raped during the Mutiny.) By 1898 the idea of the "fate worse than death" was solidly implanted in the Victorian consciousness.

The "Ghastly Murderer" panel, with its depiction of a nude, dismembered woman's body, is a reference to the *IPN*'s use of very detailed drawings of murder victims. The *IPN*'s sketches of the victims of Jack the Ripper would be deemed too graphic for today's newspaper audience.

The "Opium" panel is a perfect encapsulation of the late Victorian attitude towards opium. Although there was a certain amount of anti-opium sentiment among the general population of Britain, the press and the government, despite nominal anti-opium statements, were in favor of the opium trade. Various pretexts were given in support of the continued production and sale of the drug–its effects weren't particularly injurious, the Chinese were not being forced to use opium, the British government was simply meeting a demand– but the real reason was money. By the 1890s most opium was made in India under the control of the British government; the opium trade provided seventeen to twenty percent of the gross national product of the sub-continent. This was a significant amount of money, and the British government was unwilling to relinquish it.

As mentioned in the notes to Page 54, writers of fiction began portraying opium as evil starting in the 1860s. And the British public bought into this attitude to a limited degree. But rather than condemning the trade of opium–the reasons given by the government and parroted by the press in favor of the trade were mostly accepted by the public–the British public saw opium as evil only insofar as it was used by white men and women. Opium dens were seen as signs of decadence, and the intermingling of white opium users with Chinese and other "coloured races" was seen as socially and racially polluting, and a deliberate act on the part of the Chinese. So in a classic act of Freudian projection the British public saw opium, which was made and sold by the British government to the Chinese and Indians, as something the "heathens" used to plague "Christendom."

Likewise, the "Hindu Mariner" panel, with its glowering Nemo in front of a sinking ship, illustrates some of the attitudes of the Victorians towards the Great Mutiny, and how Nemo would be viewed by them. The Great Mutiny was deeply shocking to the Victorians, who imagined themselves to have been lenient to the Indians in the years preceding the Mutiny and who after the Mutiny gorged themselves on stories of English heroism and Indian barbarities. The British East India Company was blamed for having caused the Mutiny and was dissolved by the English government in 1858, with direct control of India reverting to the English government. The British attitude towards India became much more conservative in tone, seeing reforms and leniency as weaknesses which the Indians would seize upon. Similarly, British racial attitudes towards the Indians hardened, and crude stereotyping became the norm. In the decades following the Mutiny dozens of popular histories and novels were published which emphasized and exaggerated the atrocities of the Indians and the nobility and innocence of the English in India. The 1890s saw a new wave of novels, many a conservative reaction to the assertions of several professional historians that English women were not raped during the Mutiny. To the late Victorians a figure like Nemo, an Indian survivor of the Mutiny who was responsible for sinking several ships (as seen in his novels and in the background of the illustration here) and who had a stated enmity for the British Empire, would be sinister. He would remind them of the Mutiny and of the many atrocities which they "knew" to have been committed, and his continued survival would hint that further Mutinies and atrocities might occur.

Finally, the "Lady 'With Past'" panel, with its coy hint at a sexual scandal in Mina's past, illustrates Victorian attitudes towards sex. The common image today of the Victorian attitude toward sexuality is one of repression. But the Victorians had a very complex outlook towards sexuality. Concerns with propriety from all levels of society mixed with a very permissive attitude towards sexuality. Divorcees were scandalous, but the *demi-mondaines* and mistresses of the rich and wealthy were invited to and accepted into the most exclusive parties and occasions, idolized by many young women of means, watched with admiration by mothers and daughters, and had their fashions copied by "respectable" women. Readers were scandalized by news stories of sex–when Grant Allen published *The Woman Who Did* in 1895, about a woman who refuses to marry her lover because she feels that marriage laws are unfair to women, many in the public were horrified–but they bought in large numbers the magazines which printed such stories. Mina's appearance here would help sell many copies of a newspaper and allow to readers to pruriently disapprove of her.

Page 180. The images on this cover are meant to be from Victorian cigarette cards, which were introduced in the United States in the mid-1870s and in Britain in 1887. They were illustrated cardboard cards, roughly the size of baseball cards, which were included in packs of cigarettes. Originally the cardboard cards in packs of cigarettes were blank and intended only to strengthen the flimsy packaging of cigarette packs, but once the idea of placing advertising on the cards occurred to someone the practice became widespread. This was not a new idea; similar cards accompanied a variety of products in France beginning in 1840, and they were common across Europe by 1880.

Cigarette cards were two-sided, with an illustration or picture on one side and information about the image on the other side. One card was included in each pack of cigarettes, and each card was part of a set, with the idea being that consumers would buy multiple packs of cigarettes in order to get an entire set of cards.

The heyday of cigarette card production came between the Wars. There were plans to reintroduce them after World War II but that never happened.

A wide range of subjects were shown on cigarette cards, from animals to war heroes to Holmes and Moriarty to famous cricketers and football players. It is logical that in the world of *League* a line of cigarette cards featuring members of the League would be produced.

"Captain Nemo 1867" shows a younger Captain Nemo—note his neatly trimmed mustache and beard. As mentioned in the note to Page 17, Panel 3, both *Twenty Thousand Leagues Under the Sea* and *The Mysterious Island* take place in 1867, due to the inconsistencies in both novels. These inconsistencies are probably in part the fault of Jules Verne, who changed his mind about certain plot elements while writing *Mysterious Island*, and in part the fault of Pierre-Jules Hetzel, Verne's publisher, who changed many aspects of *The Mysterious Island* despite Verne's objections. The underwater scene shown here cannot be from *The Mysterious Island*, because in that novel Nemo dies in 1867, having lived on Lincoln Island for a decade. The scene must therefore be from *Twenty Thousand Leagues*. It may be a recreation of the moment in Chapter 21 when the *Nautilus* rams and sinks a two-decker ram which was trailing the *Nautilus*.

"Miss Mina Murray, 1897" shows an unmarried Mina Murray, from the months in 1897, before the events of *Dracula*, when she was only engaged to Jonathan Harker. Just as Captain Nemo's facial hair is notable by its absence in the cigarette card on this cover, so too is Mina's scarf, and the scars it conceals, notable by its absence. Likewise, her eyes are a much lighter green here than they are in *League*. Near the end of *Dracula* Mina is partially transformed into a vampire by Dracula before he is killed and Mina is saved. Dracula's eyes are red; Mina's eyes here are a pale green. Her eyes in *League* are stuck between the two colors, as she was halfway to being a vampire when Dracula died.

"Allan Quatermain, 1888" is, like the Captain Nemo and Mina Murray cards, meant to portray Quatermain in action at an earlier point in his career, presumably from one of his original appearances. He is holding a Zulu shield and *assegai* (javelin) and is wearing chain mail, which means that this battle scene is from either *King Solomon's Mines* or *Allan Quatermain*. Quatermain wore his chain mail vest in both novels. But in *Allan Quatermain*, Allan fought against the Zuvendi, white members of a Lost Race, and the Africans seen here are black. That leaves *King Solomon's Mines*; therefore the battle is probably the "great battle of Loo" from Chapters 13 and 14.

There is a problem with this, however; *Allan Quatermain*, the novel in which Quatermain "died," was published in 1887. Working by Moore's dating scheme, that all events take place in the same year that the stories or books about them are published, this would mean that the battle scene shown here must have occurred after both *King Solomon's Mines* and *Allan Quatermain*. "Allan and the Sundered Veil" places the events of *Allan Quatermain* in 1886. So the battle shown here must have occurred in between Quatermain's "death" and the events of "Allan and the Sundered Veil."

"Dr. Henry Jekyll, 1886" is rather generic and could be from any point in *The Strange Case of Dr. Jekyll and Mr. Hyde*.

"Blue Dwarf Cigarettes" is a reference to a penny dreadful character. Sapathwa, the "Blue Dwarf," appeared in two separate penny dreadfuls, both called *The Blue Dwarf* and both written by Percy B. St. John. The first was published in 1861 by E. Harrison under St. John's pseudonym "Lady Esther Hope." The second was published c. 1870 by Hogarth House under St. John's real name. The first Blue Dwarf dreadful was about Sapathwa, a nobleman who was denied his inheritance because of his great ugliness, his blue skin, and his generally grotesque appearance. In the words of E.S. Turner, a scholar of British boys' stories, the Blue Dwarf was "a dilapidated goblin of Gothic provenance." Sapathwa, in this story, was an evil manipulator, and the story concerned his attempt to avenge himself on his younger brother, who received the inheritance justly due

Sapathwa.

The second Blue Dwarf dreadful was actually an unauthorized sequel of Edward Viles' *Black Bess, or the Knight of the Road* (1861-1865), the extremely popular and extremely long (254 parts) penny dreadful fictionalization of the life and adventures of the English highwayman Dick Turpin. In 1861, soon after writing *The Blue Dwarf*, St. John became the editor of the *London Journal* and stopped writing for E. Harrison. When St. John wrote the second Blue Dwarf dreadful he wrote it for Hogarth House, the rival of E. Harrison, who had published *Black Bess* as well as the first Blue Dwarf dreadful. In the second Blue Dwarf dreadful Dick Turpin returns, with his best friend Tom King, and is joined by Sapathwa. Like the original Blue Dwarf the later Sapathwa was a dwarfish nobleman denied his hereditary estates due to his ugliness, but unlike the original Blue Dwarf the later Sapathwa was a noble character who was a true friend to Dick Turpin and Tom King in their adventures across England and America.

The Question Mark Man is the symbol of the League and is seen throughout the series.

The phrase "British Made by British Labour" appeared on the cigarette cards put out by James B. Duke, an American entrepreneur who began as a peddler of tobacco from a hand-cart and by 1901 had absorbed over 250 American tobacco firms. In 1901 he entered the British tobacco market, buying the Ogdens tobacco factory (outright, for £818,000) and issuing tobacco cards which bore the phrase "British Made by British Labour." Duke ceased British operations in 1902.

"Edward Hyde, 1886" is a reference to "The Story of the Door" at the beginning of *The Strange Case of Dr. Jekyll and Mr. Hyde*, in which Hyde tramples a girl:

> "Well, it was this way," returned Mr. Enfield: "I was coming home from some place at the end of the world, about three o' clock of a black winter

morning, and my way lay through a part of town where there was literally nothing to be seen but lamps. Street after street, and all the folks asleep -- street after street, all lighted up as if for a procession and all as empty as a church -- till at last I got into that state of mind when a man listens and listens and begins to long for the sight of a policeman. All at once, I saw two figures: one a little man who was stumping along eastward at a good walk, and the other a girl of maybe eight or ten who was running as hard as she was able down a cross street. Well, sir, the two ran into one another naturally enough at the corner; and then came the horrible part of the thing; for the man trampled calmly over the child's body and left her screaming on the ground. It sounds nothing to hear, but it was hellish to see. It wasn't like a man; it was like some damned Juggernaut."

"Hawley Griffin, 1897" is an ordinary scene and could be from any moment in *The Invisible Man*.

"Campion Bond, 1888" is not a reference to a pre-existing work, Bond being a character original to *League*, but Bond's outfit does contain a few clues to his background. He is wearing cricket gear in the colors of Jesus College of Cambridge University. His cap is a schoolboy cricket cap at the club level, as is his cricketing blazer. (Cricket clubs are groups of cricketers who play at the next level below professional teams.) His white shirt with an open collar indicates that this image is from an athletic event; Victorian men were rarely seen dressed this informally except during athletic events.

It is quite possible that Bond, even with his bulk, was an amateur cricket player. Several great cricketers, including the legendary W. G. Grace, were gentlemen of substance.

"C. Auguste Dupin, 1841" is a scene from Edgar Allen Poe's "The Murders in the Rue Morgue," the story which introduced Dupin. This particular scene is probably taken from Dupin's examination of the quarters of Mademoiselle L'Espanaye, the victim of the murderous orangutan.

Page 181. This cover is done in the format of a *Classics Illustrated* comic. *Classics Illustrated* was a comic book series, first appearing in 1941, which featured literary classics of the kind boys would like, from *War of the Worlds* to *Uncle Tom's Cabin* to *Two Years Before the Mast*. Each story was reduced and condensed so that it would fit into a fifty-six-page comic book. Each cover had the title square in the upper left and a symbolic or representative scene from the comic as the cover image. The cover seen here is likely of a *Classics Illustrated* version of *The League of Extraordinary Gentlemen*.

The style of art of the cover is very similar to the paintings and drawings of Westerners which Japanese artists created shortly after the American Commodore Perry forced Japan to open its borders in 1854. The wooden bridge, the depiction of the waves, Griffin's suit and waistcoat, and especially Mina, with her eyes and fan, are very mid-nineteenth century Japanese in style.

The dragon menacing the members of the League is in the Japanese and Chinese style, being long, sinuous, and snake-like unlike the bulkier dragons of Western art. This dragon also has five claws. In Chinese mythology the five-toed dragon was used only by Emperors and as iconography for deities.

Kevin O'Neill notes:
> This is not meant to be a Classics Illustrated style cover, more an attempt at an Oriental representation of the contents of Issue Three.

Pages 182 & 183. These covers are done in the style of British story papers.

Kevin O'Neill notes:
> Cover to Issue Four: Uses orange, black and white striped cover motifs found on early Arséne Lupin publications. No real reason, just sets off the painting of Hyde nicely.

> Cover to Issue Five: In the style of late Victorian book

cover, the sort that had image printed on cloth bound cover and an inset full colour image pasted on. Not based on anything, just an attempt to capture the feeling of the times.

Page 184. This format, with six panels captioned by rhyming quartets summarizing the story, was standard for British comic books of the early Twentieth century.

Ogden's, Ltd. was a cigarette company operating in the first half of the Twentieth century.

Kevin O'Neill notes:
> Cover to Issue Six: The smaller format of American comics made this attempt to produce a Victorian comic cover rather difficult. Text in rhyme under the panels was very much the style of late Victorian comics and indeed persisted in British publishing (on nursery comic) well into the 1970s, I believe. Alan did a typically wonderful job of producing apt text and in rhyme and to a consistent line length – Bravo.

Page 185. . This image brings a number of the characters of League together with their creators.

Beginning at the upper left of the page and moving left to right and top to bottom:

- Campion Bond
- Rosa Coote
- Dick Donovan
- Varney the Vampire
- Jules Verne
- Edgar Allan Poe
- A. Conan Doyle
- Sax Rohmer
- Richard Mansfield (1857-1907), an American actor whose performance as Henry Jekyll and Edward Hyde in 1887 and at the Lyceum Theatre in London in 1888 were critically acclaimed. However, Mansfield's performance as the violent Hyde was so convincing that some suspected him of being Jack the Ripper.

- Dr. Jekyll
- Si-Fan member
- Captain Nemo
- Bram Stoker
- C. Auguste Dupin
- Allan Quatermain
- Professor Cavor
- Robert Louis Stevenson
- Woman
- Mina Murray
- Woman
- H.G. Wells
- Invisible Man
- Si-Fan member
- Egyptian
- Street barker
- H. Rider Haggard
- Woman
- Man
- Policeman

Page 186. This image is similar to the cover painting of *The Fu-Manchu Omnibus, Volume 1*, published in 1996 by the British publisher Allison & Busby. The cover of the *Omnibus* has a yellow background and shows Fu Manchu's face, at a three-quarters angle (like Fu Manchu's here), with Fu Manchu wearing the same hat in both images.

Page 187. **Basil Hallward's Painting by Numbers No. 1. Dorian Gray**. This is a reference to Oscar Wilde's *The Picture of Dorian Gray* (1890). In the novel, Basil Hallward is the artist who paints the portrait of Dorian Gray and, after seeing the corruption of the Gray's portrait, is murdered by him.

Page 189. Basil Hallward's Painting by Numbers No. 1. Dorian Gray. The difference between this completed painting and the Before version on Page 187 is a reference to Dorian Gray's picture, which begins as a beautiful thing and ends with "the leprosies of sin...slowly eating the thing away."

"The American Richard Pickman" is a reference to H.P. Lovecraft's story, "Pickman's Model" (*Weird Tales* v10 n4, October 1927). In that story Richard Upton Pickman, a brilliant and disturbed painter, creates portraits of ghouls which are too vivid for comfort.

"Unorthodox Churchyard Picnic Scene-by-numbers" is a reference to Richard Pickman's most horrible painting, of a ghoul gnawing on a corpse.

"The Caligari Self-Assembly Cabinet" is a reference to the German Expressionist film, *Das Kabinett des Doktor Caligari* (The Cabinet of Doctor Caligari, 1920). In the movie a murderous sleepwalker is controlled by Dr. Caligari and kept in a coffin when not on an errand.

Page 191. **Allan has mislaid his Taduki**. This maze is similar to other mazes and games included in British comics and story papers.

The locations shown on the maze are as follows, moving left to right and top to bottom:

- Utopia, from Thomas More's *Utopia* (1516). *Utopia* was the first and remains the most important work of utopian fiction; Utopia itself is an imaginary island in which society is perfect and there are no woes.

- King Solomon's Mines, from H. Rider Haggard's *King Solomon's Mines*, the first novel in which Allan Quatermain appeared. The mines are where King Solomon hid his treasure and were the reason why Quatermain set out on his long trek in that novel.

- Limehouse, the London borough which was the cultural and business center of England's Chinese population in the late Nineteenth and early Twentieth century and so was the site of the action in, among other works, Sax Rohmer's Fu Manchu novels and Thomas Burke's Limehouse stories. For more information on Limehouse, see the note to Page 54, above.

- Zenda, from Anthony Hope's *The Prisoner of Zenda* (1894) and its two sequels. Zenda is the name of a small, rural town in the imaginary European kingdom of Ruritania. Zenda is also the name of the castle in Zenda, which is the traditional country home of the kings of Ruritania. In *The Prisoner of*

Zenda, Rudolf Rassendyll, an Englishman, visits Ruritania only to discover that the Ruritanian heir apparent is his twin. Rassendyll is forced to impersonate King Rudolf of Ruritania in order to win the King's freedom.

- Lilliput, from Jonathan Swift's *Gulliver's Travels.* In *Gulliver's Travels* Lilliput is a country of very small people.

- Morlocks, from H.G. Wells' *The Time Machine.* The Morlocks are the troglodytic natives of a dystopic future. "Allan and the Sundered Veil" reveals that the Morlocks are also the Mi-Go of H.P. Lovecraft's stories.

- Flatland, from E.A. Abbott's *Flatland* (1884). Flatland is a two-dimensional land, a place with only length and width, but no height. Its inhabitants are sentient geometric shapes.

- Vrilya, from Edward Bulwer-Lytton's *The Coming Race* (1871). Vrilya (or "Vril-ya;" both spellings appear in the novel) is the name of both an advanced race and the underground utopia, located beneath Newcastle, England, which the Vril-ya inhabit.

- Hollow Earth, from a number of sources. The tradition that the Earth is hollow dates back centuries. To explain certain magnetic phenomena the astronomer Edmond Halley, in 1692, suggested that the Earth was a series of concentric, nested spheres surrounding a small central sun. In 1741 Ludvig Holberg wrote *Nicolaii Klimii iter subterraneum* (The Journey of Niels Klim to the World Underground), in which a young Norwegian falls through the Earth's shell into the hollow interior. But the progenitor of the Nineteenth century subgenre of Hollow Earth fiction was John Cleve Symmes, an American soldier who became obsessed with the notion that the Earth was hollow. Symmes traveled the United States trying to raise money for a polar expedition to prove his theory and in 1823 appealed directly to Congress for funding for his expedition. In 1820 "Adam Seaborn" (an unidentified pseudonym) wrote *Symzonia*, the first modern Hollow Earth novel, about a trip into the land beneath the Earth's surface and the utopia found there. *Symzonia*, and Symmes' popularization of the idea of the Hollow Earth, led to many other Hollow Earth stories and novels, most notably Edgar Allan Poe's *The Narrative of Arthur Gordon Pym* (1838) and Edgar Rice Burroughs, "Pellucidar" novels, the first of which was *At the Earth's Core* (1914).

- Curupuri, from Sir Arthur Conan Doyle's *The Lost World* (1912). In the words of Professor Challenger, the Curupuri is "the spirit of the woods, something terrible, something malevolent, something to be avoided. None can describe its shape or nature, but it is a word of terror along the Amazon." Finding the Curupuri is what impels Professor Challenger to investigate the Amazon and eventually find the Lost World.

- Caves of Kôr, from H. Rider Haggard's *She*. The caves of Kôr are where Ayesha, She-Who-Must-Be-Obeyed, lives. Kôr is the capital of a long-dead civilization and the caves beneath it are where the Flame of Immortality burns.

- Wonderland, from Lewis Carroll's *Alice in Wonderland* (1865). Wonderland is the strange other world into which Alice travels.

Back Cover.

Presumably this group picture was taken in the British Museum, the League's headquarters, and the pictures on the wall are some of those which were tantalizingly shown on Pages 52 and 53.

The "Steel Giant" mechanical elephant is the Steam House. The Steam House was created by Jules Verne and appeared in *Le Maison à Vapeur* (The Steam House, 1881). The Steam House is a steam-powered vehicle in the shape of an elephant that Banks the Engineer builds so that he and his friend Colonel Edward Munro could travel around India in safety and comfort.

"Sapathwa" is better known as The Blue Dwarf. As mentioned in the notes to Page 180, the Blue Dwarf was created by Percy B. St. John and appeared in the penny dreadful *The Blue Dwarf* (1861 and c. 1870). Sapathwa was a nobleman denied his heritage because of his ugly appearance.

"Jack Harkaway, 1871" is a reference to the schoolboy hero of Bracebridge Hemyng's *Jack Harkaway's Schooldays* (1871) and its many sequels. The first significant schoolboy hero in English fiction was Tom Brown, from Thomas Hughes' *Tom Brown's*

Schooldays (1857) and its sequel, *Tom Brown at Oxford* (1861). In Hughes' books Tom Brown begins school as a shy, homesick boy, but he soon becomes an upright, robust, manly lad. All the while, however, he is moral, modest, and unassuming. Hemyng's *Jack Harkaway's Schooldays* and its numerous sequels are updated versions of Hughes' work, reflecting the ethos of Imperial Britain just as *Tom Brown's Schooldays* reflected the ethos of 1850s Britain. Although Tom Brown is originally humble, shy, and weak, Harkaway starts off as resolute, aggressive, self-righteous, and prone to violence and vicious pranks, traits which his further adventures exacerbate. Harkaway travels around the world, personifying the worst traits of Victorian jingoism and triumphing over all those who he dislikes.

The untitled painting in the upper right corner is of Phileas Fogg, from Jules Verne's *Around the World in Eighty Days*. As mentioned on the notes to Page 124, Panel 2, Fogg is the English explorer who circumnavigates the world in eighty days' time using a variety of vehicles.

"Sir Francis Varney" is the protagonist of James Malcolm Rymer's *Varney the Vampyre; or, The Feast of Blood* (1845-1847). *Varney the Vampyre*, first published in a penny dreadful and then collected into a very long novel, was the first vampire novel in English and the most famous novel of vampires before *Dracula*. Sir Francis Varney had originally been a supporter of the Crown during Cromwell's era but struck his son in a moment of passion, leading to literally divine retribution and his transformation into a vampire.

The untitled portrait next to Varney's could represent any number of Victorian characters. His profile is similar to that of Jules Verne.

The silhouette to the upper right of the untitled portrait is of Karl Friedrich Hieronymus, Baron von Münchhausen. As mentioned in the note to Page 149, Panel 3, Baron Münchhausen is best known for his extraordinarily tall tales and for the book in which they appeared.

Below the silhouette of Baron von Münchhausen is a painting of the

Question Mark Man, the symbol of the League.

"Nautilus, Basil Hallward 1870" is a reference to the *Nautilus*, from Jules Verne's *Twenty Thousand Leagues Under the Sea* and *The Mysterious Island*, and to Basil Hallward, who as mentioned in the notes to Page 187 appears in Oscar Wilde's *The Picture of Dorian Gray*. In the novel Hallward was the artist who painted Dorian Gray's portrait and was eventually murdered by him.

"Dorian Grey"is a reference to the young dandy of Oscar Wilde's *The Picture of Dorian Gray*. Gray's decadence and depravity are reflected in his painting, rather than on his face and body.

The painting below the portrait of Sir Francis Varney is the group picture of the 1787 League of Extraordinary Gentlemen seen on Page 53, Panel 2.

"Unt Allamistakeo" is a reference to Edgar Allan Poe's "Some Words with a Mummy" (*American Review*, April 1845). In the story the mummified body of Count Allamistakeo is revived via electricity. Once revived the Count shows a remarkable vitality, sophistication, and loquacity.

The headless and armless statue with the word "Ayesha" at its base is a reference to Ayesha, She-Who-Must-Be-Obeyed, the immortal goddess of H. Rider Haggard's "She" novels.

Just visible in the mirror, to the left of Mr. Hyde's image, is Alice, from Lewis Carroll's *Alice's Adventures in Wonderland* and *Through the Looking Glass*. In the latter novel Alice enters Wonderland through a mirror.

The enormous skull to the right of the Invisible Man is that of a Brobdingnagian, from Jonathan Swift's *Gulliver's Travels*.

The tiny horse at the foot of Mina's dress is one of the animals which Gulliver brought back from Lilliput in *Gulliver's Travels*. The black cat at Mina's feet is likely a reference to Edgar Allan Poe's story "The Black Cat" (1843).

Kevin O'Neill notes:
> Untitled portrait is Robur.

Material not included in the *League* hardcover.

The original issues of *League* contained some material which was not included in the hardcover and soft-cover. This material consisted of fake advertisements done in the Victorian style, quotations on the back covers, and letters pages. They are included here with the page numbering from their respective issues.

Issue #1, Page 30. "Naughty nieces? Disobedient daughters? Send them to: Rosa Coote's Correctional Academy for Wayward Gentlewoman. Let us thrash out your problems. Apply to: R. Coote, Coote's Correctional Academy, 8, Pearlspender Mews Edmonton, North London. (Please enclose recent Daguerreotype)."

This is a reference to Rosa Coote's Academy, which appeared on Pages 42-49. A "daguerreotype" was an early type of photograph, in which an image was captured on a silver plate sensitized by iodine and then developed by exposure to mercury vapors.

Issue #1, Page 32. "Crimes detected! Mysteries solved! Promising young private investigator, in the tradition of <u>Sherlock Holmes</u>, Baker Street area, seeks to fill gap left by untimely death of previous incumbent. Has own bumbling assistant, plus housekeeper with endearing working-class mannerisms. Will consider adopting violin and/or Cocaine addiction, as required. Contact S. Blake, P.O. Box 221B, London."

This is a reference to Sexton Blake, whose name appears on Page 110, Panel 2. Blake was created by Harry Blyth and debuted in the story paper *Halfpenny Marvel* in 1893. This was the same year in which Arthur Conan Doyle's "The Final Problem" was published. According to the dating scheme of *League*, the events of "The Final

Problem," including the "deaths" of Sherlock Holmes and Professor Moriarty at Reichenbach Falls, occurred in 1893. This ad is an extrapolation: Because Sexton Blake debuted in the same year that Sherlock Holmes disappeared, and because for many years Blake was very similar to Sherlock Holmes and lived on Baker Street in London, it therefore stands to reason that Blake moved in to Holmes' lodgings at 221B Baker Street in an attempt to emulate Holmes.

The Sexton Blake of *League* does not entirely match the Sexton Blake of the story papers. In the first Blake stories he has none of the physical or intellectual characteristics of Holmes, had offices on Wych Street off the Strand, and was paired with Jules Gervaise, a French detective. It was not until the late 1890s that Blake moved to Baker Street, acquired a housekeeper like Holmes' Mrs. Hudson, and began taking on Holmes-like characteristics.

Issue #2, Page 31. "Avoid eye-strain with the Edison Patented Electrical Negro. These personable fellows may be hired to stand beside your bed should you choose to sit up and read, or at your shoulder if you should wish to peruse an evening newspaper whilst riding on a darkened omnibus. Rate of hire: One Shilling per hour, or part of hour. Regent Street, London, W. Please note: Batteries are not included."

This ad is accompanied by an image of an African-American wearing a helmet with a lit light bulb. The ad is a comment on Victorian racism, but is also a reference to a real publicity stunt by Thomas Edison. When Edison first introduced the electric light bulb on a large scale in 1882, he had some of his employees stand in public areas in New York City, wearing hats with lit light bulbs on them. The public was still unsure of the safety of the light bulb, and this "living demonstration" was a way for Edison to convince the public that light bulbs were not going to hurt anyone.

Issue #2, Page 32. "For the finest teas in Limehouse, come to Quong Lee's Tea-House, 'Where there's always something' brewing!"

This is a reference to Quong Lee, who appeared on Pages 61-62.

Quong Lee was created by Thomas Burke and appeared in a series of short stories and books, beginning with *The Song Book of Quong Lee of Limehouse* (1920). Quong Lee was an elderly Chinese tea shop owner in Limehouse in London.

Issue #2, Back Cover. "'It is imperative that Britain colonize the Moon before the French attempt the same with their artillery shell device. Ideally, there should be a Union Jack flying over the *Mare Tranquillitatis* by November 1900 at the very latest.' Professor Cavor, Memo to the Minister for Scientific Progress, 1895."

This is a reference to Professor Cavor, who appears on Page 52, and to Jules Verne's *De la Terre à la Lune* (From the Earth to the Moon). In the Verne novel a group of Americans, the Baltimore Gun Club, achieve space flight by means of a ship propelled from a very large gun. The *Mare Tranquillitatus*, the Sea of Tranquility, was the location on the moon where the American flag was planted during the Apollo II mission. This quote, with its implied competition between the British and the French, is similar to the statements of American politicians during the 1960s competition between the Americans and the Soviets to reach the Moon.

Issue #3, Page 32. From the "Letters to the Editor," in response to a letter playfully objecting in the Victorian fashion to the violence of *League* #1 and its supposed effect on the letter-writer's children: "Madam, how dare you? By your own admission you are of that most disreputable and unnatural class of the female sex in that you 'act the man' and must resort to manual employment. It is almost certain, therefore that you are either a Sapphist or a harlot. As for your children, do you wish the two of them to grow up as d........ pansies? Why, you should instead be glad that our fine publication has awakened in them the appreciation of a healthy, masculine approach to life. Your worries about Benjamin are quite unfounded, as it is a well-known fact that many eight-year-olds pass harmlessly through stages of mild hemp addiction without ill effect. May we suggest that any damage to the minds or constitutions of your sons results instead from your own evident inadequacy as a mother? It is little wonder, Madam, that your husband shot himself."

Aside from the obvious humor of the response this is likely a reference to the answers given by the editors of boys' story papers. Most of the letter writers to story papers were boys, with questions about pets, their health, and their careers. The Answers to Correspondence sections of story papers could often be brusque, with Dr. Gordon Staples, the editor of the *Boys' Own Paper*, being known for his curtness. He was a firm believer in "fresh air, cold tubs, oatmeal, virol and phospherine: these are the cures for readers' ills," and his response, "Take a cold tub, sir!" became a byword not just for his responses but for the *Boys' Own* approach to its readers. However, in October 1902 he went beyond his usual severity and responded to a letter entitled "Bad Habits" with the comment, "Coffins are cheap and boys like you are not of much use in the world." This kind of abusive response is what Moore is spoofing in the letters pages.

Issue #3, Page 33. "The New Belt - for day and evening wear, made to measure. No. 1 - The Marlboro. No. 2 - The Kitchener. No. 3 - The Carlton. Madame Dowding, 8 & 10 Charing Cross Road (Opposite the National Gallery, Trafalgar Square) (All communications STRICTLY PRIVATE in Belt Dept.)"

This ad is accompanied by illustrations of three men modeling each style of corset. The man modeling the "Marlboro" corset appears to be Sir Horatio Herbert Kitchener (1850-1916). Kitchener was a British general whose career had several notable successes and failures. In 1898, at the time of *League*, he was seen as a national hero and as the archetypal Christian soldier for his reconquest of the Sudan and his victory, on 2 September, at the Battle of Omdurman, which avenged the death of General Charles "Chinese" Gordon at the hands of the Sudanese Mahdi Muhammad Ahmad. In 1900 Kitchener was appointed Commander-in-Chief of the British forces in South Africa during the Boer War. Kitchener changed British policy as a way to deal with the guerrilla tactics of the Boer leaders: Kitchener ordered the burning of Boer homes and the imprisonment of Boer civilians in concentration camps. Although this change in policy won the war for the British it also led to widespread criticism of Kitchener's tactics. Kitchener was made Secretary of State of War in 1914 and died on the *H.M.S. Hampshire* when it struck a mine during World War One.

The humor of Sir Kitchener wearing a corset lies partly in the fact that he never married, was notable at the time for being a "woman-hater," and had a number of very intense and passionate relationships with young, good-looking men, leading to widespread and persistent (though unconfirmed) rumors that he was gay.

The "Marlboro" corset is perhaps a reference to Marlborough House, the residence of Prince Albert Victor (1864-1892), Queen Elizabeth's heir, who lived at the house with a "fast-living set" which concentrated on living a fashionable life of leisure. It is thought that "Prince Eddy" was at least bisexual: according to rumor he had affairs with his tutor, J.K. Stephen, and his friend, Lord Arthur Somerset, and was nearly implicated in the 1889 arrests at a gay brothel on Cleveland Street.

The man modeling the "Kitchener" corset appears to be Prince Albert Victor.

The "Carlton" corset may be a reference to the Carlton Club, which in 1898 was the headquarters of the British Conservative Party. If this is indeed the correct reference the man wearing the Carlton corset might be A.J. Balfour, the British Prime Minister from 1902-1905 and Conservative Party leader from 1902-1914.

Kevin O'Neill notes:
> This is a genuine ad, and is simply reformatted to fit page– no other changes made– but enjoyed the scurrilous material you read into it.

Issue #4, Inside Front Cover. The Credits Page for this issue is a mock Table of Contents for the *Sunday at Home*, featuring the creators of *League*.

The *Sunday at Home* was a religious magazine which was published all through the latter half of the Nineteenth century, beginning in 1854. It was put out by the "Religious Tract Society" and billed itself as "a family magazine for Sabbath reading."

"Seven Years Before The Easel. 'My endless years of labour had reduced me to a bent, enfeebled wretch, and still it was but issue four.' Pressganged into chapbook illustration as a boy, our cautionary tale's narrator tells us of his wasted life toss'd on the woeful seas of Art. By Mr. Kevin O'Neill."

This is a reference to the books of the Nineteenth century which described shipboard life from the point of a view of a humble seaman. The archetype for this type of novel is Richard Henry Dana's *Two Years Before the Mast: A Personal Narrative of Life at Sea* (1840). "Two years before the mast" refers to the number of years a common seaman had been in service on a ship. Officers in sailing ships slept in cabins and wardrooms behind the mainmast in the stern of the ship, while ordinary sailors bunked at the bow of the ship, in the forecastle.

"Scott of the Antarctic. A person working in the editorial professions here compares his life to a bleak polar wasteland where one loses contact with one's workmates, gradually goes blind and ends up having to devour the huskies. By Mr. Scott Dunbier."

This is a reference to George Seaver's *Scott of the Antarctic: A Study in Character* (1940), which told the story of Captain Robert F. Scott's doomed expedition to the Antarctic. Scott's first trip ended around 520 miles from the South Pole, a record for the time, but his second trip, in 1912, ended in the death of all members of the Scott party, including Scott himself. Scott's team brought (and were forced to eat) horses, rather than huskies. Other expeditions to the South Pole, including Roald Amundsen's in 1911 and Douglas Mawson's in 1908, brought huskies and were forced to kill and eat them to survive.

"'I was a President of Vice.' A candid, searing true confession from the man they once called 'Soho's Sultan of Sin.' Hear how the so-called 'Vice President' ran his company of tragic, desperate harlots with an iron hand. By Mr. John Nee."

This is not a reference to a specific story but rather to the autobiographical confessional stories published in various magazines which detailed the experiences of individuals in criminal activities, especially in London during the late Victorian era.

There are four other entries on the Table of Contents:

- "Writing for Ruffians. A popular author of boys' fiction enlightens us on how we may assure ourselves a comfortable living by producing penny-dreadful trash for the more brutish classes, whilst still maintaining the appearance of a serious literary figure. By Mr. Alan Moore."

- "Passion is my Paintbox. We continue our Romantic serial narrative with an episode in which a jealous lover of our dashing young aquatint-specialist hero steals all the brighter colours from his paintbox and condemns him to work solely in a range of murky browns and greys. By Mr. Benedict Dimagmaliw."

- "Letters we have Loved, No. 17: 'Q.' Continuing our trip through the countryside of consonants and the vales of vowels, our resident lexicographer tells us why, for him, the letter 'Q' is a saucy, wanton temptress who just needs a dashed good flogging. By Mr. William Oakley."

- "Golf: The Sport of Titans. The Director of a thriving publisher of titles for young persons patiently explains to us what a Director is, and what Directors do all day, along with a dissertation upon the many responsibilities of Directorship. By Mr. James Lee."

These are not references to particular stories or novels, but are simply titles written in the typically overheated style of the penny dreadfuls and British boys' fiction of the late Victorian era.

Issue #5, Inside Front Cover. The credits page for this issue is a mock cover of the *National Police Gazette*. The *National Police*

Gazette (1845-1906) was an American tabloid newspaper whose ostensible focus was sports ("The 'Police Gazette' is the World's Sporting Authority") but whose articles were usually about true crimes, which the *Police Gazette* covered in a sensationalist manner, similar to the *Illustrated Police News* (see the note to Page 179, above).

Issue #5, Inside Back Cover. From the Answers In Brief section of the Letters Page: "Seeking Religious Advice (T.L.) - 1. On the contrary, we think God has been very clear in his personal communications with you. 2. By "filth and contagions" he almost certainly means the prostitute population of London's East End. 3. Yes, of course he means all of them. 4. Any good ironmongers."

This parody of similar columns in story papers has responses to Jack the Ripper. "Yes, of course he means all of them" may be a reference to Alan Moore's *From Hell*, in which Queen Victoria, the ultimate cause for the Ripper murders, tells Dr. Gull, the wielder of the knife, to kill the prostitutes:

> "We leave the means to you, Sir William. We would
> simply it were done, and done well."
> "All of them, Your Majesty?"
> "All of them."

Issue #6, Inside Front Cover. The Credits Page for this issue is an advertisement for the "Young Helpers' League," with the names of the creators of *League* given as "Acting Senior Enscriptuator," "Chief Petty Delineatrist," and so on. The Young Helpers' League was a charity founded in 1891 by Dr. Thomas Barnardo, an Victorian evangelical, entrepreneur, and philanthropist. Barnardo's goal was to aid homeless, needy, and afflicted children, and to this end he founded several charities. The Young Helpers' League was founded so that the children of respectable and well-to-do families could donate to help the less fortunate. The Young Helpers League still exists in England today under the name of Barnardo's.

Issue #6, Inside Back Cover. From the Answers in Brief section of the Letters Page: "Boyish Camaraderie (S.L.) - 1. It is perfectly natural to feel deep bonds of friendship for other lads in the First Eleven, or, indeed in our own experience, for a burly Rastafarian at three in the morning on Clapham Common. 2. No, we have never heard of such a practice described. Does it matter what sort of biscuit. 3. That is, of course, a matter for you and you alone to decide, although we feel that between £15 and £20 sounds reasonable."

The answer to #1 is a reference to Ron Davies, the former Member of Parliament, Welsh secretary and leader of the Wales Labour Party. In October, 1998, Davies reported to the police that he'd been robbed on Clapham Common at three a.m. by a large Rastafarian. It later emerged that Davies had picked up the Rastafarian from an area known for gay cruising.

The answer to #2 is a reference to a game supposedly common among some all-male schools in the United States, Britain, and Europe as well as in some parts of the British and American military; it also appeared in the play *Fruehlingserwachen* (Spring Awakening, 1891), by Franz Wedekind, whose creation, Lulu, appears in the Game of Extraordinary Gentlemen (see below). The game, variously called "biscuit," "wanking the bun," and "ookie cookie," involves a group of men masturbating on to a coin, biscuit or pastry. The last man to ejaculate on the coin gets the coin as a prize. The last man to ejaculate on the biscuit must eat it.

The Game of Extraordinary Gentlemen

In 2000, America's Best Comics, the publisher of *League*, published the *America's Best Comics 64 Page Giant*, an anthology of stories from various ABC comics. In the *Giant* was a *League* feature, the "Game of Extraordinary Gentlemen." The Game, done in the style of educational games for children in the 1920s and 1930s, consisted of eighty-eight squares, each illustrated and containing directions ("Advance one," "Miss 1 turn," "Return to state"). In the Game of Extraordinary Gentlemen each square contains a reference to Victorian literature, in the manner of *League*, accompanied by an illustration.

Some squares have not been annotated. Those omitted usually repeat previous squares, as with the Spring-Heeled Jack references (see Box #1 below), or have no literary references.

Box #1. "Jump 5 spaces with Spring-Heeled Jack," accompanied by an illustration of Spring-Heeled Jack. "Spring-Heeled Jack" is a reference to Spring-Heeled Jack, the subject of British folklore and penny dreadfuls. Urban and rural legends about Spring-Heeled Jack, a devil-faced creature who spat blue and white flames and attacked women, circulated in Britain beginning in the mid-1830s. A play with Spring-Heeled Jack appeared in 1863, and the first penny dreadful with Spring-Heeled Jack as the central character appeared in 1867. Several penny dreadfuls with Spring-Heeled Jack followed, the best-known being Charlton Lea's in 1890, which featured a nobleman wearing a special suit which allowed him to jump great distances and to fight crime.

Box #2. "Blackballed from the Diogenes Club," accompanied by an illustration of a dyspeptic-looking Mycroft Holmes. The Diogenes Club was created by Arthur Conan Doyle and appears in two of his Sherlock Holmes stories: "The Greek Interpreter" (*Strand Magazine*, September 1893) and "The Adventure of the Bruce Partington Plans." The Diogenes Club is "the queerest club in London," and "now contains the most unsociable and unclubbable men in town," including Holmes' brother Mycroft.

Box #3. "Refreshments with Ally Sloper." Ally Sloper, seen on Page 149, Panel 1, was a comic strip character who first appeared in *Judy* in 1867. He was a sort of heroic, roguish everyman.

Box #4. "Help Detective S. Blake solve Mystery of Edwin Drood." "Detective S. Blake" is a reference to Sexton Blake, whose name is seen on Page 110, Panel 2. Sexton Blake was created by Harry Blyth and first appeared in 1893. Blake is a gentleman detective who appeared in nearly 4000 stories through 1968 and is one of the most-published characters in the English language.

The "Mystery of Edwin Drood" is a reference to Charles Dickens' "The Mystery of Edwin Drood" (1870). "Drood," left unfinished at the time of Dickens' death, has remained a mystery because of the unclear state in which it was left; though there is an obvious suspect, the murderer's identity will never be known for sure, and because Edwin Drood's body is never found, there is the possibility that no murder was committed.

Box #5. "Fleet Street: Get tragic haircut," is a reference to Sweeney Todd, the Demon Barber of Fleet Street. Sweeney Todd is the lead character in a London urban legend which began around 1820. In these stories Todd was a barber on London's Fleet Street who killed his clients and turned them into meat pies, which Todd and his partner Mrs. Lovett then sold. The story of Sweeney Todd first appeared in a penny dreadful in 1840 and onstage in 1842, with numerous prose and stage retellings of the story following through the Nineteeth and Twentieth centuries.

Box #6. "Dr. Nikola has you in thrall." Dr. Nikola, whose name is seen on Page 110, Panel 2, is a reference to Guy Boothby's Dr. Nikola, who first appeared in *A Bid for Fortune* in 1895. Dr. Nikola was one of the first major arch-villains of fiction, but unlike Professor Moriarty, Nikola was a recurring character who appeared in four sequels to *A Bid for Fortune*.

The phrase "has you in thrall" is likely a reference to John Keats' "La Belle Dame Sans Merci" (1819), in which the lead character, enchanted with La Belle Dame, is told by her former victims, "La Belle Dame Sans Merci/Hath thee in thrall!"

Box #7. "Time Traveller: Throw again, but move backwards." The Time Traveler is a reference to the hero from H.G. Wells' *The Time Machine*.

Box #8. "Professor Gibberne slips you his New Accelerator." "Professor Gibberne" and his "New Accelerator" are references to H.G. Wells' "A New Accelerator" (*Strand Magazine*, December 1901). In the story Professor Gibberne invents "accelerator," a drug which gives the human body the ability to move three times as quickly as normal.

Box #9. "Fan-Chu Fang, Prince Wu-Ling and Wu Fang need a fourth for Mah Jong," accompanied by an illustration of three old, evil-looking Chinese men. These characters were all Yellow Peril opponents (see the "Yellow Peril" essay for more information on this character type) who plagued heroes in magazines, books, and films in the first few decades of the Twentieth century.

"Fan-Chu Fang" was the Chinese arch-enemy of Dixon Brett. Brett, whose creator is unknown, was a gentleman detective in the mold of Sherlock Holmes and Sexton Blake. He appeared in story papers and novels through the 1900s, 1910s, and 1920s. Fan-Chu Fang, the "Wizard Mandarin," was a "veritable archangel of evil;" he was an agent of the Chinese government who worked toward the downfall of the British Empire, going so far as to raid Buckingham Palace itself.

"Prince Wu-Ling" was the Chinese arch-enemy of Sexton Blake, mentioned in the notes to Page 110, Panel 2, and to Box #4 above. The Prince, the "descendant of a dynasty which could trace its philosophy back to the time when the Anglo-Saxon race was unheard of," longed "from the innermost depths of his princely nature to feel the heel of the East on the West, to carve a path of saffron through a field of white, to raise on high Confucius, Buddha, and Taoism across all the world." To achieve his goal of subjugating the West, Prince Wu Ling would stop at nothing, sending his followers, the Brotherhood of the Yellow Beetle, on many foul missions. But the Prince was honorable, after a fashion, and always treated Sexton Blake fairly.

There were five characters named "Wu Fang" during the years before World War Two. The first appeared in the 1914 movie serial *The Exploits of Elaine*. He was a standard Yellow Peril character who was the enemy of Arthur Reeve's "science detective" character Craig Kennedy, the "American Sherlock Holmes." The second Wu Fang appeared in the 1918 movie serial *The Midnight Patrol*. He was a standard Yellow Peril character. The third Wu Fang appeared in the 1928 serial *Ransom*. Although *Ransom* was written and directed by George B. Seitz, who had also written and directed *The Exploits of Elaine*, the Wu Fang in *Ransom* was a simple Yellow Peril anti-American terrorist and not the same character from *The Exploits of Elaine*. The fourth Wu Fang was the arch-enemy of Norman Marsh's Detective Dan, a.k.a. Dan Dunn, Secret Operative No. 48, who appeared in an eponymous comic strip in 1932 and eight Big, Little books beginning in 1933. Dunn's Wu Fang was the "King of the Dope Smugglers, with diabolical, fiendish cunning, aided by a horde of depraved gangsters, and an endless stream of money squeezed from human blood, corruption and degradation." The fifth Wu Fang was the protagonist of the 1935-1936 pulp *The Mysterious Wu Fang*. Created by Robert Hogan, the pulp Wu Fang was headquartered in Limehouse; he was a mad scientist who bred monstrous new species of poisonous insects and snakes and who planned to conquer the entire world.

Box #10. "Even Gunga Din's ghost is a better man than you." "Gunga Din" appears in Rudyard Kipling's poem, "Gunga Din" (1890). Gunga Din is the *bhisti*, or water-carrier, for the narrator's regiment; Din dies saving the narrator, inspiring the line, "You're a better man than I am, Gunga Din!"

Box #11. "Steal Moonstone for Dr. Nikola, or return to start." "The Moonstone" is a reference to Wilkie Collins' *The Moonstone* (1868), one of the earlier novels in the history of the mystery genre. The stone in question is a fabulous gem, a yellow diamond which carries a curse. The novel is about its theft from the forehead of a four-armed Hindu statue and the search for the diamond, as well as the efforts of three Indians to regain it.

"Dr. Nikola" appears in Box #6.

Box #12. "Mowgli mistakes you for Dr. John Doolittle." "Mowgli" is a reference to Rudyard Kipling's feral child Mowgli, who first appeared in "In the Rukh" (1892) and went on to appear in several stories, books, and films. Mowgli is raised by wolves in the forests of India and is able to speak with the animals.

"Dr. John Doolittle" is a reference to Hugh Lofting's Dr. John Dolittle, first seen in *The Story of Doctor Dolittle* (1920). Dr. Dolittle has the ability to speak with the animals, and eventually devotes himself full-time to dealing with them.

Box #13. "The Black Cat attempts to neuter you." "The Black Cat" is a reference to Edgar Allan Poe's "The Black Cat," seen in the group portrait on the back cover of the *League* hardcover. In "The Black Cat" the narrator hangs his good, black cat Pluto, only to find that the act was worse than a sin; it was a mistake.

Kevin O'Neill notes:
> My mistake. Black Cat should only have one eye (unless it's Nikola's cat)

Box #14. "Find Pip's fortune. Estelle seems restless." "Pip" and "Estelle" are references to Charles Dickens' *Great Expectations* (1860). Pip is the youthful hero of the novel. He has various misadventures as he tries to earn his way in life, and he falls in love with Estella, the adopted daughter of the wealthy Miss Havisham.

Box #15. "Oh, rotten luck! Suffer premature burial and retire from the game!" This is probably a reference to Edgar Allan Poe's "The Premature Burial" (1850), the account of several examples of being buried alive.

Box #16. "Prison. Don iron mask." This is a reference to Alexandre Dumas' *The Man in the Iron Mask*, which is one third of Dumas' *Le Vicomte de Bragelonne* (1848-1850). The novel is the last in Dumas' trilogy about the life of d'Artagnan of the Musketeers. The story is about, among other things, the famous historical mystery of the Man in the Iron Mask, the true king of France, who is held in prison with an iron mask on his face to conceal his identity.

Box #18. "Catch Moby Dick. Return to port at square 6 and see a Doctor." "Moby Dick" is a reference to Herman Melville's *Moby*

Dick (1851). Moby Dick is the great white whale which Captain Ahab and the crew of the whaler *Pequod* pursue. The "see a Doctor" comment is a reference to the mayhem caused in *Moby Dick* when the great white whale is finally caught.

Box #19. "McTeague the dentist seems distracted." "McTeague" is a reference to Frank Norris' *McTeague* (1899), a novel about a dentist, McTeague, who practices without a license and is subject to greed. These twin flaws lead to McTeague's gruesome downfall.

Box #20. "Spurt forward 4 spaces aboard Good Ship Venus," accompanied by an illustration of a ship with two large breast-shaped pieces of wood at its stern. The "Good Ship Venus" is a traditional naval and rugby song with lyrics like, "The captain had a daughter/ Was swimming in the water/Delighted squeals came as the eels/ Entered her sexual quarter." (That is one of the more printable quatrains.) The song was also recorded by the punk group the Sex Pistols in their 1980 album/documentary *The Great Rock'n'Roll Swindle*.

Box #21. "Robur shows you his Great Eyrie." "Robur" was created by Jules Verne and appeared in *Robur the Conqueror* and *The Master of the World*. Robur, mentioned in the notes to Page 39, Panel 3, is a rogue engineer who designs a new and powerful aircraft and uses it to threaten the world. Robur's "Great Eyrie" is his mountain hideaway in North Carolina.

Box #22. "Lake LaMetrie Monster stops for a chat." The "Lake LaMetrie Monster" is a reference to Wardon Curtis' "The Monster of Lake LaMetrie" (*The Windsor Magazine*, September 1899). The Monster is actually an elasmosaurus into whose body is put the brain of a human. Initially the human controls the elasmosaurus' body and can talk, but eventually the human succumbs to the body's animal nature.

Box #23. "Become obsessed with Numerology." In numerology and Illuminati conspiracy theory the prime number 23 has significance. Kabbalists define it as "union with the Godhead," Aleister Crowley defines 23 as "parting, removal, separation, joy, a thread, and life" and William S. Burroughs notes the number's significant appearances in human history.

Box #24. "Fail to recognize Nick Carter," accompanied by the picture of a pig-tailed young girl. "Nick Carter" is a character created by Ormond G. Smith and John Russell Coryell. Carter debuted in "The Old Detective's Pupil" (*New York Weekly* v41 n46, September 18, 1886). Carter, a heroic detective/adventurer, appeared in over 2000 stories and novels and went through several incarnations from dime novel detective hero to imitation Sherlock Holmes to hard-boiled private eye to ruthless spy in his century-long career. Nick Carter was a master of disguise, which is why he is not recognized in his disguise as a little girl. The girl may also be a reference to the pop singer Nick Carter, whose fan base is primarily pre-pubescent and adolescent girls.

Kevin O'Neill notes:

> Nothing to do with pop singer, I just liked the old *Nick Carter Detective Library* logo (1881). It showed Nick Carter in various disguises ranging from a Chinese boy, an old lady, fat banker, and small black boy! With such a range, it seemed amusing to show him as a little girl.

Box #25. "Great Cthulhu wants you." Great Cthulhu is the "god of elder days" from H.P. Lovecraft's writings.

Box #27. "Old Mr. Fogg offers you a lift." "Mr. Fogg" is a reference to Phileas Fogg, the world traveler from Jules Verne's *Around the World in Eighty Days*. His name is visible on Page 124, Panel 2.

Box #28. "Thrashed by Rosa Coote. Crawl like a worm to square 33." This is a reference to Rosa Coote who was created by William Dugdale and appeared in several works of Nineteenth century pornography. Rosa Coote is first mentioned on Page 39, Panel 4. Rosa Coote thrashes the player because of her predilection for flagellation.

Box #29. "Mr. Wm. Bunter Senior sends you for pies." "Mr. Wm. Bunter Senior" is a reference to William George "Billy" Bunter, who was created by Charles Hamilton and appeared in over 1500 stories and novels, beginning in 1908 in the British story paper *The Magnet*. Bunter was a greedy, cowardly, cunning, foolish, and gluttonous schoolboy.

Box #30. "If you stole Moonstone, Raffles coshes you for it." The "Moonstone" is mentioned in Box 11, above. "Raffles" is a reference to A.J. Raffles, the creation of E. W. Hornung. Raffles, who first appeared in *Cassell's Magazine* in 1898, is one of the best known of the gentlemen thieves.

Box #31. "Meet chap with dreadful appendectomy scars, on ice floe." This is a reference to Mary Shelley's *Frankenstein* (1818), in which Victor Frankenstein's final confrontation with his patchwork man occurs on an Arctic ice floe.

Box #32. "Jim Hawkins produces his wrinkled parchment." "Jim Hawkins" is the hero of Robert Louis Stevenson's *Treasure Island*, which is mentioned in the note to Page 56. Jim Hawkins is the boy hero of the novel. He and a group of pirates follow a parchment to find buried treasure.

Box #33. "At her castle in Styria, Camilla drinks your health," accompanied by a picture of a female vampire with a bloody mouth. "Camilla" is a reference to J. Sheridan Le Fanu's "Carmilla" (*The Dark Blue*, December 1871). Carmilla is a female vampire who preys on the innocent child Laura in Styria, a rural Austrian province along the Hungarian border.

Box #34. "In Ruritania Black Michael sends you to square 36." "Black Michael" and "Ruritania" are references to Anthony Hope Hawkins' *The Prisoner of Zenda*. Ruritania is a fictional central European kingdom in which Rudolf Rassendyll duels with the evil Rupert of Hentzau. "Black Michael" is the wicked Duke of Strelsau in the novel.

Box #35. "Sir Francis Varney bites you. Deuced bad show!" "Sir Francis Varney" is a reference to J. M. Rymer's *Varney the Vampyre, or The Feast of Blood.* Sir Francis Varney, who appears in the group portrait on the back cover of the *League* hardcover, is a vampire. The illustration of Varney accompanying the text here is a visual quotation from the cover of the first issue of *Varney the Vampyre.*

Box #37. "King Solomon's Mines: You can afford an extra turn." "King Solomon's Mines" refer to H. Rider Haggard's *King Solomon's Mines*, the first novel to star Allan Quatermain. The mines themselves hold the fabled lost treasure of King Solomon.

Box #38. "Hank Morgan from Connecticut seems disoriented." "Hank Morgan" is a reference to Mark Twain's *A Connecticut Yankee in King Arthur's Court* (1889). In the novel Hank Morgan is a Connecticut engineer and the embodiment of hardheaded Yankee can-do pragmatism. Through a knock on the head he is sent back in time to the court of King Arthur.

Box #39. "Meet Dr. Van Helsing. If bitten by Varney, Retire from Game." "Dr. Van Helsing" is a reference to Bram Stoker's *Dracula.* In the novel Dr. Van Helsing was the aging vampire hunter who helped Mina and Jonathan Harker kill Dracula.

Box #41. "Lilliput. Big yourself up." In Jonathan Swift's *Gulliver's Travels*, Lilliput is an island of six-inch-tall natives.

Box #43. "Join Mr. Kurtz for a drink." "Mr. Kurtz" is a reference to Joseph Conrad's *Heart of Darkness* (1899). Kurtz, an agent for a company of ivory traders, becomes corrupted by the power he gains over the natives of the Belgian Congo.

Box #44. "Curipuri: Man-apes and giant reptiles." "Curipuri" is a reference to Arthur Conan Doyle's *The Lost World.* In the novel the curupuri, which appears in the maze on Page 191, is spirit dreaded by the natives of the Amazon.

Box #45. "Brobdingnag: Suffer penile dementia. Return to 41 and regain self-esteem" "Brobdingnag" is a reference to Jonathan Swift's *Gulliver's Travels*. Brobdingnag is an island of giants whose stature might well inspire penile dementia.

Box #46. "Readestown: Frank Reade Jnr. builds you a pair of steam-boots." "Readestown" and "Frank Reade Jr." are references to the Frank Reade, Jr. series of dime novels, which ran for 179 stories beginning in the dime novel *Boys of New York* in 1879, and was the most famous and successful of the Edisonade (boy inventor) series. Created by Luis Senarens, Frank Reade, Jr. is a boy inventor and adventurer who is as successful in coming up with wonderful new inventions, like "steam-boots," as he is in exploring the frontiers and wiping out the natives.

Box #47. "Sleepy Hollow. Rest your head for 1 turn." "Sleepy Hollow" is a reference to Washington Irving's "The Legend of Sleepy Hollow" (1819), about a small town in upstate New York purportedly haunted by a headless horseman.

Box #48. "Receive white feather." This is a reference to A.E.W. Mason's novel *The Four Feathers* (1902), in which a young British pacifist refuses to fight in the Sudan, and is given four white features by his friends and fiancee as a sign of contempt for his "cowardice." The phrase "to show the white feather," or to display cowardice, predates Mason's novel, but *The Four Feathers* is likely the source Moore is referring to here.

Box #49. "Baltimore Gun Club sends you aloft." The "Baltimore Gun Club" appears in Jules Verne's *De La Terre a la Lune* (From the Earth to the Moon, 1865) and *Autour de la Lune* (Around the Moon, 1870). The Baltimore Gun Club is a group of Baltimore gun fanciers who decide to travel to the moon by shooting a manned shell at it.

Box #50. "Take Trans Atlantic Pneumatic Tube." The "Trans Atlantic Pneumatic Tube" is a reference to Michel Verne's "Un Express de L'Avenir" (An Express of the Future, *Strand Magazine*, December 1895). In this story a pneumatically-driven train carries passengers under the Atlantic.

Box #51. "The Harkaway boys don't like your tan. Thrashed and sent back 6 spaces." The "Harkaway Boys" refer to Bracebridge Hemyng's stories about Jack Harkaway and his family, who first appeared in *Jack Harkaway's Schooldays* in 1871. The Harkaway boys, whose father, Jack, appears in a portrait on the back cover of the *League* hardcover, were adventurous schoolboys who traveled around the world. The Harkaway boys would not like someone's tan and would thrash them for it because they were biased against the non-English, especially those who had darker skin than they, and often used malicious pranks and physical violence against them.

Box #52. "John Melmoth recounts an anecdote. Miss five turns." "John Melmoth" is the titular character in Charles Maturin's *Melmoth the Wanderer* (1820), the greatest of all Gothic novels. In the novel John Melmoth sells his soul to the devil in exchange for lengthened life. Melmoth then spends most of the novel bewailing his fate and looking for someone to take his place. The novel is lengthy, and Melmoth is long-winded, which is why the player misses five turns while Melmoth tells a story.

Box #53. "Join sight-seers at cylinder in crater. Retire from game." The "cylinder in crater" is a reference to H.G. Wells' *The War of the Worlds* (1898). In the novel the Martians arrive on Earth in a cylinder whose landing creates a large crater. When the cylinder opens and the Martians emerge they wipe out all those present with an "invisible, inevitable sword of heat."

Box #55. "Willie and Tim have a question. Sadly, their speech is unfathomable." "Willie" and "Tim," seen on Page 149, Panel 1, are the friendly tramps "Weary Willy" and "Tired Tim," two of the earliest recurring characters in British comics. They were created by Tom Browne and first appeared in *Illustrated Chips* in 1896.

Box #56. "Stuck in Grimpen Mire for 1 turn." "Grimpen Mire" is a reference to Arthur Conan Doyle's *The Hound of the Baskervilles* (1902). Grimpen Mire is the dangerous section of Dartmoor just north of Baskerville Hall where the notorious Hound is said to prowl.

Box #57. "Moulin Rouge. Lose virginity." The Moulin Rouge was a combination theater, concert hall, and dance hall, full of artists (like Henri de Toulouse-Lautrec), dancers, and prostitutes. It opened in Paris in 1889 and quickly became famous as the symbol and embodiment of Parisian *joie de vivre*.

Box #58. "Robbed by Arséne Lupin." Arséne Lupin, the most famous of the gentlemen thieves, was created by Maurice LeBlanc and first appeared in the magazine *Je Sais Tout* in 1905. Lupin was a mysterious master thief, similar to Raffles (see Box #30 above), who stole from society but also fought for good.

Box #59. "Rue Morgue: Assist C. August Dupin and miss a turn, or go to square 61." The "Rue Morgue" and "C. August Dupin" are references to Edgar Allan Poe's detective, C. Auguste Dupin, and his first case, "The Murders in the Rue Morgue." Dupin appeared on pages 23-36.

Box #62. "Absinthe break. Go to the dogs." Absinthe, a.k.a. "The Green Fairy," is a strong herbal liqueur, usually around 120 proof, which was popular during the Nineteenth century with aesthetes and intellectuals. Its ingredients vary: although its primary elements are alcohol and wormwood, the formula is augmented with other herbs such as anise, licorice, hyssop, veronica, fennel, lemon balm and angelica. Absinthe gained a deserved reputation for being toxic if taken in large quantities, and its use was banned across the United States and Europe from 1912-1915.

Box #63. "Broad Arrow Jack shows you the Golden Rivet, but worse things happen at sea." "Broad Arrow Jack," seen in *League* as a member of the crew of the *Nautilus*, is the hero of E. Harcourt Burrage's "Broad-Arrow Jack" serial. "Broad-Arrow Jack" is John Ashleigh, an Englishman who runs afoul of thieves while emigrating to Australia. He is branded with the broad arrow but recovers and continues with his adventures.

The "Golden Rivet" is a reference to naval folklore. Crewmen new to a ship were told that one of the rivets in the lower part of a ship's hull was made of gold and that they should find it. No such rivet existed, of course. On some ships the search for the golden rivet was also used as an excuse to sexually initiate the new crewman.

Box #65. "Sargasso Sea. Miss a turn." The "Sargasso Sea" is a reference to an area of the Atlantic Ocean where the winds, mixed by the Gulf Stream and the North Equatorial Current, move in a circle, thus causing ships powered only by sail to be trapped in it. It is known for the distinctive blue quality of its waters and its vast islands of seaweed. The Sargasso Sea appeared in the first Captain Nemo novel, *Twenty Thousand Leagues Under the Sea*.

Box #66. "Oh, no, it's Fungal Disease." This may be a reference to the William Hope Hodgson story, "The Voice in the Night" (*Blue Book*, November 1907), which is about two castaways on a North Pacific island who become infected with a fungus which transforms their entire bodies. H.P. Lovecraft's "The Shunned House" (1928) also features a fungus, this one haunting an old house in Providence, Rhode Island.

Kevin O'Neill notes:
Yes, this is a William Hope Hodgson reference.

Box #67. "Doctor Moreau will see you now. Spend rest of game on all fours." In H.G. Wells' *The Island of Dr. Moreau* (1896), the cruel Doctor Moreau attempts (unsuccessfully) to turn animals into men.

Box #68. "Treasure Island welcomes offshore investors." "Treasure Island" is a reference to Robert Louis Stevenson's book of the same name.

Box #69. "Lulu breaks your heart." "Lulu" is a reference to Frank Wedekind's plays *Earth-Spirit* (1895) and *Pandora's Box* (1902). In the plays Lulu is a German femme fatale who leaves a trail of broken hearts and fortunes behind her. She ultimately ends up destitute and plying her trade on the streets of London and is finally murdered by Jack the Ripper. The two Wedekind novels were used as the source for the silent film *Pandora's Box* (1928), in which Lulu was played by Louise Brooks.

Box #71. "Henry Hobson says go back 1 or forward 4." This is a dual reference, to Henry Hobson, of Harold Brighouse's *Hobson's Choice* (1915), and to the phrase "Hobson's choice." In the novel *Hobson's Choice* Henry Hobson is a Lancashire bootmaker who must deal with several rebellious daughters. The phrase "Hobson's choice" is a reference to Thomas Hobson (1549-1631), a hostler in Cambridge, England, who always offered his customers only that horse which was closest to the door. The phrase "Hobson's choice" has come to mean no choice, to take what is offered or nothing.

Box #73. "Buy Crystal Egg from Mr. Cave." The "Crystal Egg" and "Mr. Cave" are references to H.G. Wells' "The Crystal Egg" (*New Review*, May 1897). In the story Mr. Cave, an antiquarian, becomes obsessed with his crystal egg, through which it is possible to view Mars. The Crystal Egg makes an appearance in the second *League* series.

Box #74. "Lidenbrock Sea crossing rougher than usual." In Jules Verne's *Journey to the Center of the Earth* (1864), the Lidenbrock Sea is an underground sea, filled with various prehistoric creatures, that subterranean explorers are forced to cross.

Box #75. "Severin's been a bad boy." "Severin" is a reference to Leopold von Sacher-Masoch's *Venus in Furs* (1870). Sacher-Masoch, whose name was the source for the term "masochism," wrote *Venus in Furs* to detail his masochist fantasies. The novel is about Severin, a dissipated dilettante who falls in love first with a statue of Venus and then later with his neighbor, Wanda, who resembles the statue and who indulges Severin's taste for the lash.

Box #76. "Kapitan Mors will fly you to square 82." "Kapitan Mors" is Captain Mors, the heroic protagonist of the German dime novel series *Der Luftpirat und Sein Lenkbares Luftschiff* (The Pirate of the Air and His Navigable Airship), which ran from 1908 to 1911.

Captain Mors was a Captain Nemo-like character who fought for good and for Earth against villains both human and alien.

Box #77. "Pére Ubu screams abuse. Ignore him. He's Polish," accompanied by an illustration of a corpulent older man screaming "Merdre!" "Pere Ubu" is a reference to Alfred Jarry's trilogy of surrealist plays, *King Ubu*, *Cuckold Ubu*, and *Slave Ubu*, all written in 1896. Ubu is an unpleasant authoritarian monster given to vulgarities, including "merdre," a nonsense word close to "merde," the French word for shit. "Ignore him, he's Polish" is a reference to Alfred Jarry's speech on *King Ubu*'s opening night: "the action, which is about to start, takes place in Poland, that is to say, Nowhere."

Box #78. "Dishonored by Harry Flashman. Sting with shame for 2 missed turns." "Harry Flashman" is a character who first appeared in Thomas Hughes' *Tom Brown's Schooldays* (1857) as a bullying schoolboy who torments Tom Brown. Flashman became popular in the modern era through George Macdonald Fraser's "Flashman" novels, beginning with *Flashman; From the Flashman Papers 1839-1842* (1969). As an adult Flashman is no improvement over his childhood self; he remains an unlikeable cad and scoundrel.

Box #79. "Bed down with exotic beauty, wake up with The Beetle. Lie back and think of England," accompanied by an illustration of a ghastly old woman. "The Beetle" is a reference to Richard Marsh's *The Beetle* (1897). In the novel the Beetle is a giant, deformed beetle which is inhabited by the soul of an Egyptian princess. She can transform herself into the beetle, into a beautiful Egyptian woman, and into an ugly old man, which explains the change alluded to in this box.

Box #80. Kevin O'Neill notes:
> This should read "Flatland" – perhaps a private education might help.

> I lettered Flatland title in style of book's original title page, but for some reason this was dropped out rendering next line meaningless (restored in French edition of League).

Box #82. "The Purple Terror is starting to grow on you." The "Purple Terror" is a reference to Fred M. White's "The Purple Terror" (*Strand Magazine*, September 1899), a story about a carnivorous plant.

Box #83. "A humbling experience with Mr. Heep. Feel soiled, even if you win." "Mr. Heep" is a a character in Charles Dickens' *David Copperfield* (1850). Uriah Heep is a vile blackmailer and one of Dickens' most despicable villains.

Box #86. Kevin O'Neill notes:
> Should read: "Maiden Voyage of Titan" (Not Titanic), another reference to the novel *Futility.*

Box #87. "Professor Cavor coats you with his special paste. The moon seems awfully big tonight." Professor Cavor appears in H.G. Wells' *The First Men in the Moon*. Cavor, seen on Page 52 of *League*, is the short, fat scientist who invents a paste, "cavorite," which cancels gravity. Cavor and the narrator of the novel use it to travel to the moon.

Box #88. "Wonderland. Throw 6 to stay where you are. Otherwise, move counter in reverse." "Wonderland" is the magic land that Alice visits in Lewis Carroll's *Alice's Adventures in Wonderland* (1865) and *Through the Looking Glass* (1871). "Throw 6 to stay where you are. Otherwise, move counter in reverse" is a reference to Chapter 2 of *Through the Looking Glass*, when the Red Queen tells Alice that "Now, HERE, you see, it takes all the running YOU can do, to keep in the same place. If you want to get somewhere else, you must run at least twice as fast as that!"

Box #100. "Well, call me Kallikrates! It's the Fountain and Heart of Eternal Life! Hurrah! Jolly well done! Now join Mr. Melmoth for a long lunch." In H. Rider Haggard's *She* (1887), Kallikrates was an Egyptian who Ayesha, the immortal goddess and She Who Must Be Obeyed, loves yet slays. The "Fountain and Heart of Eternal Life" are references to the source of Ayesha's immortality.

Kevin O'Neill notes:

> As an aside, I designed the game so it is impossible to reach the end, a nice exercise in futility for the player. Unusually for a long project, because of the short deadline I had to design the game first and lay in rough copy for Alan to rewrite where essential – just as well, if I'd had this as a script it would have seemed an unreasonable task in the time we had.

ARCHETYPES

The cast of *The League of Extraordinary Gentlemen* are recognizable characters, not just visually but in terms of their literary and cultural reputations. Beyond that, however, they are recognizable to Western readers because they represent archetypal characters from Victorian literature, archetypes which are still present in Western popular culture today. Whether or not Moore chose these characters deliberately, they resonate with modern readers in large part because of their archetypal qualities.

Allan Quatermain

In H. Rider Haggard's stories and novels Allan Quatermain is a British hunter and explorer who treks across Africa, encounters various Lost Races, and fights against groups of Africans. Quatermain first appeared in Haggard's *King Solomon's Mines* in 1885. The book, about Quatermain's trek to find the legendary diamond mines of King Solomon, was immediately popular, selling over 50,000 copies in America and England in two years, a very respectable number for the time. The novel has never been out of print, and its popularity led Haggard to write a number of prequels to it: *Allan Quatermain* (1887), *Allan's Wife* (1887), *A Tale of Three Lions* (1887), *Maiwa's Revenge* (1888), *Allan the Hunter: A Tale of Three Lions* (1898), *Marie* (1912), *Child of Storm* (1913), *The Ivory Child* (1916), *Finished* (1916),"Magepa the Buck" in *Smith and the Pharaohs and Other Tales* (1920), *The Ancient Allan* (1920), *She and Allan* (1921), *Heu-Heu, or The Monster* (1924), *Treasure of the Lake* (1926), and *Allan and the Ice Gods* (1927).

King Solomon's Mines and its sequel, *Allan Quatermain*, were enormously influential, spawning hundreds of imitations. But the influence of Allan Quatermain and of *King Solomon's Mines* goes beyond simple attempts to duplicate the plot of *King Solomon's*

Mines. Quatermain and *King Solomon's Mines* had a two-fold influence on modern literature and modern writers.

The first influence was in the creation of a separate genre of stories about Lost Races/Lost Worlds. Lost Race/Lost World stories are about lost, forgotten, or hidden races, cities, cultures, and civilizations in hidden valleys or undersea or underground areas on or beneath the Earth. Stories about unknown lands and races have been written for centuries, but there was no separate, recognized genre of Lost Race/Lost World stories until Haggard wrote *King Solomon's Mines*. Historical romances using Lost Race/Lost World themes and motifs written before *King Solomon's Mines* were usually set in the past, but Haggard set his in the present. Haggard's predecessors, ranging from Lady Mary Fox, with her *Account of an Expedition to the Interior of New Holland* (1837), to Elton R. Smilie, with his *The Mantitlians; or, A Record of Recent Scientific Explorations in the Andean La Plata, S. A.* (1877), lacked Haggard's skill as a writer as well as those elements of *King Solomon's Mines* which made the novel so popular.

There are several aspects of *King Solomon's Mines* which set it apart from what came before and which explain its popularity. While Haggard is no great stylist, he is a compelling writer, and he has a genuine skill in describing battles scenes and depicting warriors like Quatermain's companion Umslopogaas. Similarly, Haggard's inclusion of realistic details were very attractive to British readers in the 1880s and 1890s. Haggard was an old Africa hand, having spent several years there as a young man, and many elements of *King Solomon's Mines* show Haggard's familiarity with Africa. Allan Quatermain is partially based on F.C. Selous, a hunter famous in the late Nineteenth century and the author of *A Hunter's Wanderings in Africa* (1881), which Haggard had read. The Kukuanas of the novel are based on the Matabele of Zimbabwe, with whom Haggard was familiar. Haggard's descriptions of the landscape of Africa, of elephant hunting, and of the equipment used on safari are all accurate. Readers responded to this verisimilitude, as they had to Jules Verne, who showed a similar concern with accuracy.

The use of Africa in *King Solomon's Mines* was another important element in its popularity. Before *King Solomon's Mines* there was only one novel of any merit about Africa: Olive Schreiner's *Story of*

An African Farm (1883), a novel of domestic realism and Boer life in the African back country. *Story of An African Farm* was only a minor success, however, where *King Solomon's Mines* was one of the best-selling novels of the century. Africa held a great deal of appeal for British readers in 1885. Earlier that year the representatives of fourteen countries, including Great Britain, met in Berlin to establish the rules for dividing and exploiting Africa. Britain was very interested in the "scramble for Africa," and many young men of the English middle class were becoming increasingly involved in imperial affairs overseas. The English had a desire to read stories about Africa, and Haggard's story, with its unabashed heroism and open masculinity, satisfied this desire in a way that Schreiner's domestic drama could not.

As well, Haggard's use of a real section of Africa as the setting for *King Solomon's Mines* allowed readers to consult atlases and find the blank, unexplored area where Quatermain discovered Solomon's mines. And, finally, *King Solomon's Mines* came at a time when archaeological discoveries, from Schliemann's excavation of Troy in 1870, to Carl Mauch's 1871 discovery of the ruins of Great Zimbabwe, to Brugsch's opening of the Valley of the Kings in 1881, were electrifying Europe and bringing to light numerous lost and forgotten cultures.

The popularity of *King Solomon's Mines* and the demand for sequels by Haggard and for similar books by other authors helped Haggard prosper as a writer also led to the rise of a flourishing industry of Lost World/Lost Race novels. These imitations of *King Solomon's Mines* were numerous in the late 1880s and 1890s and included novels whose plots were virtually identical to *King Solomon's Mines*. Examples include John De Morgan's *He*, *It*, and *King Solomon's Treasures* (all 1887), Andrew Lang's *He* (1887), and Henry Biron's *King Solomon's Wives* (1887). But even after the inital, two-decade-long wave of Lost World novels subsided, the public's taste for Lost Race/Lost World stories did not significantly diminish for several decades. Writers as diverse as Edgar Rice Burroughs, with his Tarzan novels, Arthur Conan Doyle, with his Professor Challenger novels, and Baroness Orczy, with her *The Smoky God* (1908) produced Lost World stories from the 1900s to the 1920s. The 1930s were the high point of Lost World fiction:

James Hilton's *Shangri-La* (1933) was an international best-seller. After World War Two the public taste for Lost World/Lost Race stories subsided. But Lost World/Lost Race novels are still being produced today, as with Michael Crichton's *Congo*, written in 1980 and filmed in 1995.

In a larger sense, numerous other subgenres of adventure, fantasy, and science fiction derive in part from the Lost World/Lost Race form. Stories about fantasy lands accessed by portals, doors, stairways, or wardrobes, novels about prehistoric lands, planetary romances, and stories about Ruritanian countries, all owe much to the Lost Race/Lost World form which Haggard essentially created.

The second and greater influence of Haggard and Quatermain lies in the genres of fantasy and adventure fiction and in the authors who wrote in those genres. Adventure fiction has been around for centuries with Norse sagas (The Burning of Njal) and Greek myths (the Quest of the Argonauts) and even the Babylonian Epic of Gilgamesh constituting a type of adventure fiction. In the Nineteenth century adventure fiction flourished, with Gothic novels being replaced by historical romances in England and France. Perhaps the most influential adventure novel of the Nineteenth century was Sir Walter Scott's *Ivanhoe* (1819), which brought together action, scholarship, and historical settings to create the modern historical romance. In France the works of Alexandre Dumas and Eugene Sue were similarly influential on those who followed them. But naturalist novels replaced adventure novels as the dominant form, and Scott, R.D. Blackmore (author of *Lorna Doone*), and Dumas *pére* were supplanted by the likes of Émile Zola, Dumas *fils*, Anthony Trollope, and George Eliot. The 1860s and 1870s were a low point in the century for adventure fiction. The 1880s saw a revival in the adventure fiction genre, with Stevenson's *Treasure Island* and *Kidnapped* (1886) and Haggard's *King Solomon's Mines* leading the way. While Stevenson preceded Haggard and influenced him, if only negatively (a possibly apocryphal anecdote has Haggard reading *Treasure Island* and saying that he could do better), *King Solomon's Mines* was the more influential novel. *Treasure Island* was not the immediate success that *King Solomon's Mines* was: word about the novel was slow in spreading, and a second edition of the novel was not called for until 1885. Adventure writers of the late 1880s and

1890s had earlier writers to model themselves on, from Sir Walter Scott to R.D. Blackmore, but the more recent writers, including Stevenson and Kipling and most of all Haggard, were the more influential.

Haggard was similarly influential on successive generations of American adventure writers. Edgar Rice Burroughs' debt to Haggard is obvious. Likewise, A. Merritt and Robert E. Howard read and learned from Haggard, and with Burroughs those three were models for numerous writers of American pulp-style fantasy as well as sword-and-sorcery, a genre which Haggard prefigured with his Viking fantasy *Eric Brighteyes* (1891). Finally, many of the adventure writers who penned stories for American and British pulps were influenced not only by Haggard's Lost World/Lost Race stories but also by his historical novels and colonial romances. These authors, who in turn influenced the generation of writers who followed them, included Harold Lamb, Talbot Munday, and Arthur O. Friel.

Haggard's influence on the genre of Fantasy fiction is if anything more pronounced. J.R.R. Tolkien read Haggard as a child, and the influences of Haggard on Tolkien are marked, ranging from plot similarities in *King Solomon's Mines* and *Lord of the Rings* to Tolkien's Haggardian action scenes, his descriptions of landscapes, the atmosphere of the Mines of Moria, the characterization of the dwarfs, and the use of the hidden king figure of Aragorn. Likewise, C.S. Lewis feasted on Haggard's work as a child. These two writers are among the most influential authors on modern British fantasy fiction, the "scholarly fantasy" which is counterpointed by American adventure-influenced fantasy fiction. Haggard was not the only influence on scholarly fantasy authors, nor even the largest influence of his time. William Morris was more influential than Haggard on scholarly fantasy authors. But with Haggard American-style adventure fantasy branched off from scholarly fantasy. Morris and Haggard were contemporaries and friends, and while Morris' influence on Haggard is well known–it was Morris' translation of several Norse sagas which influenced Haggard's *Eric Brighteyes*– Haggard's influence on Morris' fantasies, all of which were written after *Allan Quatermain* and *King Solomon's Mines*, is less obvious but still marked.

Finally, there is the figure of Quatermain himself. He stands as an archetype not simply of the Great White Hunter or of the African hand who is helped by a native gunbearer or friend, but of the adventurer hero who ventures into the Lost World and later into Ruritanias and other planets. Quatermain's particular brand of manliness was very influential on both his readers and on writers who followed Haggard. Its virtues were quite similar to the "muscular Christianity" which was then in vogue, the linking of healthy bodies and strong-minded Christianity, and these virtues were particularly appealing to an English bourgeoisie which had been softened, in their own eyes, by too much affluence, and to the English proletariat, who sought escape from lives filled with monotonous labor and who had developed a taste for reading through the new free circulating libraries. The figure of Quatermain was to show up, in various guises, in pulp and adventure fiction across the decades: characters from Edgar Rice Burroughs' John Carter and George Lucas' and Philip Kaufman's Indiana Jones can trace their lineage to Allan Quatermain.

Mina Murray

Mina Murray is also, in her own way, something of an archetype: she is both a satire of the Victorian view of the New Woman and an excellent example of that character type. Mina's original appearance was as Mina Harker in Bram Stoker's *Dracula* (1897), and her character in *Dracula* is somewhat different than her character in *League*, in part because of the way in which Mina has changed, in the world of *League*, since the events of *Dracula* and in part for Moore's satirical purposes. But both in *Dracula* and in *League* Mina is a New Woman, and works as an archetypal example of same.

While the term "feminism," in the sense of advocacy of the rights of women, did not come into use in Britain until the mid-1890s, feminism and "The Woman Question," about the nature and role of women in society, was debated in Britain since at least Mary Wollstonecraft's *Vindication of the Rights of Woman* (1792). The first half of the Nineteenth century saw an increasing amount of discussion about the need for radical changes in women's position in British society, and an organized feminist movement began in Britain in the early 1850s. By the late 1880s feminists were focused primarily on women's suffrage, although activists worked on a number of other issues, and women's issues were an accepted if unwelcome part of the political landscape.

The "New Woman" was a social and literary type who emerged in the 1880s. The term itself entered common parlance in the mid-1890s and referred to a group of women who took many of the theoretical ideas of feminism and put them into practice as a lifestyle. The New Woman was usually middle class and worked for a living, often at a job that until recently had been limited to men. She advocated self-fulfilment rather than self-sacrifice, and chose education and a career over marriage. (A synonym for "New Woman," the phrase "Girton girl," was a reference to Girton College, which was opened in 1869 and was the equivalent of a Cambridge college for women. The phrase "Girton girl" was was derisively used in the late Victorian and Edwardian years to refer to any woman who had completed her university courses.) She spoke directly and was forthright about her political views, arguing publicly for the destruction of class distinctions and for economic independence for women. She smoked and drank openly. She decried restrictive fashions, rejecting petticoats and corsets and instead wearing "rational" (i.e., men's) clothing. She exercised. And most alarming to the critics of the New Woman, she was sexually active, or at least advocated sexual freedom, and avoided marriage, seeing it as a trap designed to rob women of their independence.

This goes against the popular stereotype of the Victorians as sexually and emotionally repressed, but the truth is that at the end of the Nineteenth century women in England were presented with a variety of role models to emulate. Clerical, medical, sociological, literary and political spokesmen, all the mouthpieces of high culture, stressed the sanctity of marriage, family, duty, chastity, feminine modesty, and other attributes that we today think of as stereotypically Victorian. But there were a varied number and kind of female figures, from writers to journalists to activists to explorers, on which women could and did model themselves, and some of these women were notable New Women. There were, of course, the Mrs. Grundys, the morally upright, prudish figures of the popular imagination, of whom Queen Victoria might be seen as the exemplar. But there were others who were not so confined to the morality of the upper classes and who not only acted independently but flaunted their unconventional lifestyle. These women, whether or not they were open advocates for the ideas of the New Woman, lived their lives as if they were.

The reality of the late Victorian era is that men and women of all classes were much less bound by romantic and sexual restrictions than is popularly thought today. After 1860, kept women, courtesans, *demi-mondaines*, the *Grand Horizontales*, the Great Strumpets—whichever term one chooses to describe the women of the Victorian age who accepted money from their lovers in exchange for company and physical affection—were not only *not* socially ostracized by Victorian high society, but were accepted into the most exclusive parties and occasions, idolized by many young women and watched with admiration by both mothers and daughters. A large number of women went so far as to copy their fashions and dress their children in modified versions of the most characteristic styles of the *demi-mondaines*.

Society, high and low, was under no illusion as to what these women did but did not condemn them openly for their actions. Rather, they were seen as daringly unconventional as well as the living embodiments of a female fantasy: wealthy, able to speak their minds without fear of social punishment, and free to indulge in various pleasures whenever they chose while not being tied down with children, poverty, or a restrictive, soul-deadening marriage. These women were likewise able to travel when they wanted, were socially influential, and routinely engaged in activities such as riding and training horses, activities which had previously been seen as the province of men alone. These women were the New Women, and while they were criticized by would-be moral arbiters they were admired by far more people.

The New Woman appeared in literature as well. Most of the New Women were in domestic dramas, like Olive Schreiner's *Story of an African Farm* (1883), Sarah Grand's *Heavenly Twins* (1893), and Mona Caird's *Daughters of Danaus* (1894). But some New Women, or female characters with the attributes of New Women, appeared in positive roles in adventure and detective fiction, either as the heroines of the stories or as female love interests who were more independent and less subservient than was the norm. In this they differed from the heroines of the Gothic novels, who were for the most part helpless and dependent on others. The Gothic heroines appeared before organized feminism in Britain, while the female detectives and adventuresses had the benefit of a coherent feminist philosophy and movement.

The figure of the female detective is much older than most people realize. The first fictional female amateur detective, a woman whose profession is not to solve crimes but who does so in the course of a story or novel, was Mademoiselle de Scudéry, from E.T.A. Hoffmann's "Mademoiselle de Scudéry" (1818). The first professional female detective–that is, a woman employed as a professional investigator and crime solver–was "L_____" (her full name is never given), who appeared in William Burton's "The Secret Cell" in 1837. By contrast, Edgar Allan Poe's Dupin, who is generally seen as the father of modern fictional detectives and the first of the Great Detectives, did not appear until 1841. The first British novel to feature a female professional detective was William S. Hayward's *Revelations of a Lady Detective* in 1864. (By comparison, the first notable male professional detectives in English fiction were Inspector Bucket in Charles Dickens' *Bleak House*, [1853], Hawkshaw in Tom Taylor's *The Ticket-of-Leave Man* [1863], and Sergeant Cuff in Wilkie Collins' *The Moonstone* [1868]). Over the next forty years over two dozen female professional detectives appeared in penny dreadfuls, story papers, short stories, collections, and novels, with the majority of these appearing after 1890. Few of these women were as assertive and abrasive as Moore's Mina, and many of them were emphatically "ladylike," with a surfeit of personality traits that the Victorians thought were most fitting for women. But most of these lady detectives also embodied aspects of the New Woman, just as Stoker's Mina does, and all were independent and self-sufficient. Some, like Fergusson Wright Hume's Hagar Stanley and Grant Allen's Lois Cayley, were as cool, self-possessed, and tough as Mina.

Adventure fiction, too, had female characters who benefitted from the reality of the New Woman. Most of the women in adventure fiction who had the attributes of the New Woman were cast as villains. H. Rider Haggard's She (from *She*, in 1887), T. Mullett Ellis' Zalma von der Pahlen (from *Zalma*, 1895), and most memorably Irene Adler (from Arthur Conan Doyle's "A Scandal in Bohemia," 1891), all had aspects of the New Woman. Adler was The Woman to Sherlock Holmes; she outwitted him in her single appearance, and she was the only woman who he ever respected and admired ("In his eyes she eclipses and predominates the whole of her sex."). But none of these New Woman villains was presented as entirely evil, and Adler was presented sympathetically. Those New Women in adventure fiction who were not the antagonists, such as Laura de Guéran (from Adolphe Belot's *A Parisian Sultana*, 1879), are shown to be entirely admirable, despite (and perhaps because of) their New Woman attributes.

Mina, in *Dracula*, has many of the attributes of the New Woman, but Stoker takes pains to point out that she is not one of them. Mina makes several gibes at the New Woman in the novel, including the following:

> Some of the 'New Women' writers will some day start an idea that men and women should be allowed to see each other asleep before proposing or accepting. But I suppose the 'New Woman' won't condescend in future to accept. She will do the proposing herself. And a nice job she will make of it too!

Stoker's attitude towards women was complex and on the whole negative; his wife was cold to him, he may have died of syphilis, and his fiction, including *Dracula* and *The Lair of the White Worm* (1911), is often misogynistic. It is no surprise, therefore, that the heroine of *Dracula* should overtly reject the New Woman. But like many fictional and real Victorian women did, Mina vocally rejects the idea of the New Woman while unconsciously embracing her principles in her life. Even though many Victorians felt that women were not capable of holding a job as a teacher, Mina is an assistant schoolmistress and teaches "etiquette and decorum." Mina practices shorthand and typing because she wants to help Jonathan with his job. These abilities were novel for women in the 1890s, and the idea of a wife wanting to help her husband at his job was almost unheard of. Mina keeps her journal to develop her writing and vows to "try to do what I see lady journalists do: interviewing and writing descriptions." Later in the novel Mina's intelligence and willfulness helps her husband and Dr. van Helsing, and it is not until she is bitten and partially turned into a vampire that she loses her volition and becomes a passive prize for the men to fight for. At the novel's end, though she has recovered from Dracula's bites, she has become a mother and seemingly lost most of the aspects of the New Woman.

There are obvious differences between the Mina of *Dracula* and the Mina of *League*. As Moore has hinted in interviews and as is revealed in the second *League* series, the change in Mina's attitude comes from what she went through in the novel. She can no longer live with her husband, Jonathan, because he is now too much of a milksop in her eyes. Her experience, in loving and helping to kill Dracula, has hardened her. It may be that Mina, in *League*, is a parody of the New Woman; she is in some ways comically severe, acerbic, and "manly," as Quatermain himself calls her. But at the same time she is willful, independent, sexually aggressive (as with her demand on Page 147 that Allan kiss her), and verbally direct, all of which were aspects of the New Woman, and the British New Women would have recognised her, in real life or in fiction, as one of their own. Allan's reaction to Mina, on Page 22 Panel 4, would have been typical of an establishment British male when seeing a New Woman in 1898.

The Mina Murray of *League* is, therefore, archetypal in that she represents the New Woman, literary and real, and embodies so many of their characteristics.

Captain Nemo

Captain Nemo appears in Jules Verne's *Twenty Thousand Leagues Under the Sea* (1870) and *The Mysterious Island* (1875). Nemo has a very memorable character, even if the images people recall are of James Mason of the film version of *Twenty Thousand Leagues* rather than the Nemo of Verne's novels. But Nemo is more than simply memorable. In the character of Captain Nemo Jules Verne created an archetype which proved to be influential to many writers. Captain Nemo is the archetypal Man With The Machine (MWTM), the inventor/engineer character who creates a scientifically advanced vehicle and uses it on his or her adventures.

Nemo's most distinctive attributes are those of the brooding, Byronic genius combined with the Count of Monte Cristo-like avenger who stands outside of society and avenges the wrongs done to innocents. What is less often recalled is Nemo's place in the history of science fiction as the most important Man With The Machine.

There are two primary strains of science fiction which involve MWTM characters. The first is what might be called Techno-Fantasy, in which the machine replaces the magic item- sword, ring, amulet, etc- of fantasy stories. In fantasy stories magic swords are understood to be sharper and harder than ordinary swords because they are magical, and magic rings to work their spells because they, too, are magical. In Techno-Fantasies the explanation for the machine's operation and existence is that it is "scientific" or "technologically advanced;" further explanations are either non-existent or make use of pseudo-scientific jargon. Most mass-media science fiction, including *Star Wars*, *Star Trek*, and virtually all modern superhero comics, fall into this category.

The second type of science fiction in which the MWTM appears is "hard science fiction," that is, science fiction which is based on either established or reasonably extrapolated science and scientific principles. In hard science fiction faster than light travel is not possible, or takes place only through verifiable scientific phenomenon such as wormholes. In hard science fiction, travel between planets takes place at speeds slower than light. A significant proportion of modern science fiction is hard, but in the mass media it is rare and in comic books nearly non-existent.

During the Victorian era the dichotomy between Techno-Fantasies and hard science fiction was most prominently seen between H.G. Wells, whose work usually qualified as Techno-fantasy, and Jules Verne, who was far more scrupulous in his use of science. (The pair were aware of their differing approaches, with Verne speaking scornfully of what he saw as Wells' lack of scientific credibility).

Techno-Fantasies with MWTMs predate Captain Nemo. In 1868 Edward S. Ellis published "The Huge Hunter, or the Steam Man of the Prairies" in the dime novel *Beadle's American Novel* #45. "The Huge Hunter" features Johnny Brainerd, a young hunch-backed dwarf who creates a man-shaped steam engine and uses it to adventure in the American frontier. Ellis attempts to describe the steam engine in realistic terms, but the net effect of "The Huge Hunter" is of a Techno-Fantasy.

"The Huge Hunter" was the first Edisonade. Edisonades are a

genre of stories in which a boy inventor creates a vehicle and uses it to transport himself to the frontier (usually the Western frontier of the United States) and makes his fortune by helping to "civilize" the frontier, usually by slaughtering great numbers of natives. The Edisonade was one of the most popular of the dime novel forms, and Edisonades appeared from the 1870s through the 1890s, with modern descendants of the Edisonade boy inventor characters, from Howard Garis and Edward Stratemeyer's Tom Swift, Senior to John Blaine's Rick Brant to Tom Swift, Jr., continuing to appear through the Twentieth century. After the heyday of the Edisonade ended, the figure of the brilliant but eccentric inventor, whose creations were powerful weapons and vehicles, remained, sometimes as comic characters, as in Clement Fezandie's "Doctor Hackensaw" stories, but more often as heroic inventor-adventurers. The coming of the "space opera," action-adventure stories on an interstellar or galactic scale, brought the figure of the inventor-adventurer into a new context, that of outer space. In each case the MWTM, the inventor-adventurer, invented and used machines whose workings were only lightly justified (if at all) by actual science.

Hard science fiction stories featuring MWTMs also predate Captain Nemo, but they were not widely read. One of the earliest hard science fiction stories was J.L. Riddell's *Orrin Lindsay's Plan of Aerial Navigation* (1847), a novel about an American scientist who discovers that an amalgam of mercury and steel, when subjected to a strong magnetic field, creates an anti-gravity field. The scientist then uses his discovery to fly; he begins with a wooden sphere, taking it high into the sky and then returning to Earth, and then creates a larger, air-tight version of the sphere and takes it to the moon. In 1869 the Danish writer Vilhelm Bergsøe wrote *En Reise Med Flyvefisken "Prometeus"* (A Journey on the Flying Fish "Prometheus," 1869). The novel is about an engineer who builds the *Prometheus*, a winged dirigible which flies by a combination of gas and propellor. The engineer takes the *Prometheus* on an exploratory trip to the Panama Canal, where he runs into a massive thunderstorm. *En Reise Med Flyvefisken "Prometeus"* has several similarities to Verne's later *Robur le Conquérant*, and the *Prometheus* is a clear precursor to Robur's airship *Albatross*, but there's no evidence that Verne was aware of Bergsøe's work, and *"Prometeus"* is likely a case of parallel development rather than an influence on Verne.

But the genre of hard science fiction MWTM stories began with Captain Nemo, whose ship, the *Nautilus*, was described in great detail and at great length, with Verne ascribing its marvels to electricity in very realistic and plausible terms. *Twenty Thousand Leagues Under The Sea* was published in France in 1870; the first British translation was published in 1872, with an American translation following in 1873. The influence of the novel cannot be understated; it was extremely popular and widely imitated. Luis Senarens, the author of Frank Reade, Jr. Edisonades and one of the most influential and imitated dime novel authors, was heavily influenced by Verne's work, praising him in print. (Senarens later claimed to have received a letter of praise from Verne himself). Thinly veiled copies of Nemo proliferated following the British publication of *Twenty Thousand Leagues Under The Sea*, with two of the most blatant being Bracebridge Hemyng's Captain Nemo, in "Dick Lightheart; or, the Scapegrace at Sea," published in *Young Men of Great Britain* in 1873, and Edward Stratemeyer's Captain Vindex, in "The Wizard of the Deep; or, the Search for the Million Dollar Pearl," in 1895. In *Robur le Conquérant* (1887) and *Maître du Monde* (1904) Verne used another variation of Nemo. The character of Robur was influential as an MWTM, but he is in many ways a copy of Nemo.

MWTM characters influenced by Nemo appeared in both hard science fiction and Techno-Fantasies in the Twentieth century. The pulps saw a number of MWTMs, as did comic strips before World War II, and fittingly for Nemo MWTM characters appeared in adventure and science fiction stories in countries other than the United States and Britain. Captain Sakuragi, from Shunro Oshikawa's *Kaitei Gunkan* (Warship at the Bottom of the Sea, 1903), was a patriotic MWTM who was heavily influenced by Nemo. Captain Mors, a character who appeared in 165 issues of a German dime novel, *Der Luftpirat und sein Lenkbares Luftschiff* (The Pirate of the Air and his Navigable Airship, 1908-1911) and who is mentioned in *League* on Page 53, Panel 1, was another MWTM whose adventures took him into space, anticipating the space opera genre. The best friend of Anton Krechet, a patriotic bandit whose adventures appeared in the Russian newspaper *Kopeika* from 1909-1916, was a Captain Nemo-like MWTM and built a *Nautilus*-like submarine for Krechet. The character of Fédor Sarraskine, in Jose Moselli's *La Guerre des Océans* (War of the Oceans, 1929), was a very Nemo-like MWTM, as was Jörn Farrow, from Hans Reinhard's *Jörn Farrow's U-Boot Abenteuer* (Jorn Farrow's Submarine Adventures, 1932-1937). Robert Kraft's *Der Herr der Lüfte* (The Man of the Skies, 1922-1923) was a very Robur-like MWTM. Even as late as 1971 the MWTM was appearing, as in Michael Moorcock's *The Warlord of the Air*.

Captain Nemo was the prototypical Man With The Machine, first of a new archetype.

Professor Moriarty

Professor James Moriarty only appears in one of Arthur Conan Doyle's Sherlock Holmes stories, "The Adventure of the Final Problem" (1893), and his presence is felt in *The Valley of Fear* (1915), but his influence is substantial. Although Holmes faced off against a number of other notable enemies, including the very dangerous Dr. Grimesby Roylott in "The Adventure of the Speckled Band" (1892), Professor Moriarty is the first (and usually only) figure many think of when considering Holmes' enemies.

He is certainly memorable. The "Napoleon of Crime," Moriarty is (in Holmes' words) "the organizer of half that is evil and of nearly all that is undetected in this great city." A brilliant scientist and mathematician, Moriarty is a crime lord whose organization affects everyone in London, though only a handful are aware of him. Moriarty is nearly Holmes' match, almost killing him in their bout at the Reichenbach Falls. And Moriarty's reptilian description, with the protruding forehead, oscillating head, and deeply sunken eyes, creates the image of an almost mythical figure.

Professor Moriarty's influence has been extensive despite his single appearance. As Holmes' nemesis, Moriarty has become the archetype for succeeding generations of Master Villain characters, brilliant and evil crime lords who oppose an equally brilliant and capable opponent. Moriarty was not the first Master Villain, nor did he set the visual mold for the character. But Moriarty was the most influential Master Villain character.

Villains have been around as long as there have been stories of conflict. Only a few truly stand out. One of the most memorable is Iago, from Shakespeare's *Othello* (1602). Iago is an immortal character of evil, of "motiveless malignity" in the words of Samuel Taylor Coleridge. Shakespeare's portrayal of evil has proven long-lasting, and Iago was a likely influence on John Milton when he characterized Satan in *Paradise Lost* (1667-1674), the greatest of all modern epics. Milton's Satan is the figure looming over all later portrayals of master criminals. *Paradise Lost* is Milton's attempt to trace the Fall of Man and the revolt of the angels, but centuries of readers have come away with the impression that the hero of the epic is Satan, who is portrayed with a memorable combination of grandeur, dignity, heroic defiance, and ruin. William Blake wrote that "the reason Milton wrote in fetters when he wrote of angels and God and at liberty when of devils and hell, is because he was a true poet and of the Devil's party without knowing it." Whether this is true or not, Milton devoted an inordinate amount of space to Lucifer and portrayed him as a Promethean rebel, heroically defying a power he knows he cannot beat. In this Satan anticipates the Gothic Hero-Villain as well as the Master Villains of the Victorian era, who rebel against society with their crimes and eventually fall, whether through their own hubris or at the hands of their opponents.

Milton's Satan was a primary model for the Hero-Villain of the Gothics, who in turn served as a prototype for the Master Villain. The Hero-Villain was the evil-doer in the Gothics, but never purely evil. The Hero-Villain is always a paradoxical mix of passions and impulses which he knows to be evil but cannot resist or overcome. The Gothic Hero-Villain has great intellectual and physical gifts and uses them for evil ends. He is tormented by his own dark urges at the same time that he torments others. He is, in the words of Charles Maturin, one "who can apprehend the good, but is powerless to be it." The Hero-Villain appeared in nearly all of the major Gothics, from Horace Walpole's *The Castle of Otranto* (1764) to William Beckford's *Vathek* (1786) to Matthew Lewis' *The Monk* (1796) to Charles Maturin's *Melmoth the Wanderer* (1820), many of the minor Gothics, and a number of the significant post-Gothic novels, including Emily Brontë's *Wuthering Heights* (1847).

The Bandit Hero was a character who developed at the same

time as the Hero-Villain and shared many of his characteristics, and each both influenced and was influenced by the other. The Bandit Hero was the protagonist of the German *räuberroman*, or "robber novels." The three major *räuberroman* were Friedrich Schiller's *Der Räuber* (The Robber, 1781), Heinrich Zschokke's *Abällino der große Bandit* (Aballino the Great Bandit, 1794), and Christian Vulpius' *Rinaldo Rinaldini, der Räuberhauptmann* (Rinaldo Rinaldini the Bandit Chief, 1799-1801). The protagonists of *räuberroman* were patriots who were forced by circumstance or oppression into the lives of bandits, and who preyed on the rich and helped the poor, as well as fighting against the forces of the government which occupied the Bandit Hero's homeland. Though usually portrayed as straightforward heroes, Bandit Heroes also had something of the conflicted personalities of Milton's Satan and the Hero-Villains, containing both positive personality traits (bravery, patriotism, compassion) and negative ones (a capability for cruelty, violence, extravagant emotions).

Milton's Satan and the Bandit Hero of the *räuberroman* both influenced Lord Byron, whose namesake character, the "Byronic hero" or "Man of Feeling" was another influence on the development of the Master Villain archetype. Milton's Satan was a major influence on the Romantics. Many of them, most notably William Blake, Percy Shelley, and Lord Byron, saw in Milton's Satan a heroic rebel, and Shelley said that Milton's Satan was superior to his God. The Romantics saw Satan as a tragic figure worthy of admiration and sympathy, despite his evil traits. Byron in particular was influenced by Milton's Satan, recasting him in various forms in his *Manfred* (1817), *Cain: A Mystery* (1821), and *The Deformed Transformed* (1824). These characters, along with Byron himself, gave rise to the Byronic hero, the "Man of Feeling" whose passions are great and who can be both cruel and courteous, sympathetic and sadistic. He is a defiant rebel, standing apart from society and suffering for his sins.

The rise of Naturalism in Britain and France in the Nineteenth century and the corresponding focus placed on realism led to a sharp decrease in the number of Hero-Villains and Byronic Heroes appearing in popular literature, but the character type never entirely disappeared. The historical romances which succeeded the Gothics occasionally featured the Hero-Villain as protagonist or antagonist. In 1821 the Vicomte Charles-Victor d'Arlincourt published *Le Solitaire* (The Hermit). The novel is about Charles le Téméraire, a sinister hermit who controls the major events of French history for thirty years after his supposed "death." Le Téméraire is, like the Hero-Villains, capable of great good, and is shown in the novel rescuing the heroine and saving a drowning boy. He also has a doomed destiny of which he is aware and is responsible for the massacre of several monks.

The Hero-Villain made occasional appearances in penny dreadfuls and shilling shockers, inexpensive magazines sold in parts in the Nineteenth century. As early as 1845 the Hero-Villain was appearing in penny dreadfuls in the form of the lead character in James Malcolm Rymer's *Varney the Vampyre*. Varney's tormented personality is a good example of the Hero-Villain and anticipated Bram Stoker's later portrayal of Dracula.

The Hero-Villain also made occasional appearances in the French *roman-feuilleton*, serial novels which appeared in the French periodical press in the mid-Nineteenth century. Victor-Alexis Ponson du Terrail wrote the twenty-five volume "Rocambole" series from 1857 to 1870. Rocambole is a hero who began as a villain before experiencing a change of heart. By the saga's end Rocambole was a nineteenth-century version of Doc Savage, leading a group of talented assistants in a fight against evil. Rocambole was opposed by his former mentor, Sir Williams, a Hero-Villain who has a certain dignity and even grandeur to accompany his prodigious capacity for evil.

The rise in popularity of mystery and detective fiction in the Nineteenth century, accompanied by the change in readers' expectations, led to Master Villains losing the Gothic/Byronic, "tormented tormenter" aspect of their personalities and becoming less conflicted while remaining experts at crime and evil. Even before Ponson du Terrail published the "Rocambole" series, Paul Féval began publishing his "Les Habits Noir" series, which began with *Les Mystères de Londres* (1843-1844) and ran for ten novels through 1875. In that series the Black Coats conspiracy was run by the sinister immortal Colonel Bozzo-Corona, a crime lord of great ability and no conscience or redeeming characteristics.

This was also true in the dime novels, the American version of the British penny dreadfuls and story papers. The most popular and influential of the dime novel characters was Nick Carter, who debuted in 1886 and became one of the most published characters in world literature, appearing in dozens of countries and languages. Nick Carter's nemesis was Dr. Jack Quartz, who first appeared in *Nick Carter Library* n13 (October 31, 1891) and went on to bedevil Carter twenty-six times, through 1927. Dr. Quartz, the first recurring Master Villain in serial detective fiction, is a mad scientist who enjoys vivisecting beautiful women, one of the first of that type in detective/adventure fiction. Dr. Quartz also runs a crime school where he trains willing students in the criminal arts; some of his students, like Zanoni the Woman Wizard and El Sombre, went on to plague Carter in separate stories. Quartz is well-educated, very intelligent, a charming conversationalist, and honorable in his own way, but he is utterly without a conscience, feels no remorse over his acts, and enjoys his crimes.

Although Dr. Quartz provided a model for many mad vivisectors in pulp fiction, Professor Moriarty provided the model for later Master Villains. In his personality, his role, and his particular abilities, Moriarty more than any preceding villain was the dominant model for Master Villains for decades, and to a large extent remains so. Some of the Master Villains influenced by Professor Moriarty include Guy Boothby's Dr. Nikola, L.T. Meade and Robert Eustace's Madame Koluchy, Erik from Gaston Leroux's *The Phantom of the Opera*, Pierre Souvestre and Marcel Allain's Fantomas, Arthur Ward's Fu Manchu, Frederick Davis' Richard Ravenswood, Johnston McCulley's Black Star and Spider, Carl Peterson from H.C. McNeile's "Bulldog Drummond" novels, Dr. Ferraro from the "Sexton Blake" stories, A.E. Apple's Rafferty, Arnold Zeck from Rex Stout's "Nero Wolfe" novels, Ian Fleming's Ernst Stavro Blofeld (and several other villains in the "James Bond" novels), and Don Corleone from Mario Puzo's *The Godfather*.

The other members of the League, Dr. Jekyll/Mr. Hyde, and Griffin, the Invisible Man, do not individually represent archetypes of Victorian literature. Dr. Henry Jekyll and his horrific alter-ego Mr. Henry Hyde were familiar figures to readers in the late Victorian years and afterwards, and today the phrase "Jekyll and Hyde" has entered common parlance. In this sense Jekyll and Hyde are archetypal; when thinking of the Jekyll-and-Hyde phenomenon, one thinks of the character. But Hyde is essentially a doppelgänger, an alternate identity or second self which is sometimes but not always a physical twin. The doppelgänger is a recurring motif in Gothic novels and appears in works ranging from Shelley's Frankenstein to Edward Bulwer Lytton's "Monos and Daimonos" to Oscar Wilde's *The Picture of Dorian Gray* to the most prominent modern example, Marvel Comics' *The Incredible Hulk*. Like Moore's Hyde, Dr. Bruce Banner remains human while calm, but when he is enraged he becomes the Hulk, a green-skinned monstrosity of enormous size and strength. But as a doppelgänger Hyde is simply one of many, neither the first nor the last.

The Invisible Man's influence is equally small. The original story is memorable, and the notion of invisibility used for good or evil purposes continues to be interesting. Numerous superhero comics, television series, and movies have made use of the idea. This idea began with *The Invisible Man*, and so in that respect the Invisible Man is a kind of archetype. But succeeding Invisible Men and Women have had little in common with Wells' Invisible Man except the idea of invisibility. Griffin, as a character, is a human monster, a man who has gained superhuman powers and uses them for evil ends. In this Griffin is little different from various other human monsters in Victorian-era literature, like the lead character in J. Cobben's *Master of His Fate*, who had the ability to drain the life force from others and who used this ability to sustain his own youth.

Moore's choice of the six members of the League may have been simply a decision to use six very different characters to produce an entertaining narrative. It might also have been a knowing choice to make use of these Victorian archetypes as a way to invoke and make use of their symbolic and cultural capital. Either way, *The League of Extraordinary Gentlemen* is the richer for his choice.

ON CROSSOVERS

In one respect *The League of Extraordinary Gentlemen* seems to be a modern concept: characters from stories by Bram Stoker, H. Rider Haggard, Jules Verne, H.G. Wells, Robert Louis Stevenson, Edgar Allan Poe, and Arthur "Sax Rohmer" Ward, among others, interact as if they all live in the same world. This kind of crossover, when characters or concepts from two or more discrete texts or series of texts meet, is common today, or not so uncommon as to baffle readers and viewers. Most people understand the idea of Professor Moriarty appearing on a Star Trek holodeck, or Superman and Batman teaming up to stop the Joker and Lex Luthor, or Shaft helping the Jack of Spades. But the concept of the crossover is much older than many people realize. Historically there have been seven major types of crossovers: the fusion of myths; crossovers within one author's fictional universe; crossovers in which characters from different creators are brought together by another creator; the afterlife or Bangsian fantasy; the use of real people as fictional characters; crossovers in which characters from different creators are brought together as a team; and crossovers in which a fictional world contains characters from numerous authors. *The League of Extraordinary Gentlemen* is this last type of crossover, and is in fact the ultimate in crossover concepts.

The first crossover is difficult to determine. One place to begin is the Greek myths, which were a synthesis of legends from Indo-European and local, pre-Hellenic religions. One of these syntheses was the myth of Jason and the Argonauts. The myth, which dates to the ninth or tenth century B.C.E., is about the hero Jason, who sails to Colchis in search of the Golden Fleece. Jason is accompanied by a band of fifty notable heroes on his ship, the *Argo*. Many of these heroes, including Castor, Polydeuces, and Hercules, are the subjects of myths of their own. The standard account of the adventures of the Argonauts is the *Argonautica* (Third century B.C.E.) of Appolonius of Rhodes, which combines earlier scattered versions of the myth into a connected story. By bringing the heroes of various disparate myths together into one story Appolonius performed one of the first crossovers in popular culture.

This sort of crossover, in which characters from folklore and legend meet in new stories, would be repeated over the centuries in a variety of cultures. In China Judge Bao Zheng (999-1062 C.E.) was, during his lifetime, famous for his rectitude and commitment to justice. Soon after he died he became the subject of folklore, and in the centuries since then has been appropriated into various genres. *The Hundred Cases of Judge Bao* (c. 1450) is a collection of Judge Bao's legal dramas. *Five Tigers Pacify the West* (c. 1500) places Judge Bao with a group of martial artist monks. In Shih Yü-k'un's *Three Heroes and Five Gallants* (1879) he is teamed with Zhan Zhao, the "Knight-errant of the South," and with the Five Rats, five knights of renown.

In the West a similar syncretism of legend and folklore occurred. Around 150 C.E. Lucian of Samosata wrote *The True History,* a satire which features one of the earliest fictional trips into outer space. During the trip Lucian and his companions fly past Cloudcuckooland, the floating fortress of the birds from Aristophanes' *The Birds* (414 B.C.E.). In the Middle Ages, the stories of King Arthur as we currently know them were synthesized by the French author Chrétien de Troyes out of several pre-existing sources, including Celtic and Welsh stories and various legends of the Holy Grail.

The next significant type of crossover began in 1834, when Honoré de Balzac began linking his novels into a coherent, whole, individual fictional universe. Before that year Balzac's novels had possessed an internal consistency, but it was only in 1834 that he systematically began making use of recurring characters, with twenty-three of them appearing in the first edition of *Le Père Goriot* (1835). Almost 600 recurring characters appear in the nearly 90 books that make up Balzac's *La Comédie Humaine* cycle of novels.

Balzac was the first nineteenth-century author to create an ongoing fictional universe in an organized and ambitious way, but he was far from the last. Alexandre Dumas *père* linked together several of his novels into series as well as into an overarching universe, so that beginning in 1844, with *Les Trois Mousquetaires* (The Three Musketeers), his historical novels are often tied together by recurring characters. Beginning in 1866 Emile Gaboriau used a large number of recurring characters in his detective novels, many of which involved his series character "Monsieur Lecoq." Paul Féval, the greatest of the French pulp novelists, linked eight separate novels into his *Les Habits Noir* cycle, which ran from 1863-1875. Emile Zola did this as well, starting in 1868 with the first of twenty novels about the Second Empire and the Rougon and Macquart families.

The most notable example of this use of linked, reappearing characters occurs in the novels of Jules Verne. Many non-French readers are unaware of the links between his books, thanks in large part to the many bad translations of his work and to a general ignorance of his less famous work, but Verne, like Balzac, Zola and Gaboriau before him, set many of his works, famous and less so, in the same universe:

- *The Adventures of Captain Hatteras* (1864) refers to *Journey to the Center of the Earth* (1864).
- *Journey to the Center of the Earth* refers to both *Captain Hatteras* and to *Five Weeks in a Balloon* (1863).
- *Twenty Leagues Under The Sea* (1869) refers to *Hector Servadac* and *Journey to the Center of the Earth*.
- *The Mysterious Island* (1870), the sequel to *Twenty Leagues Under the Sea*, refers to *Captain Grant's Children* (1867), *Five Weeks In A Balloon*, *Captain Hatteras*, and *Around the Moon* (1870).
- *The Far Country* (1873) refers to *Captain Hatteras*.
- *Hector Servadac* (1877) and *Black Indies* (1877) refer to each other.
- *The Clipper of the Clouds* (1886) refers to *The Begum's Fortune* (1879) and to *Twenty Leagues Under The Sea*.
- *Topsy Turvy* (1889), a sequel to *From The Earth To the Moon* (1865), refers to *The Robinsons' School* (1882), *Captain Hatteras*, and *Hector Servadac*.
- *The Ice Sphinx* (1897), Verne's sequel to Edgar Allen Poe's The *Narrative of Arthur Gordon Pym*, refers to *Twenty Leagues Under the Sea*.

By the late Nineteenth century an increasing number of authors were writing more than one series with recurring characters.

Crossovers in which an author had two of his or her series characters meet grew more common in both high and popular culture. A number of these types of crossovers appeared in dime novels. Albert Aiken was the author of the Joe Phenix stories in *Saturday Journal* and *Banner Weekly* and the Dick Talbot stories in *Beadle's New York Dime Library*. Aiken brought the pair together in *Beadle's New York Dime Library* #419 (1886) in a story in which the detective Phenix pursues the highwayman Talbot but fails to arrest him. Luis Senarens was the author of the Frank Reade stories in *Boys of New York* and *Frank Reade Library* and the author of the Jack Wright stories in *Boys' Star Library*, *Boys of New York*, and *Happy Days*. Senarens had the two race around the world for a $10,000 prize in *Boys' Star Library* #375 (1896). This type of crossover continued during the years of the pulps and the story papers, with the authors of the Sexton Blake stories creating a dozen separate characters and then bringing them into the Blake series.

The first truly modern crossover, in which characters from different creators are brought together in a story by another creator, was created in 1849, when Mary Cowden Clarke published *Kit Bam's Adventures; or, The Yarns of an Old Mariner*. The novel is about Kit Bam, a retired sailor, who tells a brother and sister about his adventures. Bam's shipmates are "Will Wavelance" (Shakespeare), "Geoffrey Tabard" (Chaucer), "Edmund Faery" (Spenser), "John Paul" (Johann Paul Richter), and "Percy Shelton" (Shelley). In his wanderings Bam encounters Méala from Bernardin de Saint-Pierre's *Paul et Virginie* (1794), the falcon from William Painter's *Palace of Pleasure* (1566-1575), the barber, winged boy, and brass horse from *The Arabian Nights*, the key and the rainbow from Johann Paul Richter's *Himmelsschlüssel* (1796), Sir Lionel from Arthurian myth, the Anthropophagi from Shakespeare's *Othello* (1604), the nymph Galatea from Greek myth, Prospero's Island from Shakespeare's *The Tempest* (1612), the Monster from Mary Shelley's *Frankenstein* (1818), and the Ancient Mariner from Samuel Taylor Coleridge's "The Rime of the Ancient Mariner" (1798).

The idea of a character meeting other creators' characters while traveling was used by several authors in the Nineteenth and early Twentieth century. In 1872 Henry Lee Boyle, using the pseudonym "Theopholis M'Crib, B.A." published *Kennaquhair, A Narrative of*

Utopian Travel. Kennaquhair (a Scots words meaning "an imaginary place"), is a Utopian city in which various fictional characters live. (They die only when they are forgotten by the outside world). The narrator is escorted through Kennaquhair by Yorick from Shakespeare's *Hamlet* (1600) and meets a number of fictional characters, including Mrs. Sairey Gamp from Charles Dickens' *Martin Chuzzlewit* (1842-1844). Another author to use traveling as the vehicle for a crossover was Walter de la Mare, who in 1904 published the novel *Henry Brocken*, in which the titular character goes wandering, possibly through daydreams, and meets a number of different fictional characters, including Bottom and Titania, from Shakespeare's *A Midsummer Night's Dream* (1600), Jane Eyre and Rochester from Charlotte Brontë's *Jane Eyre* (1847), Rosinante and Don Quixote from Cervantes' *Don Quixote* (1605-1615), and Annabel Lee from Edgar Allan Poe's "Annabel Lee" (1849). Brocken also travels through the community of Sleeping Beauty and meets the Houyhnhnms from Jonathan Swift's *Gulliver's Travels* (1726).

The next major crossover is the afterlife or Bangsian fantasy. The afterlife has been used for centuries as a meeting ground for characters from different creators. One early example is Virgil's *Aeneid* (c. 29-19 B.C.E.), in which Aeneas sees a number of heroes and heroines from earlier Greek epics, including Phaedra, Pasiphae, and Deiphobus. In 1895 John Kendrick Bangs began a new vogue in afterlife fantasies when he published *The Houseboat on the River Styx. Houseboat* was the book that spawned the phrase "Bangsian fantasy," or a fantasy of the afterlife in which the ghosts of famous men and women come together and have various (usually genial) adventures. In *Houseboat* most of the ghosts are of real people, including Sir Walter Raleigh, Shakespeare, Samuel Johnson, and George Washington, but the ghosts of Hamlet, Yorick, Adam, Shem, Noah, and Ophelia also appear. In 1897 Bangs published a sequel, *The Pursuit of the Houseboat*, which took the concept further, bringing together the ghosts of fictional characters who were known or thought to be dead: Sherlock Holmes (Holmes had "died" in Arthur Conan Doyle's "The Final Problem," 1893), Shylock (from William Shakespeare's *The Merchant of Venice*, 1600), Lecoq (from Emile Gaboriau's work), Hawkshaw (from Tom Taylor's *The Ticket-of-leave Man*, 1863), and Old Sleuth (from Harlan P. Halsey's dime novels).

Sherlock Holmes' appearance in *The Pursuit of the Houseboat* was his first appearance after his"death" in "The Adventure of the Final Problem" in 1893, and the first use of Holmes by a writer other than Arthur Conan Doyle. In 1897 Holmes was referred to as deceased in Guy Boothby's "The Duchess of Wiltshire's Diamonds." But far more common were parodies of Holmes, who has appeared more than any other single character in pastiches (works done in the style of another writer) and crossovers. The first pastiche of Holmes was Robert Barr's "Sherlaw Kombs," who first appeared in a series of stories in *The Idler* in 1892. The first crossover involving Holmes and another series character is in Maurice LeBlanc's "Arsène Lupin" story, "Sherlock Holmes Arrive Trop Tard" in *Je Sais Tout* #17 (15 June 1906). (After pressure from Arthur Conan Doyle's lawyers the title of the story was changed to "Herlock Sholmes Arrive Trop Tard"). Following LeBlanc's story Holmes was often used in crossovers, either through characters like August Derleth's "Solar Pons" and Arthur Porges' "Stately Homes" or through the illegal (that is, not authorized by Doyle) use of Holmes himself. In 1908, in the first issue of the anonymously written *Miss Boston, la seule détective-femme du monde entier* (Miss Boston, the only female detective in the entire world), Miss Boston is inspired to fight crime by the murder of Holmes, which she solves, thus beginning her own career as a detective. Holmes was not the only character to be illegally appropriated and used in crossovers in this way. A 1909 Italian version of Miss Boston's adventures changed Holmes to Nick Carter as the respected elder detective whose murder was Miss Boston's first case.

Crossovers involving the use of fictionalized versions of real people became common in the last decade of the Nineteenth century and the first decade of the Twentieth century. Celebrities have often been used by authors in their stories, but before the growth of the news media in the Nineteenth century these men and women were the products of folklore rather than reality. Dick Turpin appeared in William Ainsworth's Gothic novel *Rookwood* (1834) and in penny dreadfuls (see the note to Page 180 for more information), but the Turpin used in those works was a heavily romanticized version which bore little relation to the real Dick Turpin. The growth of the newspaper in the Nineteenth century allowed individuals other than heads of state to become internationally known, and allowed them to be used by authors as supporting characters in serial fiction. Thomas Byrnes (1842-1910) was appointed Detective Bureau Chief of the New York City Police Department in 1880, and over the next fifteen years Byrnes turned the N.Y.P.D. into a modern, professional police force, one widely admired for its efficiency. Byrnes became a celebrity during these years and was seen as the personification of modern policing. He was incorporated into at least eight different dime novel detective serials in the 1890s as "Superintendent Byrnes" or "Inspector Byrnes," the "Head of the New York City Police Department" and the man responsible for giving Nick Carter or Broadway Billy or Dave Dotson or Gideon Gault their orders. Theodore Roosevelt, during the years of his presidency, was almost as popular a subject for appearances in the dime novels, as was the internationally renowned strongman Eugen Sandow (1867-1925). A fictionalized version of the Russian terrorist Evno Azef (1869-1918) fought the mystic Sâr Dubnotal in the French pulp *Sâr Dubnotal* and Sexton Blake in the British story paper *Union Jack*, both in 1909. A fictionalized version of the Japanese spy Oka-Yuma appeared as the enemy of Nat Pinkerton in the German *heldroman* (dime novel) *Nat Pinkerton, der König der Detectivs* in 1910, as the villainous lead in a serial, "Oka-Yuma, Japanese Spy" in a Russian newspaper in 1911-1912, and as the enemy of Lukas Hull in the German *heldroman Lukas Hull, Detektiv Abenteuer* in 1921.

Crossovers in French, German, and Russian newspapers and dime novels were more common than exceptional in the 1910s and 1920s. The spread of American and British popular literature through Europe and Asia in the late Nineteenth and early Twentieth century led to European and Asian authors imitating American and British authors and writing crossovers of their own. In 1921 the Chinese writer Cheng Xiaoqing began a series of crossovers between his character Huo Sang and Lu Ping, a series character created and written by Sun Liaohong. The joke of the crossovers is that Huo Sang began life as a Sherlock Holmes copy and was deliberately written and billed as "the Oriental Sherlock Holmes," while Sun Liaohong had created Lu Ping in imitation of Maurice LeBlanc's Arsène Lupin (the similarity in names is deliberate). The first duel between Huo Sang and Lu Ping was an homage to LeBlanc's first Holmes-Lupin crossover, "Herlock Sholmes Arrive Trop Tard," and like LeBlanc's story the Huo Sang-Lu Ping duel took on a life of its own and was repeated in several different stories. In 1922 the Malaysian writer Muhammad bin Muhammad Said wrote the first Malaysian detective novel, *Cheritera Kechurian Lima Million Ringgit* (Tale of the Theft of Five Million Dollars), a crossover in which the gentleman thief Lord Lister (who was created in Germany but who like Holmes was the subject of unauthorized worldwide usage) clashed with Nick Carter.

The trend continued in the 1930s, with crossovers becoming more common in European newspapers and dime novels than in American pulps and British story papers. One notable pulp crossover was the meeting between Emile Tepperman's Red Falcon and Robert J. Hogan's G-8 in *Dare-Devil Aces* (January 1935). But far more crossovers took place in the 1930s in the German *heldromans*, when numerous crossovers and team-ups between series characters were written before 1939 when the Nazi Party placed restrictions on the publishers and authors of the *heldromans*. A few examples include the following: Walther Kabel's Olaf Karl Abelsen traveling into the underworld of Jules Verne's *Journey to the Center of the Earth*; Captain Mors appearing alongside Frank Allan, Willi Sachse's Alaska Jim, Hans Reinhard's Jörn Farrow, The Four Musketeers, and Hans Stark in their respective *heldromans*; Hans Reinhard's Jörn Farrow teaming up with Captain Mors and discovering that his father had encountered Reinhard's Rolf Torring; and Rolf Torring encountering Jörn Farrow's father and the descendant of Captain Axel Holm.

The next significant type of crossover, in which characters from different creators are brought together as a team, appeared in a comic book in 1940 rather than in a book or pulp magazine. By 1940 the idea of a crossover featuring a team of characters from different creators was well known. The Argonauts were such a team, as was the group of detectives in *Pursuit of the Houseboat*. More recently, Carolyn Wells had created such a team in 1915 and 1916 in the three "Society of Infallible Detectives" stories. Presided over by Sherlock Holmes, the Society meet to solve crimes. Their membership is Jacques Futrelle's S.S. "The Thinking Machine" Van Dusen, E.W. Hornung's Raffles, Maurice LeBlanc's Arsène Lupin, Edgar Allan Poe's C. Auguste Dupin, Emile Gaboriau's M. Lecoq,

E.C. Bentley's Philip Trent, Anna Katherine Green's Ebenezer Gryce, Francis Lynde's Calvin "Scientific" Sprague, William MacHarg and Edwin Balmer's Luther Trant, E.C. Bentley's Philip Trent, Arthur Reeve's Craig Kennedy, Gaston Leroux's Rouletabille, and M. Vidocq. And in 1928 Ralph Smith wrote "Frank Merriwell vs. Fred Fearnot" in the *The Frank Reade Library*, in which two teams of characters are formed. The story is about the wedding of Harvey Shackleton's character Fred Fearnot to his sweetheart Evelyn Olcott, and the baseball game in which Gilbert Patten and Burt Standish's Frank Merriwell pitches to Harvey Shackleford's Fred Fearnot. Many of the guests at the wedding and members of the opposing baseball teams had been lead characters in their own dime novels in the Nineteenth and early Twentieth centuries: Frank and Dick Merriwell, George Marsh's Dick "the Millionaire Detective" Dobbs, sports promoter Tex Rickard, Francis W. Doughty's Old and Young King Brady, Ned Taylor's Ted Strong and his Rough Riders, S.A.D. Cox's The Three Chums, Old Joe Crowfoot, Cap'n Wiley, Bowery Billy, Frank Forrest's Dick Daresome, and Chickering Carter. Nick Carter and Luis Senarens' Frank Reade, Jr. are mentioned as having been invited but unable to attend due to active cases, and Francis W. Doughty's Young Klondike, Klondike Kit, Old Broadbrim and W.I. James' Old Cap Collier are referred to as having died in action before the wedding. Most of these characters were perennials, with some, like the Merriwells, appearing in stories for over thirty years.

The comic book crossover in 1940 was the first team crossover specifically intended to be ongoing. In *All-Star Comics* #3 (Winter 1940-1941) Sheldon Mayer and Gardner Fox, along with artists Everett Hibbard and Sheldon Moldoff, brought together characters from several DC comics: Sandman and Hourman from *Adventure Comics*, Flash and Hawkman from *Flash Comics*, Green Lantern and the Atom from *All-American Comics*, and the Spectre and Dr. Fate from *More Fun Comics*. These characters formed a team, the Justice Society of America, the first ongoing crossover team in popular culture. The Justice Society appeared in *All-Star Comics* until 1951.

All-Star Comics #3 is particularly significant in the history of crossovers because it was the single greatest vector for the concept of the crossover. During World War Two comic books had very high circulation rates, with some, like *Superman*, *Batman*, and *Captain America*, selling over a million copies per issue, hundreds of thousands more than *Time* and *Life*. Comics were bought and read by children, teenagers, and adults, and thanks to their distribution via the United States Armed Services during the war, comics were read by millions of servicemen and women. While crossovers had proliferated before *All-Star Comics* #3, significantly more men and women were exposed to the concept of the crossover through *All-Star Comics* #3 and other, similar comic book teams and crossovers.

The penultimate in crossovers was not published until 1972, when Philip José Farmer published "An Exclusive Interview with Lord Greystoke" (*Esquire*, April 1972) and *Tarzan Alive*, a "biography" of Tarzan. In the book Farmer theorized that eighteen men and women had been present when a radioactive meteor landed in Wold Newton, Britain. These eighteen men and women had been irradiated, altering their genes so that their descendants were supermen and women. Farmer went on to theorize that the members of this "Wold Newton family" included Tarzan, Sherlock Holmes, Bulldog Drummond, C. Auguste Dupin, Doc Savage, the Spider, Nero Wolfe, and many more. In the sequel to *Tarzan Alive*, *Doc Savage: His Apocalyptic Life* (1973), Farmer added a number of other fictional heroes and villains to the family tree. Farmer's idea, which eventually became known as the "Wold Newton Universe," is a world in which dozens of fictional heroes and villains co-exist and are related to each other.

The League of Extraordinary Gentlemen is an extension and furthering of this concept. Moore and O'Neill have created a world in which *any* fictional character can co-exist with any other character. The first *League* series brought together characters as diverse as Allan Quatermain, Rosa Coote, and Weary Willy and Tired Tim, and the second *League* series has expanded the cast list to include characters and places and things from hundreds of works. Anyone can appear in *The League of Extraordinary Gentlemen*. In size and scope and potential, the *The League of Extraordinary Gentlemen* is the ultimate crossover.

YELLOW PERILS

In *The League of Extraordinary Gentlemen* the threat to the League and to London is twofold: Professor Moriarty and his forces within British Intelligence, and The Doctor and his criminal empire in Limehouse. While both Professor Moriarty and the Doctor are archetypes (see the "Archetypes" essay for more on this), the Doctor is not merely an archetype but one of the oldest archetypes of popular fiction: The Yellow Peril, the evil Asian genius who schemes to conquer the West. The common perception of the Yellow Peril is that it dates to Fu Manchu, the real identity of the Doctor. This is incorrect. The concept of the Yellow Peril figure can be traced back two centuries and ultimately derives from historical sources.

There are actually two Yellow Peril stereotypes. The first is of Asians as a group. The Yellow Peril stereotype of Asians *en masse* is of a faceless horde of decadent and sexually rapacious barbarians. That stereotype, while still active in the West, is not the one addressed in this essay. This essay will sketch the history of the second Yellow Peril stereotype, that of the individual evil genius intent on destroying the West.

Although the Yellow Peril stereotype has changed over time to mirror various changing Western biases, the original source of the stereotype lies in the historical threats posed to Western Europe from Eastern Europe and Asia. In the Third century C.E. the Roman Empire began dealing with incursions of hostile Eastern peoples, with the Germanic Visigoths taking the city of Histira and crossing the Danube River in 238 C.E. In the Fourth century the Mongolian Huns, expanding west through southern Russia, forced the Goths to move west, ultimately resulting in the battle of Adrianople in 378 C.E., in which the Goths defeated the eastern Roman field army and killed Emperor Valens. In the Fifth century the Huns, under their king Attila, devastated the western Baltics, Thrace, Gaul, Italy and threatened Constantinople itself. Before Attila's death the Huns ruled an empire from the Danube to Slovakia.

The second time the Mongols threatened Europe the effects were longer lasting and the memories of the threat remained long after the immediate danger from the Mongols ended. In the Thirteenth century the Mongol armies of Temujin, a.k.a. Genghis Khan, conquered Asia and much of the Middle East and invaded Eastern Europe, destroying every European army which attempted to oppose them. Only the death of Temujin in 1227 halted the Mongol advance. After Temujin's death the Mongols moved west again, this time stopping with the conquest of Russia. Later, between 1399 and 1403, the armies of Timur Lenk, a.k.a. Tamerlane, laid waste to Azerbaijan, Damascus, Baghdad, and the Ottoman Empire, reinforcing in the Western mind the threat of an armed invasion of Mongol warriors. Although Timur was a Turkic Barlas rather than a Mongol, he claimed to be a distant relative of Temujin, a story believed in Europe.

By the mid-Fifteenth century the practical threat of a Mongol invasion of Europe was zero, but the unexpectedness of the original attacks and the vicious thoroughness of the Mongol armies, as well as the stories of the utter devastation the Mongols had wrought in the Middle East, remained impressed on the Western psyche. The records of those attacks and the years following them were set down by Christian monks, who feared the Mongols as warriors and as a threat to Christianity. Although Western Europe did not have any extensive contact with Asians for centuries afterward, the stereotype of the Eastern threat to "civilization" remained common in the West. The threat of an Asian invasion of Europe is the background, then, to the current Yellow Peril stereotype.

The modern Yellow Peril concept, the stereotype of the evil Asian mastermind who schemes to conquer the West, derives primarily from two sources: the anti-Asian biases of Americans and British in the Nineteenth century, and the British Gothic novels of the late Eighteenth and early Nineteenth centuries.

In the United States the first Asian immigrants were the Chinese who took part in the Gold Rush in California in the late 1840s. They were the first free nonwhites to arrive in the United States in large numbers, and the racial, religious, cultural, and linguistic differences between white Americans and the Chinese immigrants, as well as the perception that the Chinese were taking jobs away from white Americans, led to hostility and racism directed at the newcomers. Among the manifestations of this hostility was a new set of anti-Chinese stereotypes. (The lack of Japanese immigrants in America as well as the perception in America that Japan was an ally of the West kept stereotypes about the Japanese to a minimum until the aftermath of the Russo-Japanese War in 1905). From the mid-Nineteenth century the Chinese were seen as physical, racial, and social pollutants. White unfamiliarity with the Chinese cast their ways in the most unfavorable light. In the 1860s and 1870s, as the use of opium spread to America and as social interaction between Chinese and whites increased, the anti-Chinese movement in California mushroomed, and the Chinese were recast as drug-using sexual deviants. During the recession of the 1870s the Chinese were stereotyped as coolies who stole jobs from white Americans. In the 1880s, when the competition for jobs on the American West Coast became increasingly stiff, the Chinese were no longer viewed just as job thieves but as deliberately flooding America with their numbers; their immigration to the U.S. was now viewed as an undeclared act of war. America reacted to this with anti-immigration laws such as the Chinese Exclusion Act of 1882 and the Scott Act of 1888, but the corresponding drop in Chinese immigration to America did not stop the formation of anti-Chinese stereotypes. The Chinese were again recast, this time as a threat to overrun white America and the countries of Europe through military action and massive population growth. It was this perceived threat of an Asian conquest of Europe and America which Kaiser Wilhelm II saw as the "Yellow Peril" when he coined the phrase in 1895.

All of these stereotypes were reflected in the American literature of the time. Although there were a few positive portrayals of Chinese men and women, most of those were simple, sentimental peasants, and they were greatly outnumbered by the negative portrayals. In the 1880s the first novels were published in America which portrayed the Chinese as re-enacting the Mongol invasions, this time invading the United States. Although most of these depicted the Chinese as working as a group, one novel, Robert Woltor's *A Short and Truthful History of the Taking of Oregon and California by the Chinese in the Year A.D. 1899* (1882), showed a Chinese leader, Prince Tsa

Fungyang Tungtai, leading a military invasion of California. Although he is described as bearing "less resemblance to a human being than he did to Milton's Satan," Prince Tsa is otherwise left undescribed and uncharacterized, and so constitutes only a vague proto-Yellow Peril.

The British stereotypes of Asians were less broad, no doubt in large part because the British had far more exposure to actual Asians than Americans. The British were interacting with the Chinese in China in the Eighteenth century, with Chinese emigrating to Britain in the late Eighteenth century as employees of the British East India Company. But the British did not develop the more visceral fear of a Chinese take-over of Britain in part because of Britain's more restrictive immigration laws but primarily because of the pre-eminence of British power during the Eighteenth and Nineteenth century. With so few Chinese entering Britain in the Nineteenth century—as mentioned in the notes to Page 54 of *League,* at the turn of the Twentieth century there were only 545 Chinese officially in Britain—the threat of a Chinese take-over of Britain via immigration was non-existent. The minimal numbers of Chinese in Britain also prevented them from being widely seen as pollutants in a sexual or social sense.

This did not mean, however, that the British did not have any stereotypes about Asians in the Nineteenth century. In addition to the stereotype about the dangerous, large Mongolian, which persisted into the Twentieth century, and to the less hateful stereotypes of Chinese and Japanese, such as those in Gilbert & Sullivan's *The Mikado* (1885), there was the association, in the British mind, between the Chinese and opium, which had links to ideas of criminality and racial contagion. But the British had more stereotypes of West Asians than of Chinese or Japanese.

The Gothic novel, which began with Horace Walpole's *The Castle of Otranto* (1764), was a very popular genre in England, on the Continent, and even in America, where all of the major and most of the minor English Gothic novelists were published and avidly read within a year or two of their English publication. Although the Gothic novels written in the sixty years after *Otranto*'s debut varied in form, certain motifs were common to many, including a maiden threatened with violation and/or death, a haunted ruin, subterranean passageways, entrapment and escape, and, most especially, the Hero-Villain, a character type largely inherited from the character of Satan in Milton's *Paradise Lost* (1667) but given a new, contemporary twist. The Hero-Villain, the source of evil and the mysterious crimes which plagued the maiden heroine of British Gothics, was nearly always an extracultural Other, some non-British male who threatened the white, often British heroine. This tendency dated back to Elizabethan and Jacobean tragedies, and as in those plays the Hero-Villains of British Gothics were usually Italian: Horace Walpole's Manfred, from *The Castle of Otranto* (1764), Ann Radcliffe's Signor Montoni, from *The Mysteries of Udolpho* (1794), and her monk Schedoni, from *The Italian, or the Confessional of the Black Penitents* (1797), Victoria de Loredani from Charlotte Dacre's *Zofloya: or, the Moor* (1806), were all Italian. Even when the Hero-Villain of a Gothic was not specifically Italian, he was almost always of a markedly different nationality or race (the two were usually confused in the popular thought of the day), as with the gypsies Barbara Lovell, from William Ainsworth Harrison's *Rookwood* (1834), and Heathcliff (whose taint is his "gypsy blood") from Charlotte Brontë's *Wuthering Heights* (1847), the Arabian Vathek of William Beckford's *Vathek* (1786), and the Spanish monk Ambrosio from Matthew Lewis' *Ambrosio; or, The Monk* (1798). These figures were also usually plotters and schemers, rather than men of action, so that the innocent heroine of the Gothic was at the center of a plot designed to, variously, deprive her of an inheritance, rob her of her virginity, marry her to an unsuitable man, or all three. (This character trait would later be enhanced in the figure of the Master Criminal, whose most notable example is Professor Moriarty. See the "Archetypes" essay for more on this).

The popularity of the Gothic rapidly diminished after 1820, replaced by the newly popular genre of historical romances, and by the mid-century the Gothic genre was essentially extinct. Before it expired, however, the Gothic genre produced another non-white villain, one who was not just a murderous plotter but who was designed to remind readers of the Asian threat: the Monster of Mary Shelley's *Frankenstein* (1818). The story and the Monster are well known today, but what is generally forgotten about the Monster is that he is not Caucasian. Victor Frankenstein describes him in this way:

> His limbs were in proportion, and I had selected
> his features as beautiful. Beautiful!–Great God! His
> yellow skin scarcely covered the work of muscles
> and arteries beneath; his hair was of a lustrous
> black, and flowing; his teeth of a pearly whiteness;
> but these luxuriances only formed a more horrid
> contrast with his watery eyes, that seemed almost
> of the same colour as the dun white sockets in which
> they were set, his shrivelled complexion, and
> straight black lips.

The Monster, even before being given life, is yellow. His creator, by contrast, is specifically described as lying "white and cold in death." In the revised 1831 edition of *Frankenstein*, the only illustrated edition of the novel which we know Shelley to have seen, the Monster's yellow skin is highlighted in the novel's Frontispiece.

The Monster's ethnic coding goes beyond his skin color. The reader's first exposure in *Frankenstein* to the Monster occurs when Robert Walton and his crew, looking for a passage to China through the Arctic Circle, come across the Monster trapped on an ice floe. The next morning Walton rescues Victor Frankenstein, who is described as "not, as the other traveller seemed to be, a savage inhabitant of some undiscovered island, but an European." Shelley twice explicitly describes the Monster as not European and not Caucasian. Moreover, the Monster is found by Walton in an island north of the "wilds of Tartary and Russia" where Frankenstein has pursued him.

To the Nineteenth century readers of *Frankenstein*, a yellow-skinned, clean-shaven man with long black hair and dun-colored eyes who crosses the steppes of Russia and Tartary would be instantly recognizable as a Mongolian. Mary Shelley was a friend of William Lawrence, a vocal proponent of the theory of distinct human races, each with different moral characteristics, and *Frankenstein* shows a knowledge of then-current scientific thinking about the various human races. By 1815, thanks to science writers like William Lawrence and to travel writers like John Barrow, the image of Mongols as a separate race, yellow-skinned, black-haired, and beardless, was well established in both the scientific mind and the popular one. Likewise, the Mongols' reputation as barbaric, destructive, and innately violent continued to linger in the West, centuries after the last Mongol invasion. This stereotype is recapitulated in *Frankenstein* when the Monster savagely murders Victor Frankenstein's younger brother William, Victor's friend Henry Clerval, and Victor's fiancée Justine.

Although Mary Shelley's linkage of the Monster with the Mongols has diminished in the public imagination with the passing of time, the association was a deliberate one on Mary Shelley's part, and the Monster's role as a precursor to the Yellow Peril cannot be understated. The Monster was the first image of a Mongol in popular culture which portrayed an Asian not as a small figure but as a large one. The image of a large, dangerous Asian remained in British and American popular culture, becoming one of the motifs of the Yellow Peril.

The first true Yellow Peril figure–that is, the first intelligent, evil Asian mastermind devoted to the goal of the conquest of the West– did not appear until 1892. The American dime novel *Nugget Library* was at this time running a series of stories about "Tom Edison, Jr.," an Edisonade, or boy inventor. The stories, whose author is unknown, featured Tom Edison, Jr. adventuring around the world in a series of technologically-advanced electric vehicles: an "air-yacht," an "electric mule," a "sky courser," and so on. In "Tom Edison, Jr.'s Electric Sea Spider; or, The Wizard of the Submarine World" (*Nugget Library* #134, February 11, 1892), Tom Edison, Jr. hears about piracy in the Yellow Sea and sets out to stop it, using his "Electric Sea Spider," a spider-shaped ship. He finds that the cause of the piracy is Kiang Ho, a 7' tall Mongolian pirate and warlord. Kiang Ho is the leader of a fleet which preys on all the world's shipping in the Yellow Sea. But Kiang Ho is more than just a pirate. He is Harvard-educated and a brilliant inventor, having created the "Sea Serpent," a technologically-advanced submarine with fin-like propellers, has a rotating shell, and moves through the water in a sinuous, snake-like motion. The "Sea Serpent" is even capable of whirling in a circle and creating an aquatic vortex, what Tom Edison, Jr. calls the "spiral principle." On seeing this Tom, astonished, cries out that Kiang Ho has "outstripped us all" with this ability. Kiang Ho and Edison, Jr.

go to war, with Tom, defeating Kiang Ho's fleet and then sinking his submarine. The two battle underwater, in powered diving suits, and Edison, Jr. is saved by his cousin Georgie, who shoots Kiang Ho in the back.

Kiang Ho derives from the tradition of Genghis Khan and the Mongol invaders, but his size hearkens back to *Frankenstein*'s Monster, and his inventive genius to dime novel inventors like Tom Edison, Jr., and to inventors from science fiction like Jules Verne's Captain Nemo.

The next Yellow Peril character after Kiang Ho personified a different aspect of the Yellow Peril stereotype. In July, 1896, the American writer Robert Chambers published "The Maker of Moons" in *The English Illustrated Magazine*. "The Maker of Moons" is about a series of strange events in upper New York state. The events are eventually revealed to be the work of Yue-Laou, a powerful sorcerer who is the undisputed ruler of Kuen-Yuin, an empire in the middle of China. Yue-Laou's daughter, who he created out of a white water-lotus bud, describes him in this way:

> Yue-Laou is Dzil-Nbu of the Kuen-Yuin. He lived in the Moon. He is old--very, very old, and once, before he came to rule the Kuen-Yuin, he was the old man who unites with a silken cord all predestined couples, after which nothing can prevent their union. But all that is changed since he came to rule the Kuen-Yuin. Now he has perverted the Xin,--the good genii of China,--and has fashioned from their warped bodies a monster which he calls the Xin. This monster is horrible, for it not only lives in its own body, but it has thousands of loathesome satellites,--living creatures without mouths, blind, that move when the Xin moves, like a mandarin and his escort. They are a part of the Xin although they are not attached. Yet if one of these satellites is injured the Xin writhes with agony. It is fearful--this huge living bulk and these creatures spread out like severed fingers that wriggle around a hideous hand.

Yue-Laou's enemy describes the Kuen-Yuin as

> the sorcerers of China and the most murderously
> diabolical sect on earth....I've seen them at their
> devilish business, and I repeat to you solemnly, that
> as there are angels above, there is a race of devils
> on earth, and they are sorcerers...I tell you that the
> Keun-Yuin have absolute control of a hundred
> millions of people, mind and body, body and soul.
> Do you know what goes on in the interior of China?
> Does Europe know,--could any human
> being conceive of the condition of that gigantic
> hell-pit?

The story never makes Yue-Laou's ultimate aims clear, but he is inimical to the West, sending counterfeit gold and abnormal life forms to America as well as fighting with the American Secret Service in China itself. Ultimately Yue-Laou appears in New York's Cardinal Woods, where the story is set, and is shot by an American Secret Service agent.

Yue-Laou's ultimate origin lies in the sorcerer character type, which goes back into fable and whose members include Prospero, from Shakespeare's *The Tempest* (1611), the fictionalized versions of John Dee, such as the one who appeared in William Ainsworth's *Guy Fawkes* (1841), and William Gilbert's Innominato, who appeared in a series of short stories in the 1860s. During the Nineteenth century evil sorcerers appeared in various forms, but usually as Italians or Egyptians. Yue-Laou came from this fictional tradition but was given the Yellow Peril treatment: he was the first Yellow Peril sorcerer, a character type that would appear again, as in Allen Upward's *The Yellow Hand* (1904) and in Robert E. Howard's "Skull Face" stories in 1929.

The next significant Yellow Peril character was Dr. Yen How. In 1898 the British writer M.P. Shiel wrote *The Yellow Danger*, which featured the character Dr. Yen How. Dr. Yen How is a half-Japanese, half-Chinese scholar in London who is humiliatingly rejected by a white woman to whom he is attracted. Along with his conclusion that a race war between whites and Asians is inevitable and imminent, this humiliation fuels Yen How's determination to personally conquer the West. Yen How returns to the East, schemes his way to power in

China, unites China and Japan, and manipulates the European Great Powers into warring on each other. Yen How then unleashes the armies of Japan and China upon the West. A world war ensues, with Europe being conquered and Great Britain only barely saved through the efforts of Yen How's white counterpart, who shares many of Yen How's qualities and who agrees with him about the inevitability and even desirability of a war between whites and Asians. Yen How is eventually killed and his forces destroyed by biological warfare as the British infect thousands of Chinese prisoners of war with cholera and then set them free on the European mainland.

Unlike Yue-Lao Dr. Yen How is a military leader rather than a sorcerer; Yen How is brilliant but essentially human. And unlike Kiang Ho, Yen How's goals are global rather than local and piratical. Although Yen How's motivation can be reduced to wounded pride, he still aims at military revenge and world conquest. Dr. Yen How is the first Yellow Peril military leader whose threat is global, not local; he reflects the Western fear of the "limitless hordes" of Chinese overrunning the white countries of the West. Like *Frankenstein*'s Monster, Yen How is derived from Attila, Temujin, and Timur Lenk, the first Yellow Perils.

The last significant Yellow Peril character before the debut of Fu Manchu appeared in Dr. C. W. Doyle's *The Shadow of Quong Lung* (1900). In the novel Quong Lung is a crime lord in San Francisco's Chinatown and controls and manipulates all that is evil within the limits of Chinatown from the Tongs to muggers to opium dens. Quong Lung is more than a mere crime lord, however; he is a Yale graduate and a barrister of London's Inner Temple. His speech patterns are indistinguishable from the white heroes of the novel, apart from his boastfulness: "Whatever my shadow falls on withers— and besides being a Master of Arts, I am a Master of Accidents!" Quong Lung is highly educated, sophisticated, wealthy, and the absolute ruler of the city in which he lives. Quong Lung only has two weaknesses. The first is his lust for women, especially white women, a character trait that leads to difficulties for him. The second weakness is his pride, which leads to his death after he underestimates a man he introduced to opium for the purpose of blackmail.

Quong Lung's significance to the Yellow Peril stereotype is his role as a geographically-centered crime lord. Unlike his predecessors

Quong Lung is specifically identified with one place, San Francisco's Chinatown. The action of the stories takes place there, and Quong Lung's actions are taken to reinforce his rule over this location and the people in it. While the notion of a single man absolutely controlling the crime in one city predated *The Shadow of Quong Lung*–Arthur Conan Doyle's Professor Moriarty is the undisputed ruler of London, and many dime novel villains similarly ruled their respective cities– Quong Lung was the first Yellow Peril crime lord who filled that role.

Although the works in which the early Yellow Peril characters appeared were moderately popular, they did not start the craze for fictional Yellow Peril characters. It was Arthur Sarsfield Ward, a.k.a. "Sax Rohmer," who did that with his character Fu Manchu. Fu Manchu is the culmination of the Yellow Peril character trend and a synthesis of the unique elements of Kiang Ho, Yue-Laou, Dr. Yen How, and Quong Lung. The social environment of England in the Edwardian era contributed to the creation of Fu Manchu as well. Interest in China and the Chinese, much of it racially biased, developed in America and the United Kingdom in the second half of the Nineteenth century, and during the Edwardian years there was an enthusiasm among British readers for stories set in London's Limehouse district, as seen in the stories of Thomas Burke, among others. But Fu Manchu was immediately popular, unlike his Yellow Peril predecessors, and Fu Manchu spawned numerous imitators which his predecessors did not. Fu Manchu's first appearance came in Ward's "The Zayat Kiss" in *The Story Teller* magazine in the fall of 1911. Ward began producing novel-length works about Fu Manchu soon after the completion of *The Mystery of Fu Manchu* (1912), the first collection of Fu Manchu stories. Ward's Fu Manchu novels were *The Devil Doctor* (1913), *Si-Fan Mysteries* (1917), *The Golden Scorpion* (1919), *The Daughter of Fu Manchu* (1931), *The Mask of Fu Manchu* (1932), *Fu Manchu's Bride* (1933), *The Trail of Fu Manchu* (1934), *President Fu Manchu* (1936), *The Drums of Fu Manchu* (1939), *The Island of Fu Manchu* (1941), *The Shadow of Fu Manchu* (1948), *Re-Enter Fu Manchu* (1957), and *Emperor Fu Manchu* (1959). Fu Manchu also appeared in over three dozen movies, four radio shows, and three television shows.

Although most modern readers are familiar at least in passing with the character of Fu Manchu, few have read many of Ward's novels, and so a brief discussion of certain aspects of Fu Manchu's personality is order. In *The Mystery of Fu Manchu* Ward describes Fu Manchu:

> Imagine a person, tall, lean and feline, high-shouldered, with a brow like Shakespeare and a face like Satan, a close-shaven skull, and long, magnetic eyes of the true cat-green. Invest him with all the cruel cunning of an entire Eastern race, accumulated in one giant intellect, with all the resources of science past and present, with all the resources, if you will, of a wealthy government--which, however, already has denied all knowledge of his existence. Imagine that awful being, and you have a mental picture of Dr. Fu-Manchu, the yellow peril incarnate in one man.

Fu Manchu is the leader of the Si Fan, a secret international society of murderers which consists of Chinese Tongs, Indian Phansigars and *Thuggees*, Burmese dacoits, Syrian Hashishin, Sea-Dyaks of Borneo, and other Asian groups who are devoted followers of Fu Manchu. Fu Manchu is an elderly Chinese doctor and scholar who has been scheming towards power since the reign of the Empress Dowager in the Nineteenth century. He is distantly related to the Manchu Dynasty and tried to strengthen the dynasty and limit Western influence in China through a series of kidnapings and assassinations. After the fall of the Manchu Dynasty he broadened his war against the West, using the Si Fan to strike against his enemies and the enemies of China. Fu Manchu's ultimate goal is to

> restore the lost glories of China–*my* China. When your Western civilization, as you are pleased to term it, has exterminated itself, when from the air you have bombed to destruction your palaces and your cathedrals, when in your blindness you have permitted machines to obliterate humanity, I shall arise. I shall survey the smoking ashes which once were England, the ruins that were France, the red dust of Germany, the distant fire that was the great

United States. Then I shall laugh. My hour at last!
(*Meet the Detective*, 1935)

Fu Manchu is a Chinese patriot whose plans are all aimed at strengthening China and weakening its enemies. In addition to the Si Fan, Fu Manchu has an unmatched knowledge of both Eastern and Western medicine, a knowledge he uses to create poisons, gasses, and drugs for his plans. He makes use of non-Western creatures for his killings, from scorpions to adders to an Abyssinian half-man, half-baboon. He also has an almost supernatural ability to hypnotize. Although in the later novels Fu Manchu personally operates around the world, in the early novels his headquarters are in Limehouse, England.

Fu Manchu combines the unique aspects of his predecessors. From the Mongols he takes the Asian threat to the West. From the Gothic villains he takes the schemer/master villain trait. From Kiang Ho he takes the inventiveness and the military aspect of the Yellow Peril concept. From Yue-Laou he takes sorcery (in the form of a superhuman skill at hypnosis) and the seemingly supernatural poisons and creatures under his control. From Dr. Yen How he takes the global aim of subjugating the West. And from Quong Lung he takes the local identification; in the first several adventures Fu Manchu was located in Limehouse and did not leave it. (Later stories eventually widened in scope and became global, with *Fu Manchu's Bride* taking place on the French Riviera and *The Island of Fu Manchu* taking place in the Caribbean).

A by-no-means complete list of characters modeled on Fu Manchu will indicate the influence Ward's character has had:

- Gustave LeRouge's Dr. Cornelius Kramm, from the eighteen *Le Mystérieux Docteur Cornélius* stories, beginning in 1913
- Li Ku Yu, M.P. Shiel's reprise of Dr. Yen How, in "To Arms!" (1913), later published as *The Dragon* and *The Yellow Peril*
- Long Sing and Wu Fang, from the *Exploits of Elaine* movie serial in 1914
- Arthur Ward's Mr. King and the Golden Scorpion (the latter an agent of Fu Manchu himself), from the "Gaston Max" stories beginning in 1915
- The Chinese enemy in the movie serial *Neal of the Navy*, in 1915

- Tori, in the movie serial *The Cheat*, in 1915
- Sang Tu, from the "Nick Carter" dime novel series in *Nick Carter Stories* in 1915
- Jean de la Hire's Leonid Zattan, from the French "Nyctalope" series of novels, beginning in 1915
- Wu, from Allen Robert Dodd's 1916 comic strip "Captain Gardiner of the International Police"
- The Silent Menace, from the 1916 movie serial *Pearl of the Army*
- Ali Singh, from the 1916 movie serial *The Yellow Menace*
- The Blue-Eyed Manchu, from Alexander Romanoff's *The Blue-Eyed Manchu* in 1916
- The Mystery Man of Lhassa, from GH Teed's "Nelson Lee" stories in *The Nelson Lee Library* in 1916
- H. Irving Hancock's Li Shoon, from *Detective Story Magazine* in 1916 and 1917
- Achmed Abdullah's The Blue-Eyed Manchu, from *All-Story Weekly* in 1917
- Denison Clift's Wu Fang, from the serial *The Midnight Patrol* in 1918
- A.E. Apple's Mr. Chang, from thirty-three stories and two collections, beginning in *Detective Story* in 1919
- Prince Wu Ling, from the "Sexton Blake" stories in *Union Jack Library* beginning in 1919
- May Yohe's Wu Fang, from the serial *The Lightning Raider* in 1919
- Li Foo, Fu Canton, Sun-Fu, and over a dozen other similar characters in the "Dixon Hawke" stories in the newspaper *The Saturday Post* and the pulp *The Dixon Hawke Library* beginning in 1919
- Fan Chu Fang, from the "Dixon Brett" stories by R. Austin Freeman in the story paper *Aldine Detective Tales*, beginning in 1922
- Lin Ye Tang and over two dozen similar characters in Ernest McKeag's "Colwyn Dane" stories in *Champion Library* beginning in 1922
- The Mandarin Tang Wang, Kang-Pu, and several other similar characters in Charles Hamilton's "Ferrers Locke" stories in *The Magnet Library* beginning in 1922
- Chung, from *Succes Romans*, a Dutch dime novel published in 1923
- Ssu Hsi Tze, the "Ruler of Vermin" from "The Spider" novels, in the mid-1920s
- Fing Su, from Edgar Wallace's *The Yellow Snake* in 1926
- The Coral Prince in Frank Patchin's *Ted Jones, Fortune Hunter, or, Perilous Adventures with a Chinese Pearl Trader*

in 1928
- Wu Fang, from the serial *Ransom*, in 1928
- Kathulos of Egypt, in Robert E. Howard's *Skull Face*, in 1929
- Mendax, from Guy d'Armen's *Les Troglodytes du Mont Everest* in 1929
- Ming the Merciless, from *Flash Gordon*, beginning in 1929
- Wu Fang, from Roland Daniel's "Wu Fang" stories in *Thriller* magazine and later four novels, beginning in 1929
- Khyzil Kaya, from Guy d'Armen's *Les Géants du Lac Noir* in 1931
- Kong Gai and the Nameless One, from Sidney Herschell Small's "Sgt. Jimmy Wentworth" stories in *Detective Fiction Weekly* beginning in 1931
- Ku Sui, from Harry Bates and Desmond Hall's "Hawk Carse" stories, published in *Astounding Stories* beginning in 1931
- Botak, from the 1932-1933 radio serial "The Orange Lantern"
- Lu Wang, from Hans Reinhard's "Jörn Farrow" stories in *Jörn Farrow's U-Boot Abenteuer* beginning in 1932
- Wu Fang, from Norman Marsh's *Dan Dunn* comic strip, beginning in 1932
- Chang, from F. Van Wyck Mason's *The Shanghai Bund Murders* in 1933
- Chu-Sheng, from Eugene Thomas' "Yellow Magic" trilogy, beginning with *The Shadow of Chu-Sheng* in 1933
- Carl Zaken, "The Black Doctor," and Chang Ch'ien, from T.T. Flynn's "Valentine Easton" stories in *Dime Detective* in 1933 and 1934
- Iskandar, from Jack Williamson's "Wizard's Isle" in the May 1934 issue of *Weird Tales*
- The Griffin, from J. Allen Dunn's stories in *Detective Fiction Weekly*, beginning in 1935
- Prince Li Sin, in Nigel Vane's *The Vengeance of Li-Sin* in 1935
- Mâh le Sinistre, from Charles Robert-Dumas' *The Lead Idol* in 1935
- Wun Wey, in Anthony Rudd's *The Stuffed Men*, in 1935
- Wo Fan, in Bedford Rohmer's "Wo Fan" stories in *New Mystery Adventures* in 1935 and 1936
- Wu Fang, in Robert Hogan's *The Mysterious Wu Fang* from in 1935 and 1936
- Doctor Yen Sin, in Donald Keyhoe's *Dr. Yen Sin* in 1936
- Doctor Chu Lung, from Robert J. Hogan's "Skies of Yellow Death," in the October 1936 issue of *G-8 and His Battle Aces*
- The Red Dragon, in *Detective Comics* starting with issue #1 in 1937
- "Fui Onyui," in Jerry Siegel's "Slam Bradley" story, "The

Streets of Chinatown," in *Detective Comics* #1 in early 1937
- Chang, in Paul Chadwick's "Secret Agent X" stories in *Secret Agent X* in 1938
- Gorrah, a Chinese cyclops, in the "Tex Thomson" stories in *Action Comics*, starting in 1939
- Shiwan Khan, the "Golden Master," in Walter Gibson's *The Shadow*, beginning in 1939
- Pao Tcheou, specifically identified as a cousin of Fu Manchu, from Edward Brooker's "Le Maitre de L'Invisible" novels beginning in 1939
- Moto Taronago, the Yellow Vulture, from Frederick Davis' *Operator* #5, beginning in 1939
- The Red Dragon, in Dick Dias' *The Red Dragon* in 1941
- The Yellow Snake, from Major George Fielding-Elliot's "Dan Fowler" stories in *G-Men* in 1944
- Fen-Chu from George Fronval's *L'Enimatique Fen-Chu* in 1944
- Emperor Basam Damdu from Edgar-Pierre Jacobs' *The Adventures of Blake and Mortimer* in 1946
- Fu-Mandchou, from *Les Nouvelles Aventures de Victor Vincent*, by "Capitaine Ricardo" in 1950
- The Doctor, from August Derleth's "Solar Pons" stories beginning with "The Adventure of the Camberwell Beauty" in 1958
- Monsieur Ming, in Charles-Henri Dewisme's "Bob Morane" stories, beginning in 1959
- Al Feldstein's The Yellow Claw, from the comic book *The Yellow Claw* (1956-1957)
- Dr. No in Ian Fleming's *Dr. No* (1962)
- Stan Lee's The Mandarin, in various Marvel comics beginning with *Tales of Suspense* in 1964
- Dr. Zin, from the *Jonny Quest* television cartoon in 1964
- Dr. Khan, from Herbert Metcalfe's *The Amazing Dr. Khan* in 1966
- Ra's Al Ghul, from DC Comics' *Batman* comics, beginning in 1971
- Weng-Chiang, from the four-part "Talons of Weng-Chiang" series on the television series *Dr. Who* in 1977
- Doctor Chou en Shu, from Richard Jaccoma's *Yellow Peril* in 1978
- Hark, from Warren Ellis and John Cassaday's comic book *Planetary*, beginning in 1999

After World War II the nature of the Yellow Peril character changed. Although Communism had been associated with Asia since the 1920s, the link between the Yellow Peril and Communism had been indirect. For centuries Russia has been seen by Europeans as Asian rather than European, and the 1917 October Revolution securely linked Communism with Asia in the Western mind. But the link between the Yellow Peril and Communism did not occur until the late 1940s with the Chinese revolution. Western fears of Communism merged with pre-existing fears of the Yellow Peril so that Americans and Europeans saw the Yellow Peril masses in both Red Menace and Yellow Peril terms.

However, the nature of the Yellow Peril individual did not change, and in fact the Yellow Perils created after World War Two, when they did take note of Communism, were usually anti-Communist. Fu Manchu expressed anti-Communist sentiments in *The Shadow of Fu Manchu*, beliefs shared by the Mandarin and Ra's Al Ghul. The Yellow Peril individual is too individualistic to be a Communist and continued to be more interested in world conquest than in revolution.

The Yellow Peril individual was not immune to postmodernism, however. Parodies of the Yellow Peril individual predate postmodernism, with "Dr. Chou en Ginsberg" appearing in the BBC radio comedy series *Round the Horne* in 1966. But in 1971 James Blish wrote a moment of metatextual commentary into his novel of black magic, *The Day After Judgment*, when a crazed anti-communist American General mistakes the face of Baphomet for Fu Manchu. Yellow Peril appearances in the 1980s and 1990s have for the most part been quite aware of the racist assumptions of the character type, and at the least acknowledged it, if not played with them. Neal Stephenson's *The Diamond Age* (1995) featured Doctor X, a crimelord in a future China, who is outwardly a Yellow Peril character but is eventually shown to be humane and compassionate. The most notable recent Yellow Peril character is Hark, in Warren Ellis and John Cassaday's critically-acclaimed comic *Planetary*. Hark is a Fu Manchu homage, but with a difference: when confronted by Doc Brass, the Doc Savage analogue who pleads with Hark to join forces with him, Hark does so to benefit all of humanity rather than to gratify his world-conquering aims.

Fu Manchu is not a quintessentially Victorian character. The heyday of the Yellow Peril character came after Fu Manchu, in large part because of the popularity of Fu Manchu himself. Although there were several prototypical Yellow Peril characters before Fu Manchu, Fu was the culmination of what came before and surpassed those characters. Fu Manchu is archetypal, as the list of characters modeled on him shows, and while the ultimate source of the Yellow Peril stereotype dates back centuries, the immediate roots of Fu's archetype lie in the Victorian era.

Interview

Alan Moore is widely respected and even idolized in the comics community. But he has only attended one comic book convention in America, in 1985, and has made no further public appearances in America and only a very few in England, and so despite the many interviews he has done since then he has gained the reputation as a recluse. Combined with his formidable body of work, that makes the prospect of interviewing him an intimidating one. But the truth is that Moore is friendly, unassuming, and soft spoken, and talking with him is very easy.

In December 2002 I called Moore at his home in Northampton, England, and spoke with him about *The League of Extraordinary Gentlemen.*

- Jess Nevins

The Process of Writing

Jess Nevins: What's a typical work day for you like?

Alan Moore: If I had a typical work day I'd be delighted to answer that question. It's very very variable. I couldn't really claim to have any kind of schedule or typical kind of working day, because it all very much depends on kind of the interruptions I might get from somebody suddenly turning up visiting, or the number of phone calls I might have to field in the course of a day. That might prevent me from working. What I tend to do is try to start work as early as possible but I have to be in the right mood and that might take me 'til eleven o'clock or twelve o'clock or one o'clock. Then I will start work. If I have an uninterrupted few hours I can get quite a large amount done. If those few hours are interrupted then there'll be very little done. I kind of try to snatch whatever time I can in between the necessities of ordinary living, like sleeping and eating and occasionally going out and doing a bit of shopping or some laundry or something, and actually getting the work done. Each of the strips that I do, and I'm doing a great many of them, they all have a certain amount of things that have to be discussed, sorted out with the artist, or talked over with the editor. Then there are fanzine interviews, newspaper interviews, requests for television appearances, which despite my best attempts to shy away from all of that kind of stuff have gotten much thicker and faster lately. Things like the to my mind fairly spurious Hollywood connections with *From Hell* and the *League*, which somehow have tended to generate scores of interviews, where I basically explain that I'm not interested in film adaptations of my work. Which I wouldn't have thought was that interesting a statement in its own right, but apparently this is good enough for dozens of interviews all saying that I'm not actually interested in the films that they're interviewing me about. Somewhere in all there– it's very chaotic– but somewhere in all there I managed to do a couple of pages of a book one day, a couple of pages of another book the next day, five or six pages the day after that on some other book. The stuff gets done. I'm still, I think, just about ahead of all of the artists. So as long as I'm not keeping the artists waiting for work then my conscience is fairly clear.

JN: Disraeli is supposed to have said when he wanted to read a book he'd write one. Do you write your books for yourself, is it the joy of collaboration, or is it all of that and writing for the fans?

AM: Well, it's certainly not writing for the fans, or for an audience of any sort, really. I write primarily for myself. It's largely if there's something that I want very much to exist in the universe and it doesn't. Then, rather than wait around for somebody else to make it exist, then it generally seems to work better if I do it myself. So if I have an idea for something which I think should exist, then that is generally enough to propel me through the actual work of writing all of the issues or whatever. So that's generally the impulse. Sometimes with some of the more magically inclined works it's a similar impulse but perhaps a bit more esoteric. Occasionally I will attempt to channel works. This is mainly the things that come out on the CDs, where I have turned my attentions to a certain subject, and then tried to let the work pour into existence. Like I say, it's not a lot different to things like *The League of Extraordinary Gentlemen* or *From Hell*, but it's perhaps a slightly more esoteric process. But the basic drive is the same. Something that doesn't exist and that I want to exist.

JN: How much do you gear your writing in your scripts to your artists? How much of *League*, for example, was written with Kevin O'Neill in mind?

AM: All of it. I have been fortunate enough since my very earliest days on things like *2000AD* to know the artist that I am going to be working with. There were some of those early short stories and features where I really had no idea who the artist was going to be, so I had to write a kind of all-purpose script that would be enough information for even the least imaginative artist, but that's not a problem I've had to deal with for years now. These days I always know who I'm going to be working with, and however I try to work, the collaborative aspect is the perhaps most important part of the process, in that I will very definitely try to gear my writing to be complementary to the style of the person that I'm working with. I pride myself on having a fair degree of insight into the creative processes of the artists that I work with and whose work I'm familiar with. I can generally look at an artist's work and see potentials, often unexplored potentials in the work, that maybe the artists themselves haven't seen. There have been times when, just looking at an artist's work, I've been able to tell what that artist would probably love to do in their wildest dreams. And if you can come up with that sort of script for an artist, then you'll find that the artist in question will respond, will put much more energy into the work than they would have done if it was just another job for hire. With the *League* I settled upon the idea of Kevin O'Neill pretty much straightaway. I believe there was a brief period where contractually Kevin Eastman was asking me to do something for Tundra or for Kitchen Sink or whoever it was then. For a while he was talking about me working with Simon Bisley, and so there was a possible time when it could have been Simon Bisley doing the *League*. But that deal fell through and I ended up doing something else for Kevin Eastman instead, the Spirit books, I think. From that point I was very certain of who I wanted to illustrate it. And I think I got in touch with Kevin O'Neill straightaway, because Kevin is kind of unique in the comics field. For one thing, most of Kevin's contemporaries from *2000AD*, excellent, wonderful artists like Dave Gibbons and Brian Bolland, even Mick McMahon, these were people who, although were undeniably brilliant artists, their main influences have probably been American comic books. I can remember that Dave Gibbons' earliest work really showed the influence of Wally Wood. Mick McMahon's earliest work always looked very much like Jack Davis' to me. Kevin is an artist who has probably drawn more influence from British sources than American ones. If you look at Kevin's artwork with a knowing eye, you can see traces, very strong traces, of the often brilliant British juvenile comic book artists, like Leo Baxendale, people like Paddy Brennan, Dudley Watkins, and also great British caricaturists, people like Hogarth or Gillray. Kevin is a wonderful illustrator, he's a great comic artist in that he can tell sequential stories with incredible verve, but when you look at Kevin's illustration, then you've often got stuff that is the equal to Franklin Booth or Sidney Sime, a classic illustrator. Every one of the faces, even in the crowds, has such individuality about it, it lives and breathes. So, yes, when I'm writing *League of Extraordinary Gentlemen* I'm very consciously writing to Kevin's considerable strengths. Some of the very quiet scenes, the discussion between Mina and Hyde, in Issue Three of the second volume, I thought that was an incredible scene, and there are very few artists who could have handled it with the subtlety that Kevin did, where it's just two people sitting in a room talking, and yet it's so intensely charged, and the expressions, the nuances of facial expressions that Kevin can lend to the characters–like I say, it really makes it live, it makes it an emotional experience, it makes the *League* work upon so many levels at once. There are scenes in the issue that I'm just writing which are simultaneously sexy, emotional, funny, silly, and quite genuinely horrifying, and somehow managing to be all at once, which takes an artist of considerable versatility to accomplish, and with

Kevin I've got just such an artist.

JN: I'm looking forward to seeing how *Top Ten*, for example, changes once Zander Cannon takes over most of the art duties.

AM: Zander will be doing the *Smax* while Gene [Ha] will be doing the *49ers* graphic novel. And, yes, they've got very different styles. I've not actually seen either of the work that they've done so far yet but I've heard that it's beautiful in both interests. In working with Zander I try very much to do things that I think Zander's going to enjoy, and usually my intuitions are almost eerily exact. Like I was telling Zander the other day that in one of the final episodes of it Robyn Slinger, Smax's partner, will, because she's on a world where there is no technology and where science above the level of wheels and levers doesn't actually work, where there's no electricity, all of her electrical toys are useless, so she is pretty useless, until sometime in the final episode she will construct a massive wooden machine that is powered purely by simple ballistics and non-technological, non-electronic means, and I was telling Zander about this and he was saying that the one thing that he wanted to draw most in all the world is wooden Rube Goldberg machines. In the first "Jack B. Quick," with Kevin Nowlan, I introduced a vacuum cleaner as Jack B. Quick's way of creating a solar system. And Kevin got back to me through Scott saying that his favorite thing in the whole world to draw are old-fashioned antique vacuum cleaners. You just look at an artist's style, and all of a sudden you can see what would look good drawn in that style. Perhaps it's something that comes to you after you've been working in this medium for nearly twenty-five years like I have. You start looking at Melinda Gebbie's work, when all I'd seen of it was the black-and-white stuff she'd done for the early undergrounds, I could see what she was interested in. I could see how much she liked textures, how much she liked the female form, how much she liked faces, and lighting, and then when I saw her color work and realized what she was capable of there, I was able to craft *Lost Girls* to attempt things which Melinda on her own perhaps would not have thought of attempting, but which once she'd accomplished them are absolutely spectacular. Without wishing to sound smug about this, I was always right. (Laughs) And I always knew that these scenes, drawn in the style which I knew Melinda was capable of, would look absolutely wonderful. And the same goes for all the artists. It's like, when I do the CDs, the music is very often written first. I write my words to fit in pleasantly and comfortably with the music. There is, and I know that I'm writing the scripts first in this instance, but the artist's very style suggests a kind of music, and I am trying to write my scripts to complement the music that I perceive in that specific artist's style.

JN: I know you've done some drawing in the past–not a whole lot, certainly not comic book length work, but I know you have done some. Do you think because you have done that and you have some talent in that area, that you get slightly more insight into how an artist is going to look than an ordinary [writer]…?

AM: I think that's true. I think my drawing skills have never been any real use to me because they're very limited. If I take a couple of weeks on something I can make it look pretty good. But that's of no use at all if you're going to have any kind of commercial art career. But the one area where my drawing abilities have been useful to me is that I think it has given me an insight into drawing, into composition. I have no trouble imagining panels visually. The only trouble that I have is in rendering them quickly or well. So if I can come out with a crystalline vision of a panel that my own hands are not capable of executing, then it makes sense to work with the brilliant artists that I do work with. My layouts, in my notoriously detailed scripts, they're pretty exact, and usually they work. I always give the artists the freedom, if they can think of something better to do, to do something better. But nine times out of ten the shot as I've composed it in my panel descriptions is probably the best shot. But if the artist suddenly thinks, "Hey, this would look brilliant from overhead," then they're quite at liberty to do that, if there's something that I might not have considered. But it all seems to work out very smoothly.

The League's Beginnings

JN: How much research went into writing *League*? Did you get the idea, then do the research and read the books, and then write it, or did you get the idea and then write it, and then read the books and change how it was written?

AM: I got the idea, and I already had a certain familiarity with the books, and I could see how to make them fit together. One of the main things with the *League* is that Kevin is if anything more erudite than I am with regard to this stuff, so I'd come up with the story, I'd come up with, "Yeah, let's use this character, let's use that character," but Kevin seems to be able to pluck hard information on the characters from out of the air or to suggest characters that he's come across that might be useful, many of which I am going to be working into future stories or have already worked in. It's probably about fifty-fifty on the research for these things, like with *The War of the Worlds* I had the idea of getting all the Martian races into some sort of socio-political shape. What was the political set-up on Mars? What were the warring factions upon Mars? [Moore's Martian references are to some of the events in the second *League of Extraordinary Gentlemen* miniseries.] But on the other hand Kevin got the description of Gullivar Jones' carpet and was able to reproduce that very faithfully. Details like that, Kevin has been invaluable in coming up with them. He also brought to my attention the Wolf of Kabul, and since this was around the time when the conflict in Afghanistan was just kicking off the character seemed very pertinent. So we were able to kind of retrofit his father into our continuity. I suppose the same was true with *From Hell*, to a degree, where Eddie [Campbell] would be contributing bits of information and certainly lots of visual research, and I think we were both enjoying it. And I think that's the same thing with Kevin and the *League*. It's actually quite a lot of fun, to come up with these characters. Sometimes you'll find a character that you can't imagine how it's ever going to fit in, and then you'll suddenly find, after thinking about it for twelve months, that it's an absolutely brilliant, indispensable character that if you can pull it off will work splendidly. I can't really praise too highly Kevin's contributions in terms of throwing in ideas. It's part of the seamlessness of *League* is that we both welcome the other intruding upon our territory. I like Kevin giving me ideas, Kevin likes my panel descriptions and suggestions for pictures, and that tends, I think, to make the work organically whole, more like the work of one person, which is always the aim in these things. That is the highest compliment that you can give a collaborative work, that it looks like the work of one person, and I suppose that is the sort of standard that I'm generally aiming for.

JN: I know that you've said in past interviews that Kevin O'Neill was the one who pointed out to you that Nemo in the original Verne books was actually a Sikh–

AM: Yeah, I've since found out that in the first one Nemo is not actually specified. It's only in *The Mysterious Island* that Verne suddenly decided to make him Indian. And that's reassuring because it means that most of these great writers of the past were just as sloppy as I am. That does reassure me to some extent.

JN: Part of it was Verne's sloppiness and part of it was also his editor saying that–Verne wanted Nemo to originally be a Pole–

AM: A Pole, yeah–

JN: A Pole whose family had been killed by the Russians, but Verne's editor knew that Verne's books were selling well in Russia, so–

AM: Which would alienate them—

JN: So even a century ago, in a field other than comics, editors were making decisions that–

AM: Political decisions, right. I feel a certain kinship with those writers of the past when working on *League*, because you start to realize that some of their concerns were almost identical to your own. Like the thing about Jules Verne having picked up the ball of Poe's "Arthur Gordon Pym" and run with it in his story *The Ice Sphinx*. And of course Lovecraft was quoting from "Pym" in *Mountains of Madness*. You sometimes tend to get the feeling that all of these disparate writers were in fact already kind of knowingly contributing to this big shared world such as we're suggesting in the

Almanac sections of *League*. They were all contributing to this huge world of fiction by referring to each other's stories. God bless pulp writers, often churning this stuff out with barely time to think about it but somehow managing to often turn out wonderful things as a result.

JN: What was the inspiration of the title? There've been any number of suggestions put forward, everything from the crime film to the British comedy troupe. Was there anything in particular?

AM: It was the first thing that came into my head. It sounded right. "The League of Extraordinary Gentlemen." I wanted something formal, something that sounded Victorian and formal and had far too many words in it for a regular comic book title, and something which sounded kind of stiff upper lip, and that, the "League of Extraordinary Gentlemen," came into my mind. After I came up with that I remembered the 1940s film with Jack Hawkins, and I remembered Robert Fripp's band, the League of Gentlemen, from the, was it late Seventies?

JN: Mid-Eighties, actually.

AM: Mid-Eighties, right. But I hadn't really been thinking of them. The League of Gentlemen television show, which I've enjoyed a lot, I hadn't heard of their radio show, and the show didn't actually come out on television until we were well into working on the *League*. So, no, I think it's just that it's got a nice ring to it, perhaps because of the earlier uses of it in various things. It sounds sort of familiar. At least we bothered to add an extra word to the title, which I think is pretty creative of us.

JN: Before the book came out we'd heard that one of the potential titles was "The League of Extraordinary Gentlefolk." Was that title ever considered?

AM: I think I might have used it at one point where I was having a misguided politically correct moment where I suddenly thought, "Hang on, it's got a woman in it, shouldn't it be the 'League of

Extraordinary Gentlefolk'?" But then I thought, "No, you've got to think like a Victorian in this." It wouldn't have been called the "League of Extraordinary Gentlefolk" in Victorian Britain, they'd have just ignored the fact that there was a woman present. There might have been an afternoon where I put the title as "League of Extraordinary Gentlefolk" but it didn't last long.

JN: There's been a lot of discussion about possible influences and inspirations on the series. Some of the ones suggested were Bryan Talbot's "Luther Arkwright" stories, Kim Newman's stories, and Philip Jose Farmer's "Wold Newton" stories. Were any of those [influential]…?

AM: The Philip Jose Farmer "Wold Newton" thing, which I think was *Lord Tyger* [Actually, *Tarzan Alive*], where he's got that big genealogy? When I first read that I thought that was great, the way that he tied in all of these people into one family, and had done all of these ingenious little bits like the stuff with the Spider and the Shadow actually being split personalities of G-8 Battle Ace. There was something so mad and obsessive about that I warmed to it immediately. So, yes, certainly, that would have been in the back of my mind. I think generally what I was coming to the *League* from was *Lost Girls* in that when we started to put together the idea for *Lost Girls*, as I remember it, originally I had an idea that you could do a kind of sexual decoding of the Peter Pan story, almost in straight Freudian terms, with dreams of flying being a sort of metaphor for sex. I talked this over with Melinda, she revealed to me that she in fact quite liked stories that had three women characters in, it just seemed to be a nice dynamic. I thought perhaps we could add a couple of characters, and Alice and Dorothy from *The Wizard of Oz* and *Alice in Wonderland* sprang to mind, and then the idea kind of blossomed from there, the idea that, hey, if you've got these three characters sharing the same story, then you could say some quite interesting things, and I found it delightful, to be able to kind of refer to these previous histories of these characters. And of course this is nothing new. There's been numerous books in which, say, Sherlock Holmes has fought Fu Manchu, or defeated Jack the Ripper. I think there's a film with Arsene Lupin versus Sherlock Holmes, a

French film?

JN: There've actually been a couple. I think the first one was actually one of the Pathé silents, back in 1908 or 1909.

AM: It's kind of like Abbott and Costello meet the monsters, where you've got Frankenstein, Dracula, the Wolfman and the Mummy and the Invisible Man–there's something about the idea of separate continuities that seems to invite breaking down the picket fence, and it seems to have been a temptation to people for quite a long time. It was probably because I was enjoying so much doing *Lost Girls*, which has been ongoing now for about thirteen years, something like that, that my mind went so easily to the idea of getting a bunch of these Victorian fantasy characters and–probably lots of things played a part of it. But certainly those Jose Farmer ones, I can remember very definitely being excited by the thrill of linking up all of these disparate stories. Even if it was a kind of obsessive, fannish, mad thing to do, to work out the exact relationship between Tarzan, Doc Savage, and the Scarlet Pimpernel, I thought that you had to admire Philip Jose Farmer's fortitude and obsessive passion in working it all out. So, yeah, that would certainly have played a part.

JN: In the book I've written a couple of essays, one of which is tracing the history of the concept of the crossover, and there's a kid's book from 1849 called *Kit Bam's Adventures* in which Kit Bam talks about his sailing adventures, and it's basically Kit Bam saying, "I ran into this character from this 1790s opera, and I ran into this character from *Frankenstein*." So 150 years ago people were writing these sorts of crossovers.

AM: It's obviously been a big temptation. In fact, you could argue that this might be how mythologies build up. If you've got one set of oral traditions of stories about Hermes, say, and you've got another set of stories about Hercules or Zeus, it would have been a natural idea that if you've got heroes represented by various oral traditions, that someone would think, "Well, what if Hercules had ever met Zeus? What would have happened if Hermes and Hercules had ever gotten together?"

JN: And that's how you get your Jason and the Argonauts.

AM: Yeah, or Homer, where you've got your masses of heroes from perhaps very different traditions all ganged together in some kind of Justice League of Troy or whatever, where you've got Ajax, you've got Achilles, you've got Ulysses, you've got all of these people, or you've got Jason and the Argonauts, as you say. It's a big temptation, and I think that it's probably as old as the story itself, that when you've created these wonderful little worlds, with their wonderful little characters, it's just such an irresistible idea to put them together and see what happens.

The Characters

JN: You've mentioned in interviews that with *Tom Strong* you were trying to reel back the tape of the superhero, to go back to the pulp characters that inspired Superman. Was there any of that with the *League*?

AM: Yeah. One of the things that kick-started the idea of the League was, and ideas generally arrive from several vectors at once, I've found, but one of the ideas behind the League was that I was thinking about superhero groups and various reasons why they don't work. One set of those musings led to *Top Ten*. Another set was where I started thinking about basically how you could take the lineage of those superheroes back further than the pulps of the 1930s. It seemed to me that the fantasy fiction of the late Nineteenth century was a breeding ground for a lot of central ideas that would later surface in pulp fiction and in comics. Obvious examples, like Jekyll and Hyde slowly morphing into the Hulk over eighty years. So that led me to thinking about the characters of Nineteenth century fiction. I got to thinking about Wells and Verne and Stoker and Haggard and the rest of them, Sax Rohmer, and wondered if it would be possible to put together a Justice League of the Nineteenth century. The male characters were not difficult to come by. The female character was,

I thought that it had to have a female character in, for chemistry, but that was a little harder. I did briefly consider, what was her name, the one woman Sherlock Holmes had any respect for?

JN: Irene Adler.

AM: Irene Adler, yeah. I briefly considered her. But, I don't know, I think that there would probably be more reader identification with, I thought that probably Mina Murray was probably a better known character and that it would be interesting to speculate upon what sort of character she might have been after the events in *Dracula*, and to come up with my version of a post-*Dracula* Mina Harker. Since superheroes had evolved from characters of the Nineteenth century it seemed an interesting idea to take one of the concepts that had grown out of later superheroes, i.e. the superhero team, and then try to apply that to the characters that had been the inspiration for all of these heroes and see how it worked. When we were just writing that first issue it all seemed to work so naturally, because these characters seemed to already resonate in the reader's imagination, and you don't have to perhaps expend a lot of energy explaining who they are. You can go right into the character nuances. If this was a regular comic book and these characters had never been seen before, I would have probably had to go into the stories of *Dracula* and *Twenty Thousand Leagues Under the Sea* and explain Jekyll and Hyde and all the rest of them. Whereas I can just lightly allude to them, safe in the knowledge that the readers are going to get most of the references and will have all of that information ready to work with, and I can get on with telling an interesting story with these pre-established characters. There's turned out to be an awful lot of surprising and very pleasurable things about writing *The League of Extraordinary Gentlemen*. I'd say that along with *Promethea*, for different reasons, and perhaps even including *Promethea*, the *League* is the strip that I have the most sheer fun in doing.

JN: So when you chose the characters it was a combination of their archetypal qualities and their general recognizability?

AM: Yeah. I thought Nemo has got to be in it, because he's the science-augmented hero, he's the techno-hero, and when Kevin revealed that he was Indian all sorts of other possibilities for his character started to blossom. Griffin and Hyde are wonderful freaks and both have incredible visual possibilities. It struck me that invisibility is probably the most poorly used power in comic books because whenever you get an invisible character in comic books they always draw a dotted line around them to tell you where they are. Whereas the kind of mileage we've gotten out of Griffin being invisible in *League* so far, right from that very first scene in the girls' school, it's much better if the character is completely invisible. That's the whole point: you don't know where they are. There's a scene coming up in *League* #4 where you have Griffin beating up Mina, and it was a very difficult scene to write. I found it more disturbing than a lot of the eviscerations in *From Hell*, because seeing a woman being beaten up is a pretty horrible thing anyway, but seeing a woman being beaten up by somebody who is not apparently there kind of brings home the full horror that I think Wells intended with his original concept of an invisible man. Quatermain I wanted in there because I wanted the straightforward colonial adventurer. A guy with a gun, a guy who was handy with a gun and who was closest to the–well, it's the other way around, Indiana Jones and people like that owe a tremendous debt to Allan Quatermain, and he's perhaps not been best served by the film adaptations of *King Solomon's Mines*.

JN: That's a very diplomatic way of putting it.

AM: Well, I'm a very diplomatic person, Jess. I could see a different Quatermain. Because actually our Quatermain being a little bit craven in certain circumstances and having a tendency, he's got certain addictive qualities in his personality. None of these things actually go against the grain of what Haggard established about Quatermain. He's not the bravest soul in the world, according to Haggard's original, and there is all of that dalliance with taduki, which kind of suggests that, yeah, he could have ended up in an opium den in Cairo without too much difficulty. But he seemed like an interesting character, and I suppose that the five of them together made an interestingly volatile mix, with this incredible primness of Miss Murray, who is not unresourceful, but her view of things is very proper, and she's in this team with a Sikh fanatic, an invisible homicidal maniac, and a monster in the form of Hyde, and Allan Quatermain, who is the most human of the bunch, is not necessarily the most reliable of them. It just struck me that there were lots of interesting prospects in a mix like that. Also because the way I started to see the League meant that just because those characters were the League of Extraordinary Gentlemen for the first two books didn't preclude writing stories set in other times about an entirely different set of characters. We're already starting to think about the third book of the *League* which will probably be *Tales of the League of Extraordinary Gentlemen* and will be stories set in the Eighteenth century, the Seventeenth century, the early Twentieth century, showing two or three different incarnations of the League, with a lot of interesting new characters turning up. I can see that with the formula as we have it I could quite easily continue writing stories about the League of Extraordinary Gentlemen for years, because we've got the whole of literature, past, present, and future as this enormous technicolor playground that we can run amok in.

JN: I know that you made the announcement, a month or two ago, that you were going to be scaling back on your work for ABC [*America's Best Comics,* an imprint of DC/Wildstorm Comics] and some people were wondering if that meant the third volume of *League* would be delayed awhile. So you're thinking–

AM: Well, the third miniseries will, I'm gonna start work on it as soon as I finish this one. I'm hoping to get it finished by the end of next year, which is when I shall be going into a peculiar kind of semi-retirement. But it's worth pointing out that of all of the ABC books *League of Extraordinary Gentlemen* is the only one that me and the artist actually own, so there's no reason why I can't continue doing *League* as and when me and Kevin feel like it, from now into the indeterminate future. Like I say, we've got plans for a very, very nice 1950s League and various other sorts of ideas, which I'm very excited about, and I think that the nature of the book means that it will probably continue to suggest ideas to us the more we work upon it. Things will start to occur. It's a strip with an awful lot of mileage, and even if I am going to be more or less getting away from mainstream comic work in about a year's time I don't really necessarily see *League* as mainstream comic work. If the *League* hadn't been published ultimately by DC Comics we could perhaps not have had to think about, a few scenes, things like that, we could perhaps have been more frank–

JN: Like the Marvel ad–
[Each issue of *The League of Extraordinary Gentlemen* contains advertisements from Victorian magazines. The original version of *The League of Extraordinary Gentlemen* #5 contained an ad for the "Marvel 'Whirling Spray' Syringe" douche. Paul Levitz, the President of DC Comics, ordered the entire print run of *The League of Extraordinary Gentlemen* #5 pulped and a new edition of the issue published without the ad, reportedly because of the fear that Marvel Comics, DC Comics' largest competitor, would take offense at the ad.]

AM: Oh, yeah, well, the ad, I hadn't even noticed that before all the fuss erupted. I really hadn't noticed that it was the Marvel company at all. Marvel themselves were apparently going to publish that ad.

JN: Really?

AM: Yeah, I had Joe Quesada phone me up to ask if I minded because they were doing some Victorian book and they said, "Can we publish that ad on the inside front cover amongst others?" And I said, "Sure, it's a free world, do what you want, mate." I think they thought it was quite funny as well. But the thing is that both Kevin and me, we both come from an English comics background. We also both have a very serious respect for the underground comics. In fact Kevin is a filthy little blighter when you get to know him, and I think that we both probably enjoy immensely the thought of being able to take the *League* into more untrammeled territory, where we could ignore any of those restrictions which we haven't managed to ignore already. That said, we've been able to do quite a bit with the *League*, and I certainly wouldn't want to turn it into a sex and gore fest, but we could ignore any limits. We could be as extreme as we felt like being, which is always my general tendency in things anyway.

JN: You've mentioned before that there's a William S. Burroughs character that you may be bringing into the 1950s League. The mind reels at what you're going to do with that.

AM: Heh, yeah, well, you wait. It's not going to be in the third book of the League. This might be in a fourth book. There's also going to be a Neil Cassidy character. I'm familiar enough with Burroughs that I'm not going to have to go back to do any rereading. But Cassidy, I'm going to go back and read *The Electric Kool-Aid Acid Test*, read the first third, and his other–there are very few writings by him–so that I can actually recreate the voice and the Beat rhythm of the prose. And that would be exhilirating, to take it away from fantasy characters of the Nineteenth century, which are a surefire crowd puller, really, a sort of superhero fantasy marketplace, and take it into riskier territory, by bringing in characters from Beat literature, which I happen to like a great deal, and I don't see why, you know, there'll still be a lot of fantastic characters in the mix, there'll still be a lot of familiar characters from the earlier books still around. I think we can do a good story that might, it'll certainly be very nice if, just as we've had readers who've gone on to read Stoker or Haggard or Verne or Wells as a result of the *League*, I'd like to think that I'll push some in the direction of *On The Road* or *Naked Lunch* or *Howl* or something like that.

JN: I've had a couple of people tell me that they went on to read *The Third Policeman* because of it.

AM: Really? Oh, well, then my life has not been totally in vain. That is tremendous. Did they enjoy it?

JN: They loved it. They had never heard of O'Brien, and on the strength of the reference and, I immodestly say, my raving about it in the annotations–

AM: Well, this is why you're so invaluable, Jess, because I can rely on you. You're like a fine screen. Things that would sail by most people and references that might be lost, you can catch any of those balls and bounce them back at the readers, it's great.

JN: Thanks. I know that the readers, the ones that write to me, say that they would never have found this book if not for *League* and the annotations, they read them and they love them and they spread word of mouth, and so there are people who are out there getting turned on to all this great literature–

AM: Let's have a Flann O'Brien revival. Let's have an Alfred Jarry revival. Let's go for it. These are wonderful pieces of writing. They're fantastic. They might be outside the usual purviews of what fantasy readers interest themselves in, but...Borges. To think of someone passing their lives reading fantasy stories and not reading Borges is kind of tragic. It would be great that if through this comic we could reawaken an interest in the literature that is still my favorite art form, still my favorite technology.

JN: Were there any characters besides Sherlock Holmes that you decided explicitly not to use [as a primary character]?

AM: Dracula. That was another one. We explicitly decided not to use Holmes or Dracula. We could have brought Dracula back, but...Holmes we've referred to. We've got that really nice little Reichenbach Falls sequence in, which I was thrilled with. That was great to write. That felt epic. But we can have that as a flashback more to set up Moriarty and to give a tantalizing glimpse of Holmes without having him overshadow the story as he probably invariably would do. The same goes for Dracula. These are two such towering characters in light of their subsequent fame that even if–Sherlock Holmes was pretty big back at the time–but the films and the various related books that have been written about Dracula since that time, they far outnumber the ones written about Jekyll and Hyde or about the Invisible Man. They would tend I think to overwhelm or overshadow, say, characters that, if you've got Sherlock Holmes in the League, then that would to a degree draw attention away from lesser but more intriguing characters, like Nemo or Mina. I thought that their inclusion would probably tend to overbalance the League.

That's not to say that at some future point when we've got our world more firmly established that they won't be making cameo or perhaps even bigger appearances. But certainly in the first two or three volumes I didn't want people waiting for Holmes to show up or waiting for Dracula to show up, so we just decided that we wouldn't deal with them, at least in the initial excursions. Maybe some point in the future, but other than veiled allusions we've tended to steer clear. I must say that Dracula particularly benefits from that. He is a very powerful off-stage presence in *League*. By never mentioning his name, that gives him even more strength and charisma and aura. He's more useful to me as a terrible shadow in Mina's past that is never spoken of, because that says a lot about Mina. He's more useful to me like that than he is as a sort of red-eyed, blood-drinking caped monster at center stage.

JN: There've been a number of fans who want to insist that Nemo is actually Holmes in disguise. So I have to officially ask this: he's not, right?

AM: No. I hadn't heard that and I can't really, I don't know where that came from. No.

JN: It's wishful thinking on their part. They have all sorts of spurious rationales for it, but I think part of it is them–

AM: Them wanting Holmes to be in it.

JN: Right.

AM: We've got Holmes certainly–there will be meetings with Holmes. We've already mentioned in the Almanac that Mina goes to visit Holmes when he's doing his retired beekeeper bit. And so obviously there is some contact between the League and Holmes in the future. How much space we'll devote to that, I don't know. There might be a story where we will bring Holmes to center stage. Again, I don't know. I'm finding more interesting material by looking at less obvious figures. For example, we're going to be dealing at least in part with Bertholt Brecht and the *Threepenny Opera*. Again, if that's something that readers aren't–I'm sure that all readers could probably whistle "Mac the Knife" if you put a gun to their head but they might not know where it comes from. That'd be nice. If they want stuff on Sherlock Holmes there are a thousand places that they can get stuff on Sherlock Holmes. The sort of characters that we've got coming up, you can't get them anywhere. They're all but forgotten. That gives them, to me at least, a sort of greater appeal. Ones that are in danger of vanishing, endangered fictional species. Sherlockiana is prolific and healthy. Zenith the Albino is less well-known.

JN: Were there any characters you'd have liked to use but just couldn't fit in?

AM: Well, generally, ones that–yeah. I'd liked to have had a glimpse of Sexton Blake. But we had to stick to the story and there wasn't room, other than to make an odd veiled reference. There was some stuff that I'd have liked to have done in the second book that would have linked Gullivar Jones' flying carpet through, umm...who was it who wrote *A Child of the Jago*?

JN: Arthur Morrison.

AM: Arthur Morrison, right. Through the Gypsies or the underclass thieves of that–I would have tried to have linked Gullivar Jones' magic carpet with the magic carpet that provided the patch upon the trousers of a young British 1940s schoolboy called Jimmy who appeared in the *Beano* story "Jimmy's Magic Patch." Like I say, this is pretty obscure. Nobody would have got it apart from a few elderly British readers. Yeah, there have been things where I've been tempted to sort of tie up another little loose end. If I have got the space I will do. But generally there's so much stuff going on in the main narrative that some things get passed over. But that's not to say that as the *League* continues we won't get the chance to refer to all these things and even make them the part of the main narrative.

JN: I know you've answered this question in interviews before, but I figure that there are going to be people reading this interview who haven't read the other ones. So I apologize in advance–

AM: No, not at all–fire away.

JN: What was the particular moment when you decided to start bringing in as many different characters as you could?

AM: I think it was probably in the first issue when I suddenly realized that I had Stevenson's Hyde kill Zola's Nana upon Poe's Rue Morgue. And it suddenly struck me how poignant and funny and dramatic that was, and I think at that point I suddenly thought that, well, there's probably no need to introduce any characters by name that aren't from some form of Nineteenth-century literature or from later stories that can be retrofitted, back-engineered, to that era, so that you can have grandfathers of later characters. And once I'd struck upon that idea there was something about the purity of it that excited me. It was quite like with *Top Ten*, the moment when I had the breakthrough that everybody in this city is a superhero, and yes, that would take quite a lot of work, but the end result would be overwhelmingly dazzling and hilarious. And there was a similar moment with the *League*, where I suddenly realized that I could make this more than a fantastic Victorian romp or adventure, where I could actually have a great deal of literary fun and maybe strike a few literary sparks by juxtaposing characters from wildly different stories. That was probably the moment when the possibilities of the *League* first really presented themselves to me.

JN: This is probably not going to really be interesting to anyone but me, but how many of the non-speaking background characters were references? I know that in the second series, in one panel, in the background there are the characters from the Quality Chocolate ads.

AM: There might be, although the Quality Chocolate ads, they do show fairly generic Victorians. I'm not sure on that one. Kevin might have decided to put them in and just not–I think he likes to surprise me. A lot of it goes over my head. I know that we had Weary Willy and Tired Tim in a background panel in one of the early ones, but generally I don't think that non-speaking characters, they're never really at my specification, so if Kevin has got a character that he feels like dropping in or a background reference detail that he feels like including, then I just give him free rein to do that because I know that the end result will be mad and spectacular. But I don't think that there's been that many characters in the background–the only ones that I'm absolutely sure about are Weary Willy and Tired Tim. I can't think of any others that I'm certain about off-hand. You might be right with the Quality Street people. It's the kind of thing that would amuse Kevin and it is quite a funny idea. But, again, I don't know.

JN: There was also Ally Sloper–

AM: Oh, yeah, of course, Ally Sloper, I remember him as well. But other than those I can't think of any that I'm absolutely definitely sure about, although, actually, that Quality Street thing is quite a good idea. I've just decided that at some point in the future we'll have to get the Five Boys, from the obscure British chocolate bar Five Boys Bar, which inexplicably have the faces of five schoolboys on the back of it, each with very different expressions: one was weeping, one was beaming, one was scowling, and so on. So, yeah, we'll probably work the Five Boys into the background somewhere or other where appropriate.

JN: I can tell I'm going to have a hard time tracking that one down.

AM: Yeah, well, so you shouldn't have brought it up, Jess.

JN: Good point. In other interviews you've spoken about the rape scenes and the portrayal of the Egyptians and the Chinese as a satirization of Victorian attitudes. Were there some other aspects of the series that you intended as satire, things like the violence, the characterisation of Mina, and the Masonic control of British Intelligence?

AM: The Masonic aspect was largely–I know nobody will believe this, but it actually was largely Kevin's. I know that when we got that letter from somebody reputing to be a Freemason in one of the early issues I cravenly blamed it all upon Kevin, but actually, yeah, it was his fault. Any Masons out there reading this, it was Kevin. I think that it was him who just decided that, because the Masons are known to exert a certain influence in the British police force. And that they might not be entirely unconnected with British military intelligence, there might be the odd person in the government who is also a member of the Masons. How genuinely mysterious or threatening any of this is, I really couldn't say. Most of the Masons I've ever met are either sort of interested in it for mystical reasons or are local small businessmen who enjoy the socialization. I suppose that the dialogue and the attitudes are the place where I'm most free to satirize Victorian conventions and even some fairly modern British conventions which have probably been around since Victorian times. And also things like, in the letters pages, the extraordinarily rude and offensive tone that the people doing the responses in the letters to the editors page would use. The hectoring, bullying, public school Headmaster tone, which is very funny when you read it today. I think you quoted one particularly wonderful example, which I think was one that Kevin had actually pointed out to me already, to give me some idea as to how to answer readers' letters. Yeah, the calls to patriotism, the contempt for anybody who isn't English, the ridiculous self-importance, the hypocritical sexual prudery, all of these things, which are very much a part of the British character, and probably the American character as well, in that there might be some sort of slight genetic resemblance between the two countries–

JN: "Two nations separated by a common language."

AM: Yeah, exactly. These are things which–they're still around today. They're still as ridiculous as they were in Victorian times. But they don't dress in such funny, old-fashioned clothes any more, so we perhaps tend to take them more seriously, or give them a kind of credibility which they don't really deserve. The mistrust of foreigners, the "Mohammedan rabble," it's not difficult to take attitudes like that towards Islam and to imagine them in the mouths of a great many people in the Western world today. The attitudes towards women. They've not changed that massively, I don't think, since the

Nineteenth century. Certain cosmetic changes, but this kind of tiff of the sexes does seem to continue in one form or another. It's easier in some ways to satirize these things by transposing them to the safety of the Nineteenth century or the early Twentieth century than it is to, say, do a story about them in the present day talking about them, where everybody is very raw and jumpy about the issues and would tend to feel threatened or to perhaps overreact if presented with them in a present day context that seems to relate to their own lives. Whereas the Nineteenth century, you can have a controlled detonation of these ideas, where you can explore them, your readers can explore them, but perhaps without that initial rush of antipathy that they might feel if it did seem to be talking about the present day and present day issues.

JN: Also, along those lines, you've got the Great White Hunter in the group and you've got a sort of stereotypical Victorian heroine and you've got the Indian science pirate bad guy, and yet Quatermain is a secondary, back-up character and Mina is the leader and Nemo is probably the most able of the group. Was that a deliberate inversion of the traditional roles?

AM: I think that's just how those characters–without wishing to get into the cliche of, "After a while the characters start writing themselves," because, no, actually, I do all the writing, I think I'd be aware of it if the characters were offering to take over my typing duties. But at the same time, there is a point where you start to know the characters so well that you know what they'll say, you know what they'll think, you know how they'll react to each other. And the ways that the League seems to function kind of grew out of the characters and the interactions that I imagined them having. The fact that Mina is perhaps the strongest member of the group just seemed natural. Nemo is perhaps the most natural leader but Nemo's a fanatic. It has to be said that his plans to crush the British Empire didn't actually work. Brilliant engineer. Far-sighted visionary. But a man who has been fighting an unwinnable war for a long time and who is perhaps tired. Quatermain, he is a decent man. His role will perhaps tend to become more pronounced as things go on. He is a decent man, not without his faults, but fundamentally he is very human–other than Mina, the most human member of the group. The way that the characters play against each other and their various roles–Mina has–in some ways she is the most directed, the most focused, the most dominating, in that she is absolutely fearless and doesn't take any crap from anybody, and kind of compels a respect, even from these monstrous people all around her. It's just the way that the characters seemed to develop. It just seemed natural. It didn't really seem as if I was making some sort of labored feminist point by making Mina the strongest character. It just seemed that, in the way that I saw the character, there were only two possible roles for her. One of them was cowed, intimidated, barely daring to say a word. Much more like the Mina Harker of Stoker's *Dracula*. The other was that if she had rebelled against that victimized position and had asserted herself, and she's still a very young woman, so that assertion would be done with the vigor of youth, that in a group of men who, with the exception of Griffin, possibly, are all a great deal older than her, and who to a certain degree, some of them are rather spent forces, I think that her dynamism and her drive and passion would tend to naturally propel her, if she wasn't going to be completely subservient and a quiet little woman, I think the only alternative would be to be in a dominant and central position. And that's the way that I saw her developing.

JN: What's the significance, if any, of the Question Mark Man, the sort of symbol of the League?

AM: That was Kevin's idea as a little graphic to symbolize the League. In the second volume he tends to have been replaced by the question mark helmeted Boadicea figure. I think that it seems to fit. I think that it's the idea of something that, where, in both instances you've got the body of the figure which seems to resonate with a bygone era, y'know, the dapper evening dress of the Question Mark Man or the Britannic robes of the woman in the second volume. And these both, the costumes, seem to be talking about the past, and the Question Mark adds an element of mystery and of the fantastic to them. I think that's the general thinking. I know that I liked them when Kevin first showed me them, and we both thought that it would be a good little–it's like a trademark character, that's basically it, it's a little trademark character that we can use to graphically link the design of the various issues.

JN: What's your dating scheme with the *League*?

AM: It's a bit erratic, and we tend to sort of fudge it if we think it'll be more fun to ignore conventional dating and if we don't feel we're doing too much violence to the original stories, then we'll generally include a thing. We generally go for the date that a story was published as the date when it happened, unless sometimes there have been specific dates referred to in a story, in which case we've gone for that. Other times we've ignored specific dates given in a story. For example, the *War of the Worlds*, although it was published in 1898, was actually supposed to refer to events at some point in the future. And yet, everything in the story is very clearly talking about the kind of London that existed in 1898. So we just thought, "Oh, the hell with it, even if Wells does say that this happens at some point in the future, let's stick with the date that it was published, because that makes as much sense as any." I think it's generally that a story must have happened either on or before the date that it was published. It's a very sloppy system because we cheated, because if it was too rigid it might rule out, for the sake of obsessive continuity, some fantastic moments. So we try and keep it as consistent and loyal to the various authors as possible but given the nature of the project there are going to be times when we're going to have to do some slight fudging. But we try to do that as little as possible.

JN: What was the writing of "Allan and the Sundered Veil" like, in the Victorian, penny dreadful style? I know you've said that when you were writing "Pog," the Pogo issue of *Swamp Thing* that the portmanteau neologisms spread in your mind. Did that happen when you were writing "Allan and the Sundered Veil"?

AM: The pulp style–well, it was funny because I was just making it up as I went along. In the first issue I thought, "Well, we've got some pages to fill at the back, maybe we could have a text story." Because there have been text stories in comics before, like back in those old Stan Lee *Strange Tales* or whatever. But they've never been very good. They've never been–the language has never been exciting. I suppose with the Allan Quatermain stuff it was my idea of pulp writing, which is certainly not like Rider Haggard, it's not very much like anybody who was writing back then. But there's a kind of feel to it which resonates with that era. Very fancy, decadent writing, like I say, nothing like Haggard's, which was a lot more plain and straightforward. I more or less just decided to emulate what I thought would have been the technique of those early pulp writers, in that I would just sit down at the typewriter and pour it out. I'd start with what I thought would be a good scene and then just progress without much idea of where it was going, and know that I would have to get it wrapped up within six issues. No, it didn't, because it would probably take me two or three days to actually write an episode of "Allan and the Sundered Veil," which is not as long as the couple of weeks that I spent writing "Pog." So there isn't quite the same, and I'm doing other things at the same time, it probably wasn't a problem to stop thinking in the sort of prose terms like that because I was doing so much other ordinary comics stuff around the edges of it that I didn't have quite the time to get fixated in the way that I did with the earlier *Swamp Thing* story or with some of my other experimental usages of languages. And also it wasn't a particularly experimental use of language. Heavily mannered, and with–it was a more elaborate, more jeweled version of late Victorian prose. It wasn't really messing around with syntax or grammar or coinages in the same way that the "Pog" thing was, and I think that it's when you start to do that, when you actually start to fool around with the structure of language, that you get the most surprising mental effects, possibly because much of our consciousness is built upon language. If you start to mess around with the language, you do tend to start to mess around with your consciousness. The "Allan and the Sundered Veil" stuff was very jeweled writing, very finely considered, but most of my prose is. If I'm not going to have an artist to–it's not like a comic strip where I've got an artist to realize each of the visual descriptions, then I try to make them as compelling as I can using just the words, which probably accounts for some of the richer, more purple descriptions in "Allan and the Sundered Veil."

JN: *League* is your second extended work set in the Victorian Era, *From Hell* of course being the first. Does that particular time and place have a particular fascination for you?

AM: It didn't. Really, I think it was largely coincidence that led to *From Hell* being followed pretty much straightaway by *League*. It was sort of largely that the Victorian era was the richest in terms of the kind of fictional characters that I was interested in, and that's why it lent itself so well to *League*. That said, having explored the Victorian era, yeah, my appreciation of it as a fantastic and very involved, very charged period in British history has increased considerably. On the other hand, I realize that practically every other period of British history is just as interesting, which is why I'm very much looking forward, in the third volume, in one of the issues, where we will deal with Prospero's Men, the Seventeenth-century group, and we will be able to look at Elizabethan England, and we'll be able to talk about Gloriana, because in the fictional world of the *League* there wouldn't have been an Elizabethan period. There would have been a Glorianan period, with Gloriana as the fictional counterpart of Queen Elizabeth. I can kind of dovetail that in quite nicely with real history, like Anne Boelyn, Elizabeth's mother, had six fingers on each hand, and was generally not well liked by the British people, and was probably rumored to have connections with the faeries, so that would explain Gloriana's "Faerie Queen" attributes. I would say that in our version of Elizabethan England, people wouldn't have been so much worried about the fact that Elizabeth was a Protestant as about the fact that she was possibly a faerie. I can just see her remote cousin, King Oberon of Faerie, turning up with a retinue at her court. All of these historical periods are ones that I should love to explore in future works. The Victorian period is a very, very rich one. But I only wandered into it by accident, and while I've enjoyed my stay there I wouldn't say that it was an era that fascinated me above all others. But it certainly is a very fascinating era.

JN: After having done all this work with Victorian writers, is there any one in particular, obscure or not, that you've grown very fond of or have gotten a greater appreciation of?

AM: All of them. I think that my appreciation of all of them has grown. Rereading some of these books, rereading *War of the Worlds*, say, it reminded me that there is something very compellingly every day and bleak about British apocalyptic fiction. It seems that the main thing that you are looking at in *War of the Worlds* is not so much what the Martians are doing as what the humans are doing, how it is affecting the human characters. This reminds me of when I read John Wyndham's *Day of the Triffids*, where the scenes that affected me most were the blinded humanity wandering around getting drunk or committing suicide, because they couldn't bear this awful new reality that they'd been plunged into. There's a very kitchen sink element in British apocalyptic fiction that I think makes it all the more terrible, all the more affecting. That's certainly something that I found while looking through Wells. All of these authors. You come across people like Alexander Marsh, who did the *Beetle*–now there's a character that I wish we could have managed to fit in somewhere, and we might do at some point.

JN: I know that it was rumored that the Beetle would show up in one form or another–

AM: Yeah, that was the plan, because it's such a fascinating character, and when you actually read the work, it's got a feverish madness to it which kind of makes it–you can understand why it was more highly regarded and sold better than *Dracula*, which I believe was released in the same month.

JN: Supposedly the two of them had a bet as to who would sell better–

AM: Well, I think Marsh won. Richard Marsh, not Alexander Marsh, wasn't it, because I know that he was Robert Aickman's–

JN: Yes, Richard Marsh.

AM: Yes, Richard Marsh, who was Robert Aickman's uncle. A fascinating character, and a fascinating book. Genuinely horrible.

Phantasmagoric. I would have liked to have been able to bring that to more people's attention. But there are such a lot of jewels that lie ignored in our literary past because these things that I'm talking about are largely genre fiction, which is still by and large despised by the literary elite. You're not going to get any genre fiction really considered for a Booker Prize or for any major literary award. There is still this snobbishness which really denies anything other than variations upon Jane Austen's comedy of manners any real literary status. And that offends me. Because I think that these–Shakespeare was a pulp writer. Dickens was a pulp writer. And they weren't writing comedies of manners about the middle classes, which I have no doubt they could do, but they were writing in more vulgar forms. And more power to them. The same thing goes for most of the genre writers. Our famed, our great writers, the ones that have been given literary respectability, they are in no danger of being forgotten. But the treasures amongst our lower classes of literary status that are in danger of completely slipping between our fingers, that are no longer available in print, that are more or less forgotten–these are the real, like I say, the endangered species of the literary world that I've got a particular fondness for.

JN: Did ABC/Wildstorm express any reluctance about the series, either because it didn't seem to be automatically saleable or because of the issue of copyrighted characters?

AM: I think that the answer is pretty much "no" in both instances. The first one, I think that it's such a–if I do say so myself, it's such an obviously good commercial idea. There was nobody that I mentioned the idea to that didn't say, "Oh, that's a fantastic idea! Why hasn't anybody else thought of that before?" Although, of course, lots of people have. It didn't take much to sell the idea of *The League of Extraordinary Gentlemen*. It's got a buzz to it, even in its most simply stated form. As for the copyright things, I think that once Scott realized how we were handling stuff like, y'know, the appearance of this devilish Oriental doctor in Limehouse, things like that, that we genuinely don't want to trade off of anybody else's work. Where the authors have been living, if possible, we–like with Moorcock, where I specifically asked him if it was okay that we make the references to his Martian books, because I happen to know people who know Moorcock, so it was easy to get a message to him. And there were others. It's tribute as much as anything, and it's not like we're trading on these characters, plastering them on covers, trying to gain readers off of the readerships of these characters. It's because they were important characters and we think that they deserve a place in this attempt at a kind of definitive, playful mapping of the fictional universe. Obviously, Wildstorm's lawyers are DC's lawyers, so they're as nervous about this stuff as you might expect any lawyers to be. But generally I can't remember any specific instances of when we've strayed over the line and they've said, "You'll have to take this character out." I think if we have–I can't think of any specific instances. Like with the Devil Doctor of Limehouse, where we found that Dr. Fu Manchu was still in copyright, we thought, well, we don't have to use Dr. Fu Manchu, there's ways around these things, where, because people do have a great culturally absorbed knowledge of these characters ready to hand, then you don't have to spell everything out. You can make some feather light references that are not actionable, safe in the knowledge that somebody like you is going to be able to pick them up and explain them to the readership for me. We've got a light enough touch with this. That said, we have got a character on the cover, Kevin's just done this beautiful cover for *League* Volume Two Number Five that I think we're going to have to change because it's got some characters on the front that for one thing would tend to give away the surprise that awaits inside the issue, and I think showing them on the front cover might also be pushing our luck. Generally we tend to steer a pretty secure course between some of the reefs of litigation.

Magic

JN: In several of your works, *From Hell* and *Promethea* and your recorded words, you deal fairly heavily with symbolism and magic. Is there any of that in *League* or did you just intend that to be more lighthearted and fun?

AM: Well, no, there aren't any overt references to magic in *League*. However, particularly with the Almanac, I kind of got a feeling, I do tend to think of some bits in *League*, specifically the Almanac, but other bits as well, as a kind of magical writing, in that, to me, the world of fiction and the world of the imagination is of extreme relevance to the world of magic. Most magical events are, at least in some sense of the word, imaginary. They are, in some sense, fictional. The interplay between fiction and magic is considerable. People like McGregor Mathers, S. McGregor Mathers, who was one of the founding magicians of the Golden Dawn, over here, he seems to have been drawn in to an occult lifestyle because he had ridiculously over-identified with Bulwer-Lytton's *Zanoni*. There's a lot of romance in all of this and when you look at a lot of the writers, Algernon Blackwood, Arthur Machen, Sax Rohmer, E. Nesbit, these were all members of the Golden Dawn. A fantastic number of the ghost and fantasy story writers of that late Nineteenth, early Twentieth century period were in magical orders. There is a sympathy between the territories of the two. I would prefer to keep my actual opinions about magic confined to *Promethea*, and God knows some of the readership have enough trouble with that, so I would prefer it if magic didn't obviously permeate all of my work. But that said, particularly in the Almanac, where I actually feel that I am in some way mapping a world that actually exists in a certain sense, that this planet of the imagination which has been with us as long as our own physical planet, that in some instances the places on that world of the imagination, we sometimes know them more intimately and more intensely than we know real places that we have visited, that we may have a much firmer picture in our head of Gormenghast than we have of some office we worked at twenty years ago. In some senses the world of fiction, the world of imagination, in some senses it is real. If thoughts are real, then the products–thoughts are not real in any material sense. Thoughts are beyond the province of science. And yet I think most of us would agree that thoughts are real. We have them. They pass through our minds. And if those thoughts are real they are real in a different sense to the way that physical things are real. And it is in that same different sense that it seems to me that our fictional landscapes and our fictional characters are real. They have an affect upon us, like in the instance just quoted, with this fictional character Zanoni inspiring a real person to try and act like him and in doing so setting up one of the most important magical orders in the history of Western occultism. These fictional people actually have an effect upon the real world. I know a lot of magicians, many of them–yes, some of them have been attracted to it because they were interested in real magicians, like Dee or Osman Spare or Aleister Crowley. But I know just as many whose initial interest in the world of magic was through a fictional character like Dr. Strange. We create these ideal characters and we carry them around in our heads, we try to measure up to them, they affect our behavior. They have an effect upon our lives and thus upon our world. That would seem to me to grant them a certain reality and a certain importance beyond mere entertainment. To me, and possibly only to me, there is serious magic in working upon *The League of Extraordinary Gentlemen*, but there is no overt magic symbolism in the *League*. I suppose one way of putting it is that *Promethea* is about magic, and is obviously about magic. The *League* in some ways is a subtle kind of magic and therefore doesn't really need to be talked about overtly. The magic is in what the *League* is, what it represents in terms of giving a new way to look at this universe of fiction that we are actually surrounded by and which a lot of us have spent a large part of our lives immersed in. It offers people a new way of looking at that. If there is any magic in *The League of Extraordinary Gentlemen*, that is where it resides.